"Zealous in their pursuit of justice . . . the Cohens have played an important and valuable role. They have kept the issue before the public. They have made sure their daughter has not been forgotten, and with her everyone else who died that night."

—*The Washington Post*

"A very personal account of the aftermath of this tragedy. *Pan Am 103* is more than a book about loss and industrial incompetence. It is the moving account of a father who refused to be silenced and was determined—at whatever costs—to uncover the truth about his daughter's death."   —*Arizona Daily Star*

"The Cohens' book details the labyrinthine process of conducting their own investigation of the crime. Indeed, there are many villains in this drama. Start with the Federal Aviation Administration. Blame also falls on Pan Am for its woeful lack of security . . . and then there is the United States government, which has consistently given the impression that the deaths of a few citizens are insignificant on the international stage. The Cohens less ask for justice than demand it . . . and if you read their book, you'll want it for them."

—*The Times* (Trenton, NJ)

"Painfully sad and passionately angry."

—*The Philadelphia Inquirer*

PAN AM 103

THE BOMBING, THE BETRAYALS, AND A BEREAVED FAMILY'S SEARCH FOR JUSTICE

Susan and Daniel Cohen

A SIGNET BOOK

SIGNET
Published by New American Library, a division of
Penguin Putnam Inc., 375 Hudson Street,
New York, New York 10014, U.S.A.
Penguin Books Ltd, 27 Wrights Lane,
London W8 5TZ, England
Penguin Books Australia Ltd, Ringwood,
Victoria, Australia
Penguin Books Canada Ltd, 10 Alcorn Avenue,
Toronto, Ontario, Canada M4V 3B2
Penguin Books (N.Z.) Ltd, 182–190 Wairau Road,
Auckland 10, New Zealand

Penguin Books Ltd, Registered Offices:
Harmondsworth, Middlesex, England

Published by Signet, an imprint of New American Library,
a division of Penguin Putnam Inc.
Previously published in a New American Library edition.

First Signet Printing, April 2001
10 9 8 7 6 5 4 3 2 1

To Theo

Acknowledgments

The authors would like to thank those who, in one way or another, helped in the preparation of this book.

Jim and Rosemary Wolfe, Jack and Kathleen Flynn, Stephanie Bernstein, Eleanor Bright, Dick and Fran Kitts, Charles and Jeannie Graves, Lee Kreindler, Pat Robinson, Sheila Hershow, Chris Byron, Linda Mack, Trina Vargo, Sharon Waxman, John Bolton, Cliff Kincaid, Herb Zweibon, Harris Schoenberg, Vincent Cannistraro, Janice Osborne of *The Gazette,* and Eric Kreiger of *The Times Herald Record.* Thanks also to others who cannot be named, but you know who you are.

The best and most complete account of the early years of the Pan Am 103 case can be found in *Their Darkest Day* (Grove, Weidenfeld, 1992) by Matthew Cox and Tom Foster, two reporters from Syracuse whom we came to regard as friends as well as media contacts. Approximately the same period but from the British perspective is covered in David Leppard's excellent *On the Trail of Terror: The Inside Story of the Lockerbie Investigation* (Johnathan Cape, 1991).

Special thanks are due to Carolyn Nichols of Signet for her confidence in a very difficult project; and to Ellen Edwards, also of Signet, for her confidence, skill and ability to keep cool in the face of a punishing deadline. Also to Henry Morrison, much more than an agent.

And, of course, thanks to the animals, who did not destroy any of the thousands of pieces of paper that were scattered about within easy reach during the preparation of this book—at least not anything vital.

Introduction

At 7:02 P.M. local time, on December 21, 1988, a bomb exploded aboard Pan Am flight 103. It wasn't a large bomb. It contained less than a pound of the plastic explosive Semtex and had been concealed inside of an ordinary brown Samsonite suitcase. The suitcase was in baggage container AVE 4041 PA, which had been loaded into the left side of the plane's front forward cargo hold.

The explosion itself was a comparatively small one. But the shock waves it created inside of the Boeing 747 literally tore the aircraft to pieces.

The destruction of Pan Am 103 had been tracked on radar. The plane, bound for New York, had left London's Heathrow Airport at 6:25 and headed north. By 6:56 it had cleared the congested airspace around Heathrow and had leveled off at an altitude of 31,000 feet, cruising altitude and usually the safest part of any flight.

That something was terribly wrong was first noticed by Alan Topp, an air traffic controller at Scotland's Prestwick Airport. Flight 103 had just crossed into Scottish airspace when he saw that the green box, which represented the plane on his radar screen, had broken into four smaller boxes. At first he thought that he was seeing some sort of false image that would soon be corrected. Seconds passed but the multiple images did not fade; they seemed to be fanning out.

Topp tried to contact flight 103's crew by radio telephone. There was no response. Other air controllers had also lost the image of flight 103 and were unable to contact the crew. Then came a report from a British Airways shuttle from Glasgow to London of seeing an explosion off the ground in southern Scotland.

The unthinkable had happened. A Boeing 747 had been ripped apart in midair, nearly six miles above the ground, and pieces of the plane, luggage, and the bodies of passengers and crew rained down on the small Scottish town of Lockerbie.

One of the passengers was Theodora Eugenia Cohen—everybody called her Theo—a drama and music student at Syracuse University, returning home after spending the first semester of her junior year in England with the school's Study Abroad program. Theo had turned twenty on September 10.

When she boarded the plane at Heathrow, she was assigned to seat 21 H, an aisle seat over the wing. Whether she was actually in that seat when the bomb went off is unknown. Also unknown is whether she was killed or rendered unconscious immediately, or had some awareness of the horror that had occurred.

What is known is that the following day her body was found in a sheep pasture in Tundergarth east of Lockerbie, not far from the much photographed wreckage of flight 103's cockpit.

Theo was our daughter.

Chapter 1

SUSAN: The day Theo died, and my life came to an end, got off to a cheerful start. The weather was mild for December, so there would be no worries about driving to the airport. It would be one of those banner reunions, the kind families mark with photos in the album. We had never been so far away from each other for so long. The house, which had been a quiet, two-working-adults place for months, would again be transformed into a headquarters for the young. There would be parties and endless gossip and chitchat about trips and school and boyfriends. The phone would ring constantly. Theo would tell me about the plays she had seen, her plans to start an experimental theater in Syracuse, and when tryouts for summer theater would begin. Could she have the car to go visit her friends? One of life's ironies: I'd always been edgy about giving her the car. Teenagers and cars are a scary mix.

I expected her to greet me with some witty comment, made in an English accent. I expected her to take a long shower no matter what time we got home that night. One of her biggest complaints was the rotten water pressure in the apartment she shared with friends in London. I knew she'd sing in the shower, and I would once again hear that beautiful soprano voice, so good her voice teachers always urged her to study opera. She'd come out in a warm robe with a towel wrapped around her head, sit in our big kitchen, and tell me one fascinating story after another about the great trip. Fascinating to me, that is. Once, on one of her quick stop offs at home between school and a summer theater job, I sat on the steps for an hour with her, drinking in every word she had to say about ordinary things. She said things well. She was witty and clever. She had to be, in our house. We zinged one-liners at one another all the time. It was expected.

I had last heard from Theo two days before. She called to tell me how she'd gone to Scotland the previous weekend and bought new leather boots and a stuffed sheep. She loved stuffed animals, and even had a small teddy bear collection born from her love of the television version of Evelyn Waugh's *Brideshead Revisited,* which she watched when she was thirteen. Before she hung up there was a pause, and she said, "I miss you and I love you." "I miss you and I love you too," I said. When we hung up I danced a little jig in the kitchen. I was so happy she'd told me she loved me and missed me. Gone was teenage cool and teenage sarcasm. She was homesick and could admit it now that she was twenty. For the past few years she had sneaked looking at the photo album, looking at her own past. This year she might be ready to sit down with us, risking the sentimentality and intense emotion, and look at pictures with us.

All was in readiness in our big Victorian house. The Christmas tree, covered with ornaments, most of which were small souvenirs we had picked up on our travels or on special occasions, to mark our past along with the photo album, looked beautiful reflected in the glass den door and the large living room windows. As was our tradition, we had covered the pictures and the prints on the wall with evergreens. The cards hung on strips of ribbon on the latticed side of the staircase. Ornaments, including a gold-colored wreath, were on the mantelpiece of our red fireplace, a fireplace capable of a blaze so magnificent it looked like a Norman Rockwell Christmas card.

Because Theo had missed Thanksgiving, it was going to be a feast of a dinner with turkey, two kinds of potatoes, real cranberries—in short, the works. The silver plate, a wedding present that I used once a year, was polished and ready.

I had put a lot of thought into presents. When she left for the trip that would take her not only to England but also on side excursions to Amsterdam, Greece, and Paris, we'd given her a camera and a tape recorder. I had bought the usual winter stuff, like mittens and slippers, for a cold Syracuse winter, but we'd been to the Miami Book Fair and I'd picked up a poncho and silver beads. Dan had found an amusing cow object, because Theo liked cows, especially she said, for their long lovely eyelashes. And, because she now claimed to be practically a vegetarian, we had picked up an electric juicer. We wondered who she would be, this person we were meeting at the airport, this person who was at the age when change comes quickly and abundantly, and whom a semester abroad would certainly have affected.

I remembered when we took her to the airport back in September. We'd gotten stuck in a traffic jam, and I was concerned we'd miss the plane. There was a warm wind that night, which I noticed as we walked down the stairs from where we had parked the car at the airport. Theo was sad about leaving because she'd had to say good-bye to her latest boyfriend, Oz, at the MacHayden Theater, where she had sung the role of "the girl" in *The Fantastiks*. Before she went off to the lounge with the other Syracuse students waiting for the flight, I hugged her and said, "Have a good time." "I will," she said. I gave her the return ticket. We had arranged in advance for her to come back on December 21 because we were afraid the holidays would make it hard for her to get a seat on a return flight. "Don't lose it," I said. It was Dan's idea to book an advance return flight, and mine for it to be the twenty-first. That was the last possible day to get home on a return ticket, and I thought I'd give her as long as possible, since she'd wanted to stay over and travel. This gave her at least an extra day.

The day before, I had called Pan Am and was told that she was on a morning flight. Then I was called back and told, no, it was the evening flight. That morning Theo's friend from babyhood, Megan, had called to find out what time Theo would be home. On a spring day, many months earlier, Theo had told me how Megan had taken Pan Am home when she went to Europe. I had worried about charter flights and rinky-dink airlines. I hadn't worried any more than I always worry about Pan Am. When I was a little girl, I dreamed over pictures in magazines of the glamorous Pan Am clippers; it was America's airline.

On the twenty-first I had work to do. Dan and I were writing a kids book on rare-breed dogs. But excitement was building. Tonight I would see Theo again. She was small, but so animated, so full of life, with a zest for living. P. G. Wodehouse had a wonderful description of a character named Sue Brown. It described Theo: "She was a tiny thing, mostly large eyes and a wide happy smile. In every movement of her was Youth."

I called Pan Am and was told that the plane had got off late but was now on its way.

DAN: Most people believe, at least subconsciously, that if something truly terrible is going to happen, they will have some sort of warning, a premonition, a hunch, a feeling, however faint, that will later allow them to say they knew, or feared it was going to happen.

I had no such warning. I wasn't even anxious about making the three-and-a-half-hour drive from Port Jervis, New York, to Kennedy Airport to pick up Theo, and then making the return drive in the middle of the night. There was no rain or snow in the forecast, and the weather was quite warm for the first day of winter.

I was taking an afternoon nap, in preparation for the long drive, when the phone next to the bed rang. It was a friend of ours, the mother of one of Theo's closest high school friends.

She said she had just heard something on the radio about a U.S. bound airplane having crashed in England. She knew Theo was scheduled to come back from England that day and wanted to know if everything was all right.

I told her that we hadn't heard anything, but I didn't think Theo's plane had even taken off yet. In fact, I didn't know when her plane had been scheduled to take off, but my immediate reaction was: "It can't be Theo. There must be lots of planes flying from England to New York every day, no reason to panic and assume it was her plane."

Susan was in her office working. When I told her about the phone call, she was much more alarmed than I had been.

We rushed downstairs and turned on the TV. There were pictures of houses in Lockerbie, Scotland, that had been set ablaze by the burning aircraft fuel from the crash. Across the bottom of the screen was the flight number of the downed plane—Pan Am 103.

On the large wall calendar near the TV set, Susan, a diligent list maker and note taker, had printed next to the date not only the time of Theo's expected arrival at JFK but the flight number, Pan Am 103.

It was her plane.

SUSAN: I was sitting at my desk when Dan burst into the room and said that Clem had called, saying a plane from England had crashed. "It can't be Theo," I said, jumping up and running out of the room. "That must be the morning flight, the one she wasn't on." I rushed downstairs to the calendar next to my kitchen desk. There it was, glowing in huge numbers, "Pan Am 103." "It *is* Theo's flight," I screamed. I turned around and looked at the television facing me from the den. That horrible picture of the flaming wreckage. She was in that. My Theo was in there. Dan looked at me and said, "Susan, I don't see how anyone could have survived."

DAN: We didn't make a reasoned decision about going to JFK. But since we weren't being told anything, we thought we might get more information there. Anyway, we couldn't just sit around the house and wait.

Susan talked wildly about going to Scotland. I didn't know how that could even be arranged. I don't recall we even took our passports.

SUSAN: I went nuts. I ran upstairs, grabbed an overnight bag, and threw in a toothbrush, pajamas, but no underwear. I would go to Scotland. I would find her. I would go to the hospital and there she would be. I would stay with her. I would make her well. She couldn't be dead. Didn't I always say that Theo was lucky? I used to say I got lucky with Theo, and Theo got lucky with me. An only child, adored by her parents. A little girl growing up first in a woodland paradise with writer parents, then in a safe little town full of kids. Books floor to ceiling. Trips to New York for museums and plays. Summer camp. Six Augusts in Nantucket. She once said to me that when she had to think about something sad in drama class, all she could think about was one of our cats who had died.

I started phoning. I called the Syracuse travel agency that booked the flight. "The crash hasn't been confirmed," the woman at the other end of the line said nervously. "What do you mean, hasn't been confirmed. I can see the wreckage on television." I hung up the phone. I picked up the phone again and tried to reach Lockerbie. I'd never heard of the place before; now it was the only spot on earth that mattered.

I couldn't get through. The line was busy, busy, busy. I called the AT&T operator. She put me through to a man who was an operator in Scotland. He told me he couldn't get through. I shouted at him that he had to help me. I told him I didn't know whether Theo was alive or dead. The AT&T operator interrupted and angrily said, "Stop yelling at him. He can't get through, you're hysterical."

"But my daughter was in a plane crash. Wouldn't you be hysterical?"

"Me, never," she said with contempt, and cut off the call.

Then it really hit me. Theo was dead. I knew it. I believed it. I had no hope. We didn't know what to do. So we decided to go to the airport. No one called. No one gave us any information. We didn't want to just sit at home until morning.

DAN: Before leaving, I called a neighbor who had a key to the house and told her to be sure and come over and feed the cat. I then called the kennel where we always boarded our dog when we took a trip and arranged to bring her over for the night. Fortunately, even though it was the Christmas holidays, there was space available. The cat could be fed, but we had never left the dog alone, even for a single night.

Like so much else that was to follow, the drive to the airport was surreal. I felt very calm and was conscious of having to stay under control. I drove carefully, never exceeding the speed limit, even though there was little traffic.

Susan was hysterical. She was crying and threatened to throw herself out of the moving car. She actually opened the door on her side a couple of times. I put a restraining arm on her and got her to close the door. The car never even swerved.

SUSAN: It was when we reached the thruway that my numbness started to dissolve. I watched the headlights of so many cars, all moving normally, carrying people along on their normal Wednesday routines. We should have been driving with light hearts and eagerness to pick her up. A few hours ago we had a normal life. How could it be that in such a short time everything changed and we were going off to the dreaded airport to find out more about our daughter being dead. The human body isn't made to take such a shock. The human mind isn't constructed to survive it.

As the numbness subsided, the hysteria increased. I wanted to die. Without Theo, there didn't seem to be any point in staying alive. If I searched for her, I wouldn't find her. She wouldn't be anywhere. Billions of people in the world, but without her it was empty. While we were on the thruway, I tried to open the car door and jump out. Dan restrained me. I never had imagined killing myself. Now it seemed the logical and inevitable thing to do.

DAN: The worst moment came while we were listening to news on the car radio. One report said that thirty-five

Syracuse University students had been on the flight. I turned off the radio.

We had not entertained any serious belief that Theo had somehow survived. She was not the sort of person to miss a flight, and if she had she would certainly have called us to let us know about the change of plans. She was that kind of kid.

The news reports didn't come right out and say everyone aboard had been killed. In fact, for the first few hours they didn't say anyone had been killed. But they didn't say anything about survivors either, and the tone of the reports, plus the pictures from the crash scene that we had seen on television, left little doubt in our minds that everyone was dead.

Once at JFK I drove directly to the Pan Am Terminal, from which Theo had departed some four months earlier. In front of the terminal was a collection of police cars with flashing lights and television satellite trucks—the inevitable trappings of a major, modern disaster.

Suddenly it wasn't a picture on a screen or a voice over the radio anymore. It was real and it was right in front of me. The control I had maintained in arranging for the animals and throughout the long drive fell apart. I abandoned the car in the roadway in front of the terminal. I don't even think I turned the motor off. I certainly didn't take the keys. We jumped out of the car, without bothering to close the doors, and rushed into the brightly lighted terminal building.

From our appearance it must have been obvious why we were there because before we said anything we were taken in hand by Pan Am employees and guided to a large lounge area for Pan Am 103 families.

We were ushered through a gauntlet of cameramen and reporters. Later there was to be a lot of criticism of the media for vulture-like and intrusive behavior. Months afterward I saw news videotape of our arrival at the Pan Am Terminal—and we were surrounded by what looked like a media mob. But at the time I was barely aware of them. Theo was dead—that thought filled my mind and blotted out everything else. What was going on around me was blurred, muffled, and supremely unimportant.

The lounge was large and filled with people. As far as I could tell, only a few of them were family members or friends of Pan Am 103 passengers. There were a lot of Pan Am or other airport employees. Many of them were quite young and inexperienced. They seemed puzzled and frightened by the scene; they tentatively but repeatedly offered me coffee and sandwiches.

The mayor didn't come to the airport. There were no phone calls from the President. I doubt if a message from the mayor or the President would have been of any help at all at that moment. More significantly, while there were plenty of lower-level airline employees wandering about, no official airline spokesmen ever came to the lounge. They may have been somewhere else in the building briefing the press, but we were never personally told anything about the fate of Pan Am 103 and its passengers.

I kept grabbing people and asking them if Theo's name was on the passenger list. Though the crash had taken place hours earlier, I was told they knew of no official list. I asked if there were any survivors. No one knew. Indeed no one would even admit to me that anyone had been killed.

Finally a Pan Am stewardess ushered me over to a quiet corner and told me that everyone who worked for the airline knew there couldn't possibly be any survivors in such a disaster; they just were not allowed to say it officially. That was what I had expected to hear, what I had really known, but I was deeply grateful for her honesty.

SUSAN: We were taken to a large lounge filled with other relatives of those on Pan Am 103. It was a trip into hell. Everyone was stunned. I began crying and they began moaning. Someone was fanning me. It was Flo Bissett, whom I would get to know later. She was silent then. The screaming would begin later. Some woman appeared, standing in front of me, someone official, from JFK's emergency team. She told me she had seen many tragedies. There seemed little beyond this that she could do or say. I wandered around mumbling that Ronald Reagan, who was finishing up his presidency, had caused this by deregulating the airlines.

DAN: I couldn't sit still. I spent much of the time pacing back and forth across the lounge. I must have looked like a zombie. I certainly felt like one. Someone told me I had a phone call. It was my father calling from Chicago. He had no idea we were going to the airport, and I never found out how he located us or how he managed to actually get through. For a usually quiet man, he could be remarkably persistent and persuasive when necessary. All I could tell him was that we had to assume that Theo was dead. He had no words of comfort for me, nor I for him. We both accepted the fact that death is very final.

I began to feel claustrophobic. Even though the lounge itself was large, I needed to get out of there, if only for a few minutes. The airline employees who were guarding the doors to the lounge tried to talk me out of leaving. Perhaps they were really concerned about the state I was in, or perhaps they thought my distressed appearance would scare passengers on other flights. They didn't really try to stop me; they just warned me that there were lots of reporters out there, and I shouldn't talk to them. In any case, none of the reporters and cameramen near the door to the lounge approached me.

As I scanned the crowd in the terminal, I saw two familiar faces in an ocean of strangers, Dick and Fran Kitts, friends of ours from Staten Island. They had heard about the crash and knew when Theo was coming home. "We knew you would be at the airport," Fran said, "and we had to be with you." At that moment no sight could possibly have been more welcome. Fran grabbed me and hugged me. I hustled them past the guards at the door to the lounge. The guards protested mildly that since the Kitts were not family members they really shouldn't be in there, but they didn't press the point.

Though I had driven to the airport with great precision,

there was no possibility that I was going to be able to drive back home that night. Arrangements had been made to put some of the family members up at an airport motel.

We were bussed over, and as I was getting off the bus, I saw a small group of reporters and cameramen standing in front of the motel. One of them came up and asked if I was willing to talk to them.

I had graduated from journalism school, and though I never had been what could properly be called a reporter, I had been a magazine editor and later a writer for my whole professional life. I had interviewed lots of people and had often been interviewed myself by print reporters and on radio and television. I was comfortable with reporters, and I liked them. I wanted to talk, though I'm not sure what I wanted to talk about, probably about Theo. I never got the chance.

I was spotted by airline employees who had been on the bus. They rushed over and tried to chase the reporter away, shouting, "Don't bother him. Can't you see he doesn't want to be bothered." I protested that I wasn't being bothered and I had agreed to talk, but the airline employees weren't listening to me. They kept on shouting and physically pushed me into the motel and shut the doors. I was too weak and fuzzy-headed to resist.

Over the years I've thought about that incident a lot; its almost violent and certainly unexpected nature made it stick in my mind. Was it the case of a few airline employees acting overzealously in an attempt to protect a distraught father (which I certainly was) from media vultures? Or were the employees told to keep members of victims' families away from the media? Seeing what happens to people when they find out that their child has dropped six miles out of the sky, after a 747 has disintegrated in midair, is not going to be good for airline business. Considering the way Pan Am attempted to manipulate and soften public perceptions of the disaster makes suspicion natural and inevitable.

In the Holiday Inn, we were put on one of the lower floors that was taken entirely by people connected with the

Pan Am disaster. As far as I could tell, however, there was
only one other family member on the floor. She was Georgia Nucci; her son Christopher had been one of the other
Syracuse University students returning on the flight. She
was a short, heavyset woman with large glasses and amazingly, an almost continual smile. She was very controlled
and tried to keep busy by, among other things, trying to
comfort Susan and me. I was astonished by her control.
Then during that long night, she told me that less than a
year earlier her daughter had died suddenly while partici-
pating in an American Field Service program in Ecuador.
I was no longer astonished at her control. I was astonished
that she had survived at all.

There was a motley assortment of people on our floor in
the motel. Some were obviously Pan Am employees in uniform. Others appeared to be airport security people wearing khaki uniforms with matching baseball caps. There was
a sad and rumpled-looking doctor, who like so many others was confused and overwhelmed. Susan was still hysterical, and I asked him if he could give her something that
would allow her to sleep. He said he wasn't authorized to
give anyone anything stronger than an aspirin. I wondered
why he was there at all.

Susan's condition had become increasingly alarming.
There was a rumor, untrue but not entirely implausible,
that she had tried to throw herself out of a window. Finally
someone, perhaps the doctor but I don't know for sure,
gave her a shot of something that put her to sleep, at least
for a while.

SUSAN: I calculated the distance to the ground from our
hotel room. No, I would not die if I jumped out the window.
I couldn't stand. I couldn't sit still. I started crawling along
the corridor floor. Back and forth I went. Georgia Nucci,
taking pity on me despite her own sorrows, hugged me. "It
feels like something's being pulled out of you, doesn't it?" It
did. I went back to crawling.

Sometime during the night a man came in, reputedly

some sort of counselor. He badgered me with questions.
How old was Theo? What year in school? I answered for a
while, but I wanted him to go away. In the enormity of this
tragedy, did I have to have psychobabble 101 thrust upon
me? Dan ordered him out of our room. He refused to go.
Dan practically had to assault him to get him to leave.

DAN: At the best of times I am a poor sleeper, so I didn't
even try to lie down. I walked up and down the corridors
and got into a long conversation with one of the uniformed
flight attendants. I think we talked about Chicago. And finally it began to get light outside—it was morning, December 22, 1988, the first full day of a new life that was to
be as gray and chilly as that winter dawn.

SUSAN: After a hundred years, morning came. How happy
December 22 mornings had been in the past. How bleak,
how black was this one.

Chapter 2

DAN: I was still in no shape to drive back to Port Jervis. Whatever Susan had been given had worn off, and she was hysterical again. A car service was arranged to take us back home, and somebody followed driving our car.

All the way back Susan cried and screamed, and there was nothing I could say or do to help or comfort her. I couldn't tell her that everything would be all right, or that Theo was in God's hands or at peace or any of the other conventional phrases that are trotted out in these situations. She screamed that Theo was dead and our life was in ruins, and she was right.

I was worried that the driver would say something to try to be helpful and would only make things worse, but he hunched over the wheel, pretending not to hear, and never said anything more than, "Do I turn off here?"

SUSAN: When we got home, I was startled to see that some of our friends were already inside the house. I was in shock and confused, unable to grasp even the simple and obvious, that everyone who owned a television set knew of the Pan Am 103 crash, and those who could help were there for us. They cleaned up, did laundry, went shopping, ran errands, and they continued to do so for weeks. I was incapable of gratitude at the time, but they were invaluable. A lesson in how to truly help the grief-stricken and the lost.

Throughout the day the house began to fill up. Theo's friends from high school came over. They took down all the Christmas decorations, which now seemed so horribly inappropriate.

They slept on the living room floor, so that we wouldn't have to be alone at night.

DAN: Port Jervis is officially called a city, but it is really a small town with about 8,000 inhabitants. Located on the Delaware River, it had once been a canal town, hence the title "Port." The "Jervis" part was the name of the engineer who had designed the canal. After that it became an important railroad town, but when the railroads died nothing replaced them and Port Jervis just became a poor town. Local legend held that the depression era anthem "Brother, Can You Spare a Dime?" had been inspired by the plight of the unemployed railroad workers in Port Jervis.

Port was never one of those places that attracted upscale émigrés from New York City; it remained a very insular town, with few outsiders. Though we had lived there for nearly fifteen years, we were not considered natives—to be a native your grandfather had to have attended Port Jervis High School. We had come to Port because I could easily drive from there to New York and back in one day, and mainly because it was cheap. We had a huge house with plenty of room for two offices and several thousand books. Friends called it "the Writers' Castle." Since Theo had gone off to school, it was really much bigger than we needed and we were always talking about moving.

Theo had grown up in Port. She had never taken a school bus. When she was little she lived a block from the elementary school. Later, when we moved to a larger house, she was four blocks from the middle school. High school was a twenty-minute walk in good weather. In bad weather she bummed a ride from friends or talked me into driving her.

With no other relatives in the area, she wasn't really a native either. But everybody in town knew who she was. She was the actress. In the fourth grade she got the lead in a class production of *Hansel and Gretel,* loved it, and never looked back. By the sixth grade she was in the chorus of the high school's annual musicals. By high school she was starring in musicals and plays. In her senior year she was Gypsy in *Gypsy* and Anne Frank in *The Diary of Anne Frank.* She was in community theater and spent several summers working in a professional summer stock company about fifteen miles up the road from Port. She was flamboyant. At one point she wore only purple to school; at another it was all black. No one in town had to ask, "Theo who?"

Port was a place that had seen more than its share of misfortune, and people knew how to respond. The doctor made house calls, and now when the washing machine broke, the local repairman put aside all his other appointments and got to our machine first. It seems a small thing, but at that moment it was a very big thing indeed. A friend rushing to our house got a speeding ticket. When the judge found out where he was going, he voided the ticket.

As soon as I got home, I went to get the dog out of the kennel. It is often said that dogs can sense their owner's moods. Not this dog. She was an unusual breed, a Clumber Spaniel, seventy pounds of solidly built white spaniel with speckles of light brown on the face and ears. Her name was Fergie—it seemed a good idea when we got her back in the fall of '87. She was aggressively friendly—she loved people, and she was excited to find the house full of them. She ran from one to another, wagging her stubby tail and waiting to be patted. Better still, most of these people had brought food, and they were careless about where they set it down. She cheerfully stole from everyone.

When Theo's friends camped out on the living room floor in front of the fireplace, Fergie curled up with them. She was having the time of her life.

As time passed and the house emptied out and we were left largely alone, Susan would be upstairs asleep, and I would sit with the dog for hours. When you are in a state of despair, as I was, you become a burden to people, even to your close friends. After a while you drag them down and wear them out. And they wear you out. You try to keep up a conversation, try to show them you appreciate their help or concern, but you just don't have the energy to be convincing. A dog is much easier to be with. You don't have to talk to a dog, though I did. I had long, rambling, one-sided conversations with Fergie. She didn't care what I said, or if I didn't say anything at all, she was just glad to be with me, no matter how I felt. And I needed her always happy and totally accepting presence. Even when she just fell asleep with her head in my lap, she was more comforting than any human being.

I was too enervated to do much of anything. But I could accomplish small and simple tasks, like walking and feeding the dog. These were jobs that had to be done; they were something to organize the day around, and they made me feel like I was doing something useful. More than anything else, the big white Clumber Spaniel helped me to survive those first few terrible weeks.

SUSAN: Help came to me in the form of Max, our silver tabby, as sensitive to nuances of feeling as Fergie was impervious. Theo had first seen Max when she came home for a weekend that summer. "Oh, the kitten's adorable," she'd said. Now the kitten was grown up. I lay in bed, sometimes sobbing, sometimes falling apart and screaming, sometimes just staring ahead in mute depression. I was alone. No one mattered. Not Dan. Not anyone anymore. Certainly not me. I imagined myself rowing alone in a boat on the water, watching a shore that was crowded with people. And I didn't want anyone to touch me.

Max would have none of this. "You can take this attitude toward people if you choose," he as much as said, "but you can't get away with that with me." Whenever I started crying, no matter where Max was in the house, he would rush up to the bedroom and curl up with me on the bed. Showing extraordinary sympathy and persistence, he would nudge me with his head, insisting on getting my attention. I would find myself patting his head, despite myself, running my hand along his back, feeling his slightly bristly fur.

Max wasn't demanding affection simply for himself. He seemed to understand and wanted to express his unhappiness that I should be suffering so. "Let me help you," he would meow in his tiny voice, and swish his tail across my face. I would put my face against Max's forehead and rub it cat style, push his nose with mine. And I would talk to him, as I cried, telling him about Theo, since he hadn't known her very well. Telling him how Theo had found a red tabby Jack O' Dandy when she was three. And telling him about Punch, the gray cat who had been wild and who came out of the woods to settle down with us when we lived in the country. And about Boris, the complex, interesting Russian Blue, who became the toughest cat in the neighborhood, who liked to eat cantaloupe seeds, and curl up in bed with us at night.

I generally sneered at sentimentality, but one part of my life where I let it in was animals. Anthropomorphizing, so what? I would swear that Max did, in some sense, grasp that a tornado had blasted his comfortable world, and that the humans who loved him and had treated him with the utmost kindness and respect were in deep trouble. And if people couldn't reach me, he could and did. Max kept a warm spark alive in me when all else was cold and dead.

When I talked about killing myself, Dan would say, "I would never abandon you. How could you abandon me?" Well, when the desperation and panic and fear and rage and loneliness overwhelmed me, I could have abandoned him, despite catastrophic results. But I couldn't abandon Max and Fergie. I couldn't leave them to face the results of what my killing myself would do to Dan.

DAN: Christmas Day was bizarre. Most of the ingredients for Christmas dinner, including a large turkey, were in the refrigerator. One of those who had been camping out on our floor was Theo's friend Michelle Graves from New Jersey. She had heard about Pan Am 103 while she and her parents were getting ready to go to Texas for Christmas. She decided (demanded, I was later told) that she'd cancel the trip to spend Christmas with us. On Christmas morning she decided that she was going to make Christmas dinner for all of us. Michelle was a determined young woman, but after she was in the kitchen for a few moments, I realized that she had rarely seen the inside of an oven. I wasn't going to be of much help. Nor were Theo's other friends, who stared at the large uncooked turkey with a sort of puzzled wonder.

Susan was the only person in the house who could avert the potential disaster. She had been barely able to get out of bed for three days. I didn't want to bring her any bad news, but I had to tell her what was happening. As I described the situation, I could almost see the machinery click into place. There was going to be a Christmas dinner that day, no matter what. And she was going to cook it.

SUSAN: I was sleeping at night only because my doctor had given us knockout sleeping pills. You closed your eyes, and when you opened them an instant later, it was morning. On Christmas Day I lay in bed asking myself how I could get through the next hour, the next few minutes. A Christmas without Theo! It was incredible; days before, actually inconceivable. Years earlier Dan had said to me, "Can you imagine life without Theo? Does it seem like there was a time when she wasn't here?" I had laughed and said no. Now I kept repeating, "Theo is dead. The little songbird is dead."

What was it like up in that plane before it crashed? There must have been one moment, maybe more than one, of terror. I was up there as I would be many times. I could see Theo chatting with friends, everything normal. Then a noise, an explosion, the lights go out, the plane breaks apart. I see Theo dressed in black, her favorite color for clothes, choking, dying in pain. Falling into the bitter cold airless sky. Her body twisting and turning.

I was convinced that I would not be able to get out of bed. The kids downstairs offered to make Christmas dinner. Everything was in the house, ready to be prepared, some of it already made.

It must have been very hard for the kids to see me like that. Powerful adult and authority figure of their teen years turned into a crumpled wreck. The person who organized a fight against the school board when the music department was going to be abolished, who wrote a weekly column about kids who sang and danced or played a musical instrument and painted pictures, for a local paper which up to that time had covered only the Port Jervis High School football team. Who spoke out loudly and uncompromisingly for gay teens, eccentric teens, and who was forever badgering everybody under the age of twenty to leave town and go away to college. That person had vanished. Now I was weak and helpless and must have seemed very, very old.

I would have stayed in bed if Dan hadn't come up and told me the kids didn't know what they were doing in the kitchen. Michelle popped her head through the door and asked, "How do I cook the potatoes?" Then I knew I had better get up.

I cooked the dinner. We set it all out on the big dining room table and ate it. Afterward I distributed the presents I got for Theo to her friends.

Despite tears and pain, I was still protected by the cushioning of shock that mercifully comes over one when catastrophe first strikes. I went to bed that night thinking things couldn't get worse, but one year later I couldn't make Christmas dinner. I couldn't sit at the table, couldn't have even the minimal conversation I'd had on that first bleak Theo-less Christmas.

DAN: Because of the investigation none of the bodies were being returned from Scotland, and signs pointed to a considerable delay. We decided that there should be a memorial service for Theo on December 29. It was held at the First Presbyterian Church, about a block from where we lived.

The service was to be nonsectarian, indeed nonreligious. The First Presbyterian Church had a little theater group called Presby Players. Theo had been in several of their productions. It was the nearest thing to a cultural center that Port Jervis possessed. That night several hundred people packed the church. They filled a balcony that had not been filled in years. The music was mostly show tunes from local productions Theo had appeared in.

Some of Theo's high school friends came in what looked like costumes. Donald Somerville, one of her closest and most theatrical friends, wore a sequined white tuxedo. It seems that at one time Theo and some of her friends had a discussion about how they would like to be remembered if they died. It wasn't a morbid discussion. It's the sort of thing that kids who are sure that they are never going to die sometimes talk about. Theo had said that she would like her friends to remember her by dressing for her funeral as if they were going to a fancy party; and that's what they did.

I wore a rather threadbare and stained khaki field jacket. It was inappropriate for a memorial service, but very appropriate for Theo. It was a jacket she had admired. She'd told me that if I ever got tired of it, she would love to have it. Once I wore it when we visited her in Syracuse, and she said that all her friends thought I looked cool because I looked just like Jerry Garcia. I was touched and flattered, even though at the time I didn't know who Jerry Garcia was.

There were a lot of media representatives at the service, reporters, microphones, and TV cameras. It was a bit of a circus. I told people in the crowd that while this might have looked undignified and disrespectful, Theo would have approved. She was flamboyant, always craving the spotlight. This was a hell of a way to get it, but I was convinced that she would never have wanted to let her death pass in quiet obscurity. There were some shouts of "Yes!!" from where her friends sat.

Susan: I was able to face the memorial with dignity in spite of myself. Every step I took on the short walk to the

Presbyterian Church brought a flood of memories, for those were familiar streets. I had walked them so often with and without Theo. I'd taken Fergie this way. She loved to carry a milk carton in her mouth when she walked, and stopped to be patted by everyone she met, drooping if someone ignored her. I'd ridden my bicycle this way almost every day in good weather, going down the sloping hill. I'd walked past the church to the library, the drugstore, downtown, sometimes as far as the A&P. I'd sat in the small park in front of the church in the spring, been in the Methodist Church across the street when they'd honored the novelist Stephen Crane, who had lived in Port Jervis, an event I'd organized. The kind of community thing you do in a small town because a small town really is a community.

And now I was walking to a community memorial to honor my daughter, a daughter barely out of her teens. It was all wrong: It was terrible. I was in a parallel universe. How many times had Theo walked along the main street to the middle school, passing the funeral home where her ashes ultimately went. The newspaper ran her obituary. Her obituary! Why, a year and a half from now there should have been a graduation notice. How could this be? How could it happen? Everything was completely and irrevocably wrong.

The church was packed. The whole town and people from rural places beyond seemed to be there. Fran and Dick Kitts had come from New York. Fran was on one side of me. Carol Forbes Jones, a friend from town, was on the other. They were holding me up. Theo's voice teacher played a medley of tunes in her honor, songs she had sung in that beautiful voice. I would hover in the hall listening to her sing in her room, knowing if I were caught I'd hear an indignant "Mothurrrr!" He also played "Memories" from *Cats*. I'd gone along on the bus, one of the parents always considered necessary on such field trips, when the high school music department went to Broadway, in Theo's junior year.

There were speeches at the memorial. Odes to and descriptions of Theo. The minister of the church spoke.

Regina Leone from high school, both touching and suit-
ably, affectionately funny.

Boyfriends past and present were there. A friend from
Syracuse sang "Sing Happy" in a lovely voice. Dan spoke.
It was my turn, but I couldn't. I shook my head and stayed
in my seat.

Afterward I stood calmly and greeted everyone as they
came past. I recognized some old friends from New York,
theater people who had summered on the property where
we lived in Forestburgh, New York. Congressman Benjamin Gilman was there. Port Jervis in Orange County was
his home turf, and he had lost several constituents on Pan
Am 103, more than any other congressman in the United
States. Dan and I had been active supporters of his Democratic opponent. That didn't matter anymore. Nothing mattered anymore.

We went home, back through those familiar, memory-
plagued streets. We went into the house. It would soon be
empty of our friends and Theo's friends. People had lives,
people had commitments and responsibilities. When the
last person left the large house, it felt like an abandoned
castle. Dan and I were alone, in the house, in the world.
Theo was real and warm to me still. Everyone else may as
well have been a ghost.

Chapter 3

DAN: In the days immediately following the twenty-first, neither of us thought much about the possible cause of the disaster. We both had some sort of vague idea that it was the result of sloppy maintenance due to airline deregulation. But at that point we didn't know and really didn't care—Theo was dead, that was the overwhelming fact. The cause was immaterial.

We didn't watch television, read newspapers, or listen to the radio. We were never contacted by anyone in the government. None of the reporters who had come to the house said anything about sabotage, nor did any of our local friends. Considering the state we were in, it seemed to be a subject that was best left alone.

The first I ever heard of the possibility that Pan Am 103 had been brought down by a bomb came in a phone call from a relative in Florida.

I finally began to follow the news again. I saw President Ronald Reagan being questioned about the bombing. I clearly remembered his commanding and masterful performance after the explosion of the space shuttle *Challenger* because Susan and I had written a book on that disaster. Three years later, when confronted with Pan Am 103, Reagan looked very old, very tired, and very confused. Yes, he said, it was a terrible tragedy, and the United States should respond somehow if they ever found out exactly who did it. He didn't sound as if he thought that was going to happen. If president-elect George Bush had a reaction, it didn't make the nightly news.

The most shocking revelation in those early reports was

that there had been a warning that a Pan Am plane from Frankfurt, Germany, where Flight 103 originated, was going to be bombed shortly before Christmas. This was the "Helsinki warning," received on December 5. A male caller with what was described as an "Arabic accent" contacted the U.S. embassy in Finland. The call warned of a bomb on a Pan Am flight to the United States from Frankfurt sometime before Christmas. After the bombing of Pan Am 103, U.S. officials insisted the call was a hoax. Hoax or not, the State Department cabled embassies and diplomatic posts all over the world. The warning was not withdrawn before December 21.

The threat was taken most seriously in Moscow because Americans returning to the United States generally went through Frankfurt and generally flew Pan Am, the main U.S. carrier out of Frankfurt. A notice about the threat was distributed to all Americans in Moscow, including journalists, and was posted on bulletin boards in the U.S. embassy. That's why the world found out about the warning so quickly after the twenty-first.

The Federal Aviation Administration (FAA) had been notified of the threat, but no warning was ever issued to the general public. Would things have been different if the warning had been made public? Theo would probably have chosen to ignore it; most twenty-year-olds think they are immortal. Her parents, however, would have been very alarmed and insisted that she change airlines. Perhaps a public warning would have resulted in increased security by the airline, or possibly the terrorists themselves would have been forced to change their plans. These are some of the "what-ifs" that became an obsession and continue to prey on our minds to this day.

When I first heard about the Helsinki warning, I thought it must have been one of those sensational rumors that inevitably accompany every disaster. I've never been a great fan of the government, but even I couldn't believe that they would be so callous as to warn one another but not tell the general public. I called the office of our congressman, Benjamin Gilman, who had attended Theo's memorial service.

I was given the number of a "Hotline" established by the State Department that was supposed to supply information to members of victims' families. After about four hours and a dozen tries, I managed to get through to the "Hotline." When I asked about the warning, the voice at the other end sounded harried and defensive. Yes, the voice admitted, there had been such a warning. But then the voice went on to add that several members of the State Department "family" had been on Pan Am 103 and that State was grieving their loss, just as we were grieving ours.

I responded that the State Department employees had known about the threat, and they had had a choice whether to fly Pan Am or not. Grudgingly the voice admitted that was true. "My daughter didn't have that kind of choice, did she?" I said. Grudgingly the voice acknowledged that too was true. Then I hung up. It was years before I could bring myself to even talk to anyone connected with the State Department without calling them names.

SUSAN: A bomb! So it wasn't an accident, a screwup by some faceless underling. Somebody had deliberately done this thing; somebody had bombed an American plane. Theo had been murdered. One victim in a mass murder. Suffering was spreading in waves across the lives of hundreds of people, maybe more, and it had all been planned by someone. Someone wanted this to happen.

I was madder than I'd ever been in my life. All the clichés: a boiling rage, a seething rage, they were all true, and they barely did justice to what I felt. I had always felt hurt when Theo was hurt. To think that someone had purposely set out to kill whoever was on Pan Am 103, and that meant Theo, made me so mad I couldn't stay in bed. I would collapse over and over in the course of a day. I would retreat to bed. But in between I would get up, go down to my kitchen desk, and desperately think about what I could do. I had no goals then, no plans, and no idea what I was doing or why I was doing it. I didn't even know how to begin.

Dan and I had some political savvy, a lifetime as news addicts and our share of marching and carrying signs against the Vietnam War. I had written one of the early women's liberation books. But for many years my battles had been against the powers that be in a small town, and really, a fight to get better lighting in the high school auditorium didn't exactly equip me for taking on the United States government.

DAN: The more closely we followed the news, the more awful it became. It turned out that there wasn't just one warning of a possible airline bombing—in the fall of 1988, the atmosphere was thick with credible threats to U.S. commercial aircraft.

On the morning of July 3, 1988, the USS *Vincennes*, patrolling the Persian Gulf during the Iran-Iraq war, shot down Iran Air Flight 655, a commercial airliner loaded with Muslim pilgrims going to Mecca. All 290 people on board—including 227 adults and 63 children—were killed. The Reagan administration called the tragic loss of civilian life an unfortunate miscalculation in a war zone.

The Iranians saw it differently. Images of bloated bodies floating in the waters of the gulf were broadcast around the world. At a funeral for some of the victims, thousands of Iranians chanted, "Death to America," and the president of Iran called for vengeance. "The Iranian nation and officials assert that they reserve the right to take revenge in any manner and at any place, and God willing, they will exact revenge with force."

A few days later a warning was posted on a U.S. State Department computer bulletin board available to U.S. businesses that operated overseas. It said that in response to the downing of the Iranian plane, "threat to U.S. interests worldwide has increased significantly . . . we believe Iran will strike back in a tit-for-tat fashion—mass casualties for mass casualties. . . . Targets could include aircraft, airports. . . . We believe Europe is a likely target for a retaliatory attack . . ."

That wasn't all. During the fall of 1988, the German domestic intelligence service had been conducting surveillance on a cell of a particularly violent Middle Eastern terrorist organization, the Popular Front for the Liberation of Palestine/General Command (PFLP/GC). The surveillance operation was called Autumn Leaves.

The PFLP/GC was led by a former Syrian army officer named Ahmad Jibril and operated out of Damascus with the full approval and protection of Syrian dictator Hafez al-Assad. Jibril also had close ties with Libya and increasingly with Iran. His group had been implicated in a number of terrorist attacks in the past, including airline bombings. In a February 1986 press conference in Tripoli, Jibril proclaimed, "There will be no safety for any traveler on an Israeli or U.S. airliner."

In October 1988, the German intelligence service began to suspect that Jibril was preparing to make good on that threat. The PFLP/GC cell in Germany was headed by Hafiz Kassem Dalkamouni, one of Jibril's key aides. In mid-October an old Dalkamouni associate, a Jordanian named Marwan Khreesat, arrived at Dalkamouni's apartment in the town of Neuss. Khreesat was well-known to intelligence agencies throughout the world as a master bomb maker. He was suspected of fashioning several bombs that had exploded aboard airliners.

Agents of the West German Internal Intelligence Agency trailed Dalkamouni and Khreesat as the two men went on a shopping trip where they bought electric and digital clocks, switches, batteries, screws, and glue, all of which could have been used in building bombs. They also taped hundreds of hours of phone conversations between Dalkamouni and Khreesat and people in Damascus. Khreesat said things like, "I've made some changes in the medication. It's better and stronger than before."

By October 26, German authorities were convinced that the terrorist group was about to carry out some sort of violent action. Starting at 7:45 in the morning, teams swept down on apartments and businesses in Frankfurt, Berlin, Hamburg, and Neuss. In an apartment in Frankfurt they seized a huge cache of weapons, including submachine guns, hand grenades, dynamite, TNT, and eleven pounds of the powerful Czech-made plastic explosive Semtex, enough to make more than a dozen bombs.

A dozen German agents surrounded Dalkamouni and Khreesat outside of a shopping mall in Neuss. In the trunk of Dalkamouni's car, the police found a Toshiba radio-cassette recorder (chillingly called a BomBeat) that had been converted into a bomb containing 10.5 ounces of Semtex connected to a timer and a barometric switch. The only possible use for such a device would be to blow up a commercial airliner in flight. It was remarkably similar to the bomb that less than two months later would destroy Pan Am 103, right down to the type of radio-cassette recorder that had been used.

In all, sixteen men were arrested on what appeared to be overwhelming evidence. Two of them, innocent bystanders, were released at once. But within twenty-four hours the inexplicable began to happen. Most of the other suspects were released as well, for reasons that have never been adequately explained. Within two weeks only three suspects, including Dalkamouni and Khreesat, remained in custody, and Khreesat himself was soon released, though he had actually been found with a bomb in his possession.

The German judge who released the suspects insisted that there simply wasn't enough evidence to hold them. Rumors hinted that some of those arrested, including bomb-maker Khreesat, had been double agents, working for German intelligence as well as the PFLP/GC. More than a decade later, this episode has remained shrouded in secrecy and still casts a long shadow over the entire Pan Am 103 case.

The German authorities apparently believed that they had been able to head off a major terrorist incident. News of the arrests and particularly of the bomb in the radio-cassette player were not kept secret. The news prompted the Federal Aviation Administration to send out a warning to all U.S.

airlines. On November 15, the Germans held a press conference during which the Toshiba radio-cassette was put on display. Two days later the FAA issued another security bulletin. It told airlines to be especially diligent in following basic security procedures of matching each bag to a passenger on the plane, because a bomb of this type, powered by Semtex, would be very difficult to detect by X-raying the bags alone. The British Ministry of Transport sent out warnings of its own, and a model of the Toshiba bomb was shown to security officials at Heathrow Airport in London.

Still no general warning was given to the flying public, and there was no indication that any airline anywhere in Europe tightened its security procedures as a result of the discovery in the trunk of Hafiz Dalkamouni's car. The British Ministry of Transport drafted a second and more detailed warning on December 19, but they delayed sending out the warning because they said they couldn't get a color photograph of the device. This warning was finally mailed out in mid-January.

The shock and outrage that we both felt at this stream of revelations is indescribable. The warnings were all out there. Why was nothing done? Why weren't we warned?

To top it off, all those TV and newspaper interviews with security "experts" and terrorism "experts" claimed that the public couldn't be warned because that would frighten people and disrupt airline travel, and that would hand the terrorists a victory. What was the successful bombing of Pan Am 103 supposed to be, a defeat for terrorism?

SUSAN: My rage would not be denied. I began by making phone calls and writing letters. Good citizen stuff, but it was the only thing I could think of. Have you ever tried to call a government office cold? I didn't even have one of those guides to Congress books. At first I couldn't get anywhere. Low-level aides answered the phones. I was told to write my congressman. I was put on hold, cut off by mistake, passed on to other aides; they would put me on hold and it would all start again. I was in such terrible shape I couldn't think clearly, but I kept calling. In early January I was wandering through a nightmare maze or hall of distorted mirrors. One lone, helpless voice trying to break through an indifferent bureaucracy.

The inauguration festivities for George Bush were underway in Washington when I reached some poor guy stuck in one of the congressional offices late on a Friday afternoon. I never got his name. I don't even remember where he worked. He was just one of the people I was handed over to down the chain of pass-alongs. He said to me, "Look, nobody here cares about this. Nobody's talking about it. If you want to get anything done, go to the media. That's all they pay attention to here. Get to the press." Oh, a tip of the hat and raise a glass of champagne in honor of that unknown man. Because whoever he was, he was so right.

I had already had some contact with the media. Just a day or so after the twenty-first, when I could barely talk coherently with anyone, I had given a long phone interview to Rich Lamb at CBS radio, talking about the house shiny with lights for Christmas and the loss of my only child. I gave that interview because even that early in the tragedy, I was afraid that America would soon forget Pan Am 103. As has often been said, America is an amnesiac country: forward-looking, glancing backward only in search of nostalgia. A friend of mine was told by a reporter sitting next to him watching the coverage of the crash in a New York bar on December 21, that you could give Pan Am 103 a few weeks in the news, and it would be gone. Not if I could help it. I started making phone calls, not to Congress anymore but to reporters.

DAN: Someone, perhaps it was that supreme political cynic Joseph Stalin, said, "One death is a tragedy. A million deaths is a statistic." Susan and I agreed, almost without discussion, that if there was to be a human face put on the tragedy it would be Theo's. Gravestones, statues, and monuments are quickly forgotten; they become roosting places for pigeons, not reminders of a life. Our memorial to Theo was going to be to try and keep this story and thus Theo's memory alive for as long as possible. We had no idea how long that would be, but it would be more than a couple of weeks anyway.

Almost immediately we opened our house to the press, and they came. The *Today Show* was there. A CNN crew did a special on Theo and one other Pan Am 103 victim. I don't recall many of the others, but they were almost without exception polite, considerate, and as nonintrusive as was possible under the circumstances.

There were a few odd incidents. This was the time when tabloid TV shows like *A Current Affair* and *Hard Copy* were just getting started. The producer of one of these shows called me and asked if I would go on television with a terrorist, Yasser Arafat! I had no idea what I would say to Arafat or what Arafat would say to me, but I agreed, though I was troubled by visions of Arafat and me arriving at the studio in bulletproof limousines with the shades drawn. A couple of days later the producer called back to apologize and these, I swear, were his exact words: "I'm sorry, Dan, Yasser can't make it. But don't worry. We'll get you another terrorist." He never did, and frankly I was relieved.

SUSAN: I didn't know the other families whose lives had been shattered by this catastrophe. The airline did not release what is called the manifest. Syracuse University was planning a memorial for January 18, and I had the list of names and addresses of the parents of the thirty-five Syracuse students who had died. I called the University and arranged for a place to hold a meeting after the service. Then I wrote to all the parents and asked them to come to the meeting. I couldn't hold a pen without my hand shaking, so my writing came out a scratchy scrawl. No matter, I was writing lots of people letters like that. Journalists. Columnists. Anybody who wrote about Pan Am 103. At some point I even sent a letter to the writer Graham Greene. God knows why.

Someone suggested I talk to Paul Hudson, an Albany, New York, lawyer whose sixteen-year-old daughter, Melina, had been on the plane. To die at sixteen is even more horrible than to die at twenty, and I was quite wrenched thinking about Melina. But I did talk to Paul. He was one of a handful of relatives who had gone to Lockerbie immediately after the disaster. He had somehow found the strength to cut through all the red tape and fight the exhaustion of despair, so that on December 24 he stood looking at the devastation of Sherwood Crescent in Lockerbie, where much of the wreckage of Pan Am 103 had fallen and where the eleven Lockerbie residents had been killed.

Paul told me the Syracuse families could form the nucleus for a group, and he wanted to come to the meeting, even though his daughter had not been a Syracuse student. He also gave me the name of Ralph Nader's airline security person, Chris Witkowski, who also wanted to attend the meeting.

Dan and I arrived in Syracuse, and how different everything seemed. Each time I'd gone to Syracuse before, I'd been happy, simply because Theo'd been happy there. She was always performing in something, and I loved to watch her onstage. Now I took one look at the student theater and knew this was the last time I would ever go to Syracuse.

The important memorial, as far as I was concerned, was the one the drama students put on for the six drama school students who had been killed. It was separate from the main university-wide memorial, and held at the theater. I looked at the pictures of those who had died that were on display in the lobby. Theo in costume. As Rumpelstiltskin in summer stock. As the bird in *Once Upon a Mattress* at Syracuse. There were pictures of others that I had remembered from shows. I was in a trance as I wandered around looking at all the pictures. It seemed so unreal, so impossible. Little more than a year ago I'd been here with other parents watching *A Midsummer Night's Dream*. Theo had been only nineteen. All of these kids had been so young, so talented. It was unthinkable that they were dead.

I brushed past Rosemary and Jim Wolfe. Jim was the father and Rosemary the stepmother of Miriam Wolfe. Theo and Miriam had been good friends. When we bought the Pan Am ticket for the twenty-first Theo had even said that her friend Miriam was coming back on the same flight. She looked forward to long hours of gossip with her. In London Theo and Miriam made plans to start an experimental theater when they returned to school. Would they have done it? Who knows? But they had energy and enthusiasm and the dreams that go with that. On December 21, they sat together on Pan Am 103.

At the theater there were individual tributes to each of the six students who died. Annie Lareau, Theo's friend and roommate, did Theo's tribute. She finished up by saying, "Wherever you are, Theo, I hope you're tall and blonde." I smiled through tears. Theo had always complained about being short. "Is this it?" she'd wail when she was sixteen. As for being blonde, well, all you have to do is walk into a theater or watch a movie to see that being tall, blonde, bosomy, and beautiful has smoothed many performer's career path, and Theo well knew it.

"I sing of the body electric," the kids at the memorial sang. I remembered the song from the movie *Fame*. "Theater is my life," Theo would say, joking around, but she meant it too. And as those who love performing do, she immersed herself in it. This was the memorial that touched me deeply, though sometimes I barely knew where I was. The kids onstage and in the audience laughed and cried, moving from one emotion to the other and back again in an instant, as the young can do. The tributes were affectionate, funny, and they vividly celebrated the lives of their friends.

DAN: In her tribute Annie Lareau related a story I had never heard before. It was an account of how Theo had tried to stop someone from leaving a party by rushing out of the apartment, across the street, and then throwing herself over the hood of the moving car. She was never passive. That was the Theo I knew. That was the Theo I lost.

SUSAN: The other memorial was very different. Donald Somerville had come with us. He was at the state university at Cortland, not far from Syracuse, and he knew several of the drama students through Theo, and had been at parties with them. As Donald and I entered the large chapel for the main memorial, Governor Mario Cuomo was there, and we caught his eye. Senator Pat Moynihan was there too. He spoke well, but rushed out early. It was a day for officials, a place where the politicians had to show up. It was like all such ceremonies: speeches and soothing words from people who had never known Theo or the other kids, and could not possibly be in mourning for them. A ritual performance, carried live in its entirety by CNN. Some people found comfort in it. I didn't disapprove or resent it. I just didn't care about it. I have never liked empty ceremonies. I sat alone with my grief. I barely listened.

As for the parents' meeting, I wondered if they'd come. They did, about fifty of them. They were all stunned and in pain. They had loved their children, and lost them. When everyone was together they looked at us, since we had arranged the meeting, and my heart sank. I had no idea what to say. Beyond writing letters to the newspapers and congressmen, I didn't know what to do next. Neither did Dan. Then, a bit late, and rather like the deus ex machina, Paul Hudson appeared. And he did know what to do.

Paul was a mild-looking, very soft-spoken man whose most prominent feature was the thick, dark-rimmed glasses he wore. He seemed shy and self-effacing, hardly the image of a leader. But in the emotional wreckage that was most of the victims' families in that room, Paul was very much in control, and he had a plan. He wanted to form an organization of family members to pursue certain goals, which he had listed. For example, he wanted to press for the prompt return of victims' belongings that had been recovered from the crash. We didn't care about that, but it was vitally important to many others. He had longer-term goals as well. A campaign for improved air security was among them. He asked for suggestions, and people who had been sitting mute began to speak up. Paul took all the suggestions down, often converting a confused and vague wish into a concrete proposal. He carefully collected everybody's name, address, and phone number.

Later there would be bitter discord among the families, clashes of personality and viewpoint. But in the beginning we were all united. Without Paul Hudson there would never have been an organization of Pan Am 103 families at all.

DAN: In January of 1989, neither Susan nor I was functioning very well. It took all the energy we could muster just to get through a day; long-range planning was impossible. Even at the best of times we weren't the sort of people who could have started an organization. We had both worked as freelancers for years—we worked on our own and preferred it that way. We were too disorganized to be leaders, too impatient, unsociable, and imperious to be followers.

Chris Witkowski, the executive director of the Aviation Consumer Action Project, a Nader-associated group, also came to the meeting. He passed out copies of *After the Crash*, a brochure filled with useful information about legal and insurance issues following an air crash, and he answered a variety of questions about airline security, terrorist threats, and other issues that no one in the government had been willing to talk to us about.

We left the meeting with a feeling that at least something concrete had been accomplished.

SUSAN: At 8:00 P.M. on a Friday late in January, the phone rang. A voice said, "This is Governor Cuomo." I was startled. I had called earlier and left a message that I wanted to talk to him. I didn't expect this, no secretary, no aide, just a direct, personal, "This is Governor Cuomo."

We talked for a long time. He asked me if I was religious and I said no. He didn't push it. I told him that I wanted to die, and he asked me what my daughter would want me to do. She would want me to live. He told me how his brother had lost a small child in a terrible accident, and how hard that had been. We talked about philosophy and ideals and whether there was a meaning to life. At the end he asked me what he could do to help. I asked him to do whatever he could with the State Department in getting victims' personal possessions back to the families who wanted them. He said he would. And he did. It was an amazing conversation. Very human and intimate and intense and not very political. I was a fan of Mario Cuomo anyway, but as we spoke I became more of a fan. I was impressed by his intelligence, the range and depth of his thought and his humanity. He was so unlike so many of the other powerful political officials I was to meet.

Chapter 4

DAN: A lawyer friend told me that after every commercial airline disaster there is going to be a lawsuit—no matter what. "You may find that too painful to think about right now, but the airline started thinking about it the moment the plane hit the ground. As far as Pan Am is concerned, you are now the enemy, and you have to protect yourself. Get a lawyer who is an expert in this kind of litigation—not me, I do mortgages, wills, and minor marijuana possession cases."

The lawyers were already gearing up for the Pan Am 103 case, and in the days immediately following December 21, we received several phone solicitations. Since friends were monitoring most of our calls, we never talked directly to any of these lawyers. A relative of Susan's, a woman she had not talked to for many years and barely knew anyway, called to offer her sympathy, and to put in a pitch for her son-in-law the lawyer.

Other Pan Am 103 family members were pursued much more aggressively. As parents of a student, we were not going to be one of the big-money cases. The big money would go to the widows of men who had held high-paying jobs. And a hefty percentage of that money would go to their lawyers. Some widows received personal visits from celebrity lawyers. We didn't get that treatment.

At Syracuse, Witkowski had warned us all about airline representatives. Typically after a crash airlines assigned one company representative to the family of each victim. The representatives were supposed to provide useful information and help guide a grieving and distraught family through the inevitable red tape associated with a sudden and violent death. These representatives could be genuinely helpful in small matters and appear to be a real friend, with your best interests at heart. But in the end they were employees of the company you were soon going to sue for a great deal of money, and therefore not to be trusted.

I recalled a *60 Minutes* broadcast I had seen some years earlier. It showed how the representatives of another airline—not Pan Am—had gathered information about crash victims that could be used against them in a trial. After a crash, people are emotionally shattered and very vulnerable, likely to pour out their hearts to anyone who seems sympathetic. In one case, a widow had told her friendly airline representative that her marriage had been on the rocks, and shortly before the crash she had been contemplating divorce. In court, defense lawyers could use this information to argue that since divorce was imminent, the widow could not reasonably have expected a high level of financial support, therefore her compensation should be less than if the marriage had been a stable one. In another case, parents of a boy who had died confided to their sympathetic airline rep that their son had been gay. Airline lawyers then argued that since a gay person was not likely to provide the couple with grandchildren anyway, compensation for his death should be lower.

A few days after the crash, I got a call from a woman who introduced herself as our personal Pan Am rep. She asked if there was anything she could do to help. At that moment Susan was just a few feet away, sobbing that her life was over. I just held out the phone so the rep could hear. Then I asked her if she could help with that. We never heard from our Pan Am rep again.

In talking to other family members, I found that most of them had been deeply suspicious of Pan Am reps from the start and would have little or nothing to do with them. One woman who did talk to her rep over a period of several weeks, and had come to regard her as a friend, found the rep scribbling notes after what she thought had been a purely private and personal conversation between friends. She immediately cut off all contact.

Virtually all of the families quickly came to hate Pan Am. For a while we hated the airline even more bitterly than we hated the terrorists who had actually planted the bomb. The terrorists seemed distant and shadowy figures, who might never even be positively identified. Pan Am was right there, and evidence of their deadly negligence began to unfold dramatically almost immediately after the twenty-first.

An Israeli named Isaac Yeffet, who had once headed security for El Al airline, began appearing regularly on television news shows. Yeffet now ran a security consulting firm, Ktalav Promotion and Investment or KPI. He had been commissioned by Pan Am to prepare a report on their security procedures. His detailed confidential report, submitted in September 1986, was devastating. He said that most of Pan Am's security was a mess and that its planes were particularly vulnerable to bombs placed in the luggage compartment—exactly where the bomb was placed on Pan Am 103. "The fact that no major disaster has occurred to date is merely providential," the report concluded.

Pan Am filed this scary report and then ignored it. Later Pan Am executives insisted that some of Yeffet's suggestions had been followed. In fact, Pan Am had done virtually nothing. Now Yeffet was telling the world about what he had told Pan Am.

SUSAN: I didn't want money from Pan Am. I wanted Pan Am executives and Pan Am employees who were responsible for the lousy security thrown in the slammer. Our lawyer friends warned us that a civil suit was only about money. It had nothing to do with justice; no one in Pan Am would go to jail. But I did know that continued bad publicity was going to damage Pan Am severely, maybe even put it out of business. And I very much wanted that.

I didn't know anything about what one lawyer did and another one didn't; what kind of law they specialized in. I had seen Alan Dershowitz on television for years, had read his articles and knew that he took up causes. I knew he had strong Jewish feelings, and this was a case of Arab terrorism. I knew he wasn't afraid to use the media to wage his campaigns. Dershowitz had a column in a newspaper about Pan Am 103 that seemed to beg for a response from victims' families. So I tracked him down at Harvard, where he was a professor, and left a phone message for him to call me. He did.

Dershowitz made it clear that he specialized in appeals cases and couldn't bring a civil suit against Pan Am himself. But his brother Nathan could. He said that he himself would be there in the background, though, someone we could turn to. He was very interested in the Pan Am 103 case. He also recommended Speiser and Krause, a firm that specialized in aviation law. When I hung up the phone, I was very excited and called my mother-in-law to tell her we had the famous Alan Dershowitz. But doubts crept in quickly.

I had friends who were lawyers in upstate New York who knew Nathan Dershowitz and warned me against going with any lawyer who was not specialized in the correct branch of law. I spoke to other lawyers I knew. They all said the same thing. They spoke very kindly and slowly to me, as if I were an idiot child. They made it clear that in spite of my intentions and desires, the law was the law and I didn't know anything about it. The law was unswerving, rigid. Those at the top of Pan Am were hedged round with legal protections. That was the way it was, and that was the way it would stay. Not Dershowitz, not the ACLU, not Clarence Darrow himself, should he return to Earth and take the case, would do any good. This was a civil suit, and it would follow the rules and it was about money.

I needed a top civil suit lawyer who specialized in aviation law. I was stubborn. I kicked. I thrashed around. I even called Nathan Dershowitz, who told me I could ignore all the advice I was getting and "march to a different drummer." But in the end I listened to my friends. I was worn out, sick with grief, and they were kind and caring and generous with their time. Anyway, everyone told me the case would be settled, not quickly, for nothing in the law is quick, but in the usual way. I was lost, miserable, and the lawyer, the suit, and everything connected with it didn't seem worth the bother. I'd stick to politics and the press.

DAN: By late January we figured we had better settle the lawyer business, so we went down to New York to do some lawyer shopping.

One of the lawyers we talked to was a famous old trial attorney and former judge. The wall behind his desk was plastered with photos of the judge and FDR. We decided to see him because he seemed to have a flair for publicity—and that was what we were looking for.

We told him about this. He smiled and said sure, as soon as he filed his lawsuit on our behalf "we can call a little press conference." We left unimpressed.

We talked to a prominent personal injury lawyer whom we had seen on television. He was cheerfully cynical. He told us it wouldn't make any difference if we got the best attorney in the world or the worst attorney in the world because all of the lawyers for both sides would finally gather in a room and settle on the amounts of money to be paid out and that would be that.

We told him about how the families of the Pan Am 103 victims were getting together to form a lobbying group. He just shrugged and said that he had seen family groups before. "They come and go," he said. They weren't going to affect the outcome of the case, but if attending meetings for a while made us feel better we should stick with it.

Another name on our list was Lee Kreindler. His firm, Kreindler and Kreindler, was on a short list of aviation law specialists that Witkowski had passed out at Syracuse. Our local attorney had told us he was the dean of aviation law in America. Our lawyer said that what would happen is that all the separate cases would be combined, and all the individual lawyers would form a plaintiffs' committee with Kreindler as the lead lawyer, because he would have the most clients.

Kreindler had a big suite of offices on Park Avenue, with a dizzying compass design in the carpeting. Lee Kreindler himself was a grandfatherly looking figure, who could appear benign, distracted, even a bit pathetic. This, we were to discover, was simply a pose that he adopted when there was something he didn't want to tell us or we were asking him to do something he didn't want to do. That persona could change in seconds in a transformation worthy of Jekyll and Hyde. Instantly his hearing and eyesight improved, his voice became strong and assertive, and he could overwhelm you with an avalanche of information called up from memory.

When we first met Lee that January day, he was in his assertive, confident mode. I asked him about the KPI report. He slapped the top of his desk and said, "I've got it right here in the drawer." He then briskly outlined how he thought the case was going to proceed. He said that since Pan Am 103 was an international flight, it was covered by an international treaty called the Warsaw Convention. According to these agreements, Pan Am was required to pay only $75,000 per victim even if they were found negligent. This, he said, was an antiquated and unrealistic figure and there would probably ultimately be a settlement in the case. The reason was that if a jury found Pan Am to be guilty of willful misconduct, the $75,000 cap no longer applied and the airline was liable for "compensatory damages." In short, if the jury found that Pan Am merely screwed up, it would cost the airline practically nothing. If the jury decided they really, really screwed up, it would cost them a lot more. Compensatory damages were supposed to be based on the amount of money that the victim could reasonably be expected to give to the person who was suing during a normal lifetime. The widows of high-paid executives were going to get a lot, the parents of children a lot less. For parents there were no provisions for emotional distress or what the lawyers called "loss of society." There was a remote possibility of receiving punitive damages, which could be huge, but Kreindler said a more realistic estimate based on past experience was a settlement of a few hundred thousand dollars for children.

We told him that we were less interested in the money than we were in trying to keep the memory of Pan Am 103, and hence Theo's memory, alive, and we thought publicity was essential. We wanted to hurt Pan Am; we wanted to put them out of business. A settlement wouldn't do that because they were covered by insurance. Bad publicity would hurt a lot more. Lee was visibly not too pleased with our approach. It wasn't that Kreindler was media shy; in fact, we discovered he was extremely adept at using the press for his own purposes. He just didn't want his clients going off on their own. But he allowed that there was really very little he could or would do to control our talking to the media at this point. If and when there was a trial, that would be another matter.

Normally before making any major decisions, Susan and I like to discuss things carefully, take time, sleep on it before coming to a decision. But it had been a very long day, and we were very tired. We just wanted to get the distasteful business of lawyer shopping finished. There was only one other name on our list, and this law firm had offices in the Pan Am Building. We couldn't bear to enter the Pan Am Building.

Kreindler must have sensed our weariness. Miraculously a letter was produced. I signed it without reading it. I still don't know what it said, but I guess it made us Kreindler's clients.

We were then politely but efficiently hustled out of the office. There was another potential Pan Am 103 client waiting to be interviewed. Getting people out of his office or off the phone without offending them was another of Kreindler's talents. We knew that Lee Kreindler was a bigtime lawyer and we were small-time clients. We assumed that our case would be turned over to one of the junior members of the firm and that we probably wouldn't see or talk to the big man again until the case went to trial, if it ever did. Boy, were we wrong.

SUSAN: I didn't want to go see lawyers at all. It meant getting up, getting dressed, and riding for a long time in the car. It was like going shopping. The lawyers would do their seductive best to impress us, and we were supposed to decide whether we liked the style of lawyer A or lawyer B— like those old movies where the customers sit in the store and models are paraded before them in different dresses for them to choose what they like.

We were so depressed, we might have been vulnerable to the seductiveness of the soft sell. But because we were so depressed, we were also indifferent. We knew we had to get someone. If nothing else, then the lawyers would go away and leave us alone. The last names on our list were two of the most important airline aviation lawyers in the country. One of the firms was located in the Pan Am Building. I couldn't face going into it. So we skipped them and went to Kreindler and Kreindler. They were on Park Avenue, overlooking the Pan Am Building, which was bad enough.

From one big room we were taken into another to meet Lee Kreindler, head of the firm. He seemed aggressive and strong, which I liked, but really I paid scant attention to anything he said. I had been done in by the Broadway theaters we had to pass on our way over. Pat Robinson, Lee's secretary, gave us a letter to sign. We signed. And that was that. I didn't think we'd ever talk to Lee again.

DAN: It was already dark when we went to pick up our car at the parking lot. The attendant recognized me from seeing me on television. He expressed his sympathy. I thanked him and told him that we had spent the day visiting lawyers.

"That's right," he shouted. "Sue 'em, sue 'em. Those bastards let your kid die. Take every penny they got."

A small group of people waiting for their cars overheard this. Everybody started nodding in agreement. I thought they were going to applaud. It seemed as if everybody hated Pan Am.

During early 1989 the media was doggedly pursuing Pan Am. New information about the airline's lack of security, its violations of regulations and downright deceptions, just kept rolling out. The lawyers like Kreindler must have been delighted because their case was getting stronger by the moment. On the other hand, we were devastated by every new revelation. It was so obvious that this disaster could have been prevented easily—yet so little had been done.

Perhaps because of its size, or its reputation as America's semiofficial airline, Pan Am had been the target of an unusually large number of terrorist threats and attacks. In 1970 a Pan Am plane in Cairo was attacked by hijackers. In 1973 terrorists in Rome attacked a Pan Am plane killing thirty and injuring many more. In 1975 there was an attack on a Pan Am plane in Burma. A bomb exploded on a Pan Am plane en route from Tokyo to Honolulu in 1982. One person was killed and more than a dozen injured, but it could have been lots worse.

In order to counter all the bad publicity and resulting loss of business, Pan Am stepped up its public-relations campaign. They tacked an extra five-dollar fee on every one-way international ticket, claiming that this would help to cover the cost of increased security. Security became one of the airline's main advertising points. Ads said they "would screen passengers, employees, airport facilities, baggage, and aircraft with unrelenting thoroughness." In a TV commercial that began airing in 1987, Pan Am's chairman boasted, "We at Pan Am are determined to provide a secure environment for our passengers." A highly visible symbol of Pan Am security was a team of "bomb-sniffing dogs" and their handlers, which were to be stationed in front of the airline's gates at JFK.

What could be more reassuring to the nervous air traveler than the sight of a team of well-trained bomb-sniffing dogs? But it was all a sham, a fraud. The dogs, as it turned out, were just a bunch of well-trained but quite ordinary German shepherds that had been leased from a Long Island kennel for a televised press conference. They might have detected someone trying to hide a bunch of hamburgers in a suitcase, but they couldn't have found Semtex or any other explosive.

The front line of Pan Am's defense were not well-trained bomb-sniffing dogs, but minimum-wage security personnel, who had received little or no training. The KPI report noted, "Most security officers have never seen explosive devices, whether real or dummy, nor have they handled explosives."

These badly paid, poorly trained, and often indifferent employees were working with equipment that couldn't do the job that it was supposed to do anyway. An X-ray machine will detect a handgun in a suitcase, but it won't detect a bomb if it is made from plastic explosives and concealed inside of a common object—say a radio-cassette player. On the screen it will look like an ordinary radio-cassette player.

Since not every single piece of luggage can be opened and checked, the Federal Aviation Administration had come up with a simple but logical security procedure. Everybody who checked in a piece of luggage had to be on the plane. That would assure that all attempts to use a luggage bomb would be a potential suicide mission. Not a perfect defense, but one that would certainly cut down the number of willing bombers. If a piece of luggage could not be matched to a passenger, then it would be taken off, opened and examined, or simply left behind.

That was supposed to be the rule, particularly at high-threat airports like Frankfurt. That was the rule contained under section 508 of Pan Am's own security manual.

It was, however, a rule that Pan Am, and indeed all airlines, resented and still resent. It can be troublesome and time-consuming and expensive to implement. For example, if luggage from a connecting flight cannot be matched with a passenger, it must be removed, even if it is already buried deep within a luggage container inside the cargo hold. Retrieving that luggage could delay the flight and might cause costly schedule disruptions, particularly at major airports like Frankfurt, where there were many connecting flights from all over the world.

Airlines complained that strict enforcement of such a rule could create chaos and bring international air travel to a halt during busy times, like the week before Christmas. But the rule was still on the books. In March 1988, Pan Am sought to get around this rule by purchasing more X-ray machines and X-raying all the baggage from connecting flights. The fatal flaw, of course, was that X rays couldn't detect bombs made with plastic explosives like Semtex, which were the explosives of choice for international terrorists.

In a telex Pan Am's top security executive, Daniel Sonenson, exulted that if a passenger failed to show up for a Pan Am flight, and his or her baggage was already on the plane, "We go!!!!" There was apparently no thought of applying the stricter baggage-matching standards in the tense and threat-filled late fall of 1988, when everybody involved in airline security knew or should have known that terrorists in Germany were building bombs made with X ray–undetectable Semtex. This was a decision that nine months later was to result in Theo's death and the deaths of 269 others.

Just who made the decision to rely completely on X rays was never entirely clear. The ultimate responsibility, however, would have been with Martin Shagru, who was at that time Pan Am's temporary top executive. Shagru insisted that he knew nothing about the change.

Like most people, we had assumed that a rule was a rule even if it was an inconvenient one. Pan Am was claiming that FAA security chief Daniel Salazar had agreed to allow them to waive the rule and rely solely on X rays. Salazar denied this. To be official, such a waiver would have to have been made in writing, and Pan Am was never able to produce that piece of paper. The airline argued there had only been a verbal agreement.

However, FAA inspectors had visited the Pan Am facilities in Frankfurt in the fall of '88. They either were unbelievably careless and failed to notice that Pan Am was violating the baggage-matching regulation—or they simply looked the other way. We never knew, and still don't.

Salazar was quietly moved out of his position as security chief to another position in the FAA. A "sideways promotion," one knowledgeable reporter told me. No one involved in the fatal decision to rely solely on X rays was ever really punished, or even properly identified. The bureaucracy of both the FAA and the airline were doing what they did best, not protecting the public, but protecting their own.

This was absolutely maddening.

Chapter 5

DAN: In the months that followed Theo's death, I kept seeing her. I thought every young girl with long dark hair was Theo—at least for a second. I've been told this reaction is a common one after someone you love dies. The mind lets you see what you want to see, and I wanted to see Theo more desperately than I had ever wanted anything in the world—a thousand times more. I couldn't imagine how someone could want something so badly and not have it.

She was in my dreams too. Not once did I ever dream of crashing planes and violent death. I dreamed about picking her up at the airport. I dreamed repeatedly that her death had been just a dream and she was really still alive. When I woke up there would be a moment of confusion—what was dream, what was reality. Then reality flooded in and destroyed the dream. I hated to wake up.

I felt her presence all over the house. In my career I had written a lot about ghosts. I never believed in them. To me they were always just good stories, and I had wondered how anyone could believe in ghosts. Now I knew.

One afternoon, late in the winter, I went into Theo's room. It had been left essentially unchanged, as if she could move right back in when the school year was over. Suddenly I felt—no, I *knew*—she was there. I looked over at the bed and could see the top of her head just peeking out from under the covers. She often slept with her covers pulled up to her ears. The image was so solid it knocked me back against the wall.

Of course, she wasn't there. It was an illusion sharpened by the bright sunlight that had warmed the room in that cold season and released hints of scent, perfume, makeup that clung to the carpet or to clothes still hung in the closet or folded in drawers. Yet the impression was so overwhelming, it remains with me today, more forceful and more real than practically any other memory from that time. I call it up in an instant.

SUSAN: I phoned the organization named "Parents of Murdered Children." What they had been through was ghastly. People whose daughters had been raped and murdered, sometimes as much as ten years ago. Sometimes the murderer hadn't been caught. Sometimes the murderer had been caught but hadn't been found guilty or hadn't served much time. Often, as with Pan Am 103, the crime had been preventable if the bastards who worked in the system had only done their jobs. Parents of murdered children's lives had been shattered. Yet they were still standing. They had survived. During the times when I didn't want to die, I fought to live. So I talked to them.

They were kind and savvy and patient, and spent hours listening to me and telling me their stories. I liked them. I liked the name of their organization too. The name told the brutal truth. One man I spoke to whose son-in-law had been stabbed to death praised me for fighting back. It was years later for him, and he was still enraged. Before the murder he had been a liberal and opposed the death penalty. Now he favored it and loathed Governor Cuomo for vetoing the death penalty in New York state. I defended Cuomo, and we had a brief chat about politics. "You'll change," he warned me. "You'll become a different person because of Pan Am 103."

"Not me," I said to myself as I hung up the phone. "That could never happen to me."

Another Parents of Murdered Children member told me he had become a minister and political activist after his daughter's murder because he couldn't go on doing the same work he did, living the same life he had, before the murder. He too encouraged me to fight back. I asked him if the black nightmare I was living in would ever lift. "Life will get easier," he said, "but it really doesn't get all that much better. We fought hard to make sure our daughter's murderer was caught. When he was found guilty, everyone came up to me and said, 'Congratulations, don't you feel great?' Glad, yes, but I didn't feel great. My daughter was dead. How could I ever feel great about anything again?"

I knew instinctively that this was true. I had just learned a useful lesson. You don't fight back to win when you've already lost, because you can't win. You fight back because it is the right thing to do. And you fight back because your rage will not allow you to do otherwise.

I fared less well with the organization called Compassionate Friends. This was a group where members had lost children or others through illness and accident. Very nice people, but the soft, schmaltzy religious glow of the people I spoke to from that group put me off.

My friends tried to help me by giving me grief books and including me when they got together, though I was no fun to be with. The books were either squishy, sentimental greeting-card tomes on grief, or they clinically described the "stages" of grief in a sterile way, then poured on the psychobabble.

As for the social occasions, I wasn't ready and wouldn't be for a long time. In early May of 1989, we went to a small party at a friend's house. I couldn't join in the chitchat, and when they talked about plans for Mother's Day, I fell apart and had to lie down and cry. My friends were very sad, and did their best. I saw them again later. Tried once more. Tried several times with friends. But conversations just floated past me. I may as well have been a log dropped down in the middle of the living room. I could contribute nothing. I was grieving and needed to grieve. I had to cry when I had to cry. Lunch one on one with friends didn't work any better. I was too depressed, always had a miserable time, and was miserable to be with. Even my in-laws, who called constantly and did their best to help in any possible way, seemed to be on another planet. I was far away from everyone. Nothing was helping. What to do?

We weren't rich people. As freelance writers we had to work hard every day just to stay ahead of the bills. Now work was impossible. I didn't have any money to pay a therapist, so I was stuck with whoever would see me for free. Neither the federal government nor the state of New York gave victims of violent crime money for therapy, or anything else for that matter, even though it was through the federal government's abominable neglect that the tragedy had occurred. Thanks to someone in Parents of Murdered Children, I got the name of a therapist in up-state New York, Eileen Leary. In addition, for a while I saw two therapists not far from where I lived.

One was a psychologist who very decently offered his services pro bono. He assured me that though he had never encountered anyone who had gone through what I was going through, he had treated people who had lost children from illness or accident. His was a tough, no-nonsense approach to grief. There would be no mollycod-dling from him. The sessions were loose and free-form. I would talk and talk, becoming more confused and frus-trated while he said nothing. Sometimes he'd interrupt and tell me he sensed I was "attempting to seduce him into an argument" and he wasn't going to allow that. I was always very angry in his office. My torment and pain bounced off him as if he were a statue. In between sessions, when I felt I had to talk to him or would grab a razor blade and slit my wrists, I would leave frantic messages at his office. It took him hours to call me back.

In the spring of '89, Dan was invited to speak at a school in the Midwest, and I was invited to come with him. It would mean getting on a plane. I didn't want to fly. I talked it over with this therapist. He told me he was all for people struck by disaster getting back into the flow of normal life as quickly as possible. He thought I should go.

When Dan and I reached the airport (deliberately not Kennedy) and stepped out of the car in the parking lot, I fell to the ground shaking. Dan got me to the terminal. I had stopped crying by then, but when I looked at the gate with its X-ray machine, I couldn't walk through it. So Dan and I wandered back and forth in front of the gate, rehearsing going through security until I felt strong enough to face it. Every minute of the flight, Pan Am 103 was in my head, and I could hear Theo screaming.

The other therapist I saw in those early months after the bombing was an ex-priest, a very humane and decent person. The problem was I scared him. He stared at me from frightened, rabbity eyes as I unleashed powerful emotions of rage and sobbing pain. His was a very quiet office, and the women who worked there spoke in soft voices. I couldn't have been more different.

He wasn't happy with our by now deep involvement in the Victims of Pan Am 103 group. "What are you going back there for?" he'd ask. He didn't want us to "stay" in the tragedy. "You have a lot to give," he said, and urged us to adopt a child. He and his wife had just adopted a child. If we didn't want to do that, he had a friend who worked with disturbed teenagers at the modern equivalent of a reform school, who needed placement in foster homes. Knowing I had a masters degree in social work, he suggested we take in some of those kids and try to help them. As a fellow social-worker friend of mine pointed out when we told him about this suggestion, taking in hostile teenagers who had been through hell themselves, and who might injure us, our animals, or burn down the house, wasn't a very useful suggestion.

The ex-priest wasn't the only therapist making the "find your salvation through helping children" suggestion. Flo Bissett had gone to a therapist who told her to "involve herself with other people's children." Flo had adored her son. "I can't look at children," she said. I understood because I couldn't either. When I looked at babies and small children, I saw Theo and bled pain.

Friends also urged us to adopt. I didn't want someone else's child. I wanted Theo. As Jim Wolfe said about Miriam, "I took her on camping trips in the mountains when she was little, and she never got so much as a scratch, because I protected her. She was my flesh and blood."

DAN: I always resented people who told us that because Theo had been murdered we should therefore go out and do good deeds, like feed the hungry on Thanksgiving. That is a noble thing to do, but the people who made such suggestions weren't feeding the hungry on Thanksgiving. They were having a big dinner with their families. They seemed to assume that if we went out and found people who were even more miserable than we were that would make us feel better.

One of the great myths of all of this, and you read about it a lot, is that tragedy is ennobling. It makes you a better person. Oh no, it doesn't. I was a kinder, better person before December 21, 1988. Now I'm angry and bitter. Early on, after we found out this was a bombing, we had a press conference, and I remember myself saying I don't want any bombing in retaliation for this act. A couple of years later we were talking to a group down at the United Nations, and I found myself saying, maybe I was wrong about that because nothing else has happened. We should retaliate. We should bomb them. I wasn't even aware that change had taken place till I heard the words coming out of my mouth. This change is not something I'm proud of, it's not the way it should be, it's just the way it is.

SUSAN: The therapists kept trying to get me to take drugs— oh, excuse me, the proper word to use is the far more respectable "medication." Ironically, alcohol is viewed as a horror by every therapist I have ever encountered. They all sound like teetotalers. Avoid the fatal glass of beer. But legal drugs are the great American cure-all. Prozac was the drug of the hour, no doubt to be replaced someday by some other wonder drug. The therapist as Prozac pusher.

I took Xanex in a small dose for a while. A psychiatrist somewhere in the mix got me to take the antidepressant for a few months. It didn't help me, and I got off it. I can still see that same psychiatrist gazing out the window at a vivid sunset and saying, "Pan Am 103 is like fate." At which point she lost me. Pan Am 103 was not "fate," it was deliberate mass murder.

The ex-priest told me I should go into a hospital. "Get some rest. You need quiet. Maybe they can help you." I'd reach down for strength, and there was no strength. Just as in the case of giving in and getting on a plane when I didn't want to, I was too weak to resist the therapist's suggestion, so I went to a hospital.

The beautiful grounds were inviting. They were actually one of the main selling points of the place. Of course, one could only stay a month. No lengthy hospitalization in this well-maintained facility would be possible. Was this the result of some great change in clinical theory? No. Insurers would only pay for a month. Rich people could stay longer. But for us poor hangers-on of the middle class, there would be thirty-one days, and out.

I talked to two women psychiatrists. One was pregnant. I felt terrible about what I was doing to Dan. He had the burden of Theo's death and of my, as they would have said at one time, "nervous breakdown." Like a tape recorder I would go over and over incidents from the past, lament selecting the twenty-first for Theo's return from London, yell at him for every small thing that went wrong, like the time he put the garlic press in the dishwasher and took off its protective coating. "I'm afraid I'm going to kill him if I keep going on like this." That tore it. They exchanged looks. I tried to explain what I meant: Not that I was going to shoot him, but that he was going to have a heart attack. Just the other day I was flailing him so cruelly that he put his hands to his head and shouted to himself, "Hold on, hold on!" But the psychiatrists wouldn't listen.

They called Dan in, and he fought for me like a shining knight. It took a few minutes to get going, but soon I began fighting for myself too. The psychiatrists talked up a storm to persuade me to sign myself into the hospital and get on medication pronto. No question it was a temptation to chuck everything, and be taken care of. I looked out at the beautiful grounds. I thought about escape into peace and quiet, escape into the numbing effects of medication. Forget the politics. Forget trying to get justice. Just escape. Be passive. The world loves passivity.

Passivity is what the media pushes with almost every story about overcoming tragedy, "moving on" and finding "closure," that anemic word that is appropriate for getting a mortgage, not for losing a child. That's what the rabbis, priests, and most of the ministers I had encountered so far pushed. That's what grief therapy pushed. I had gone to one group therapy session with Pan Am 103 families where the therapist, a Southerner wearing a huge cross, couldn't work hard enough to encourage in the families one of the few psychobabble words I do like, "denial." She didn't hold with fighting the government or anything else. Depression was okay. Raw anger wasn't acceptable.

"I'm worried about you, Susan," she said in front of the entire group. "Open your heart," she said, making the word "heart" two syllables. She sounded exactly like a Baptist preacher trying to get a sinner to see the light. I held my ground. At the end of the session, she came up to me to smooth things over. "We need our fighters," she said weakly. Who was she kidding? Fighters were persona non grata.

Years later I wrote an article for *Time* magazine in which I coined the phrase "the grief industry." It is that combination of therapists, drug companies, and clergy who, while hypocritically acknowledging anger as a grief symptom, really do everything they can to take anger away, or to reduce rage over a horrible injustice to something that can be overcome by hitting a punching bag or riding an exercise bike. They work to keep anger private. They are all like the Borgs in *Star Trek*. Their motto: "Resistance is futile."

But anger is a saving emotion. It surges through you and makes you strong and energetic. When you're mad, you do brave things. That makes anger dangerous. The powers that be never want anger. Never want resistance. How convenient for them that the grief industry and the media preach acceptance, forgiveness, and resignation.

So there I was facing the two psychiatrists in a hospital with a clear-cut choice before me. Be a passive victim or stand up against evil. But I didn't really have a choice. By a policy of deliberate neglect and calculated indifference, the government was doing what it could to silence the Pan Am 103 families and get the bombing out of the news so that nothing would have to be done about it. As Dan had said to me, "They count on people being too destroyed to fight back." Well, they couldn't count on me. I would stay angry. Whatever hell I was in, it was going to be an active hell. If Dan and I died from fighting, then we'd die. We were going to die anyway someday. Might as well die a mensch.

My decision was made. Dan and I walked out of that hospital, through those beautiful grounds, and came home. I hugged Fergie and Max as soon as I got home. They needn't worry. I wasn't going to leave them. I wasn't going to run away.

DAN: I never had much faith in therapy. Talking about my feelings to a stranger seemed a waste of time, a sign of weakness, an exercise in futility. I doubt I could talk honestly to a therapist if my life really depended on it. I went with Susan to some of the sessions, but after a while I was reduced to a hostile and sullen silence. What particularly bothered me was a perceived subtext to all the therapy talk. We were told that we had to "let go" of Theo, allow her to become "only a memory." No one was quite crude enough to say "put it behind you" and "get on with your life," but they were close. I had no intention of "letting go" or allowing Theo to become "only a memory." She had been brutally murdered. I wanted justice. Hell, I wanted revenge—on Pan Am, on the terrorists, on anyone who had done this or allowed it to happen. The message I was hearing was one of resignation and passivity. I hated it. I wasn't interested in "feeling better" or "finding peace." If that's what I had been looking for, I would have gotten a bottle full of pills or a bottle full of gin.

Finally I couldn't even go to the sessions anymore. I just sat out in the car and waited. Sometimes I would bring the dog to keep me company.

At winter's end Susan had been advised to talk to someone at a large mental health facility in Westchester County. I didn't like the idea, but she made an appointment and I drove her there.

As usual I sat outside in the car. After about an hour Susan came out and told me that they wanted to talk to both of us. The talking was done by a young woman psychiatrist. She said that in her opinion Susan should be hospitalized immediately. The hospital was on the other side of the parking lot, and she could be walked over there just as soon as the proper papers were signed. I could bring personal items like pajamas and toothbrush later.

I was horrified and frightened. I was convinced that institutionalization—that's what it would be—would shatter Susan's fragile self-confidence. And for purely selfish reasons, I didn't want her to go away because I didn't know how I could survive without her, even for a few days. I was no shining knight, I was just damn scared.

"No one here cares about you like I do," I told her. I was absolutely opposed to her going into the hospital, and I talked her around to rejecting the idea. It wasn't that hard, because I think I was only reinforcing what she already had decided.

I just wanted to get out of the place as quickly as possible, but we were told that the director had to talk to us first. He was a very thin, sinister-looking man (or so he appeared to me at the time). He listened to us for a few moments, and then very deliberately and obviously picked up the forms that had been filled out and tore them up, leaving no record of Susan's visit. To this day I don't know what that gesture meant. All I wanted to do was go home.

That was the lowest point. After that I think we both realized that if we were going to make it at all, we would have to make it on our own.

A few months later the psychiatrist from the hospital called to find out how things were. I talked to her. She seemed surprised and, I felt, almost disappointed to discover that Susan was still alive. I was not friendly, and we never heard from her again.

SUSAN: I didn't give up on therapy. Perhaps it's not accidental that the best therapist was the person I'd found through Parents of Murdered Children. Eileen Leary was a grief therapist who worked mainly with parents whose children had died. She lived far away from me. I called her early that spring, hoping she could recommend a therapist nearby, but instead she offered to take me on at no cost except the phone bill.

From the start Dan noticed that I felt better after I talked to Eileen. I liked her. She had a strong streak of Irish rebel in her, and she didn't give a damn about respectability. She was religious, in a quirky, mystical way, which made her tremendously optimistic and confident, yet the optimism was leavened with a strong dose of down-to-earth good sense and think-fast inventiveness. "I have never put a grieving parent in a hospital," she said firmly when I told her about the psychiatrists at the hospital. Her response to the overpowering emotions I sent down the phone line to flood her? "I am not afraid of grief." I met her in person once at a Victims of Pan Am 103 group therapy session. She saw me on television from time to time. Years later we would meet once again. We didn't need to see each other. Our voices were enough.

What was different about Eileen from the other therapists? First of all she listened, really listened and didn't answer in jargon. She had no hidden agenda. No rigid routine response. She sized me up, then shaped herself to what I needed. Add experience and natural talent, and you have Eileen. When I said I wanted to kill myself, Eileen told me to lean on her and call her any time day or night when I needed to talk. She was true to her word, getting back to me within minutes to give me one of her "prepackaged pep talks." Sometimes I could only get through an hour and it was back on the phone.

She fought my depression by building me up. "Susan, you are in better shape than you think you are. You are facing the truth. You are fighting back. You're a survivor. It's those survivor skills that are going to save you. I worry a lot more about grieving people who don't show emotion, who don't get angry enough, than I do about you. Keep fighting." My war wasn't her war, and we didn't talk much about the specifics of the Pan Am 103 fight for justice. But she never tried to stop me from doing what I had to do. She was proud of me for doing it.

She fought my panic. "You've got no place to stuff. So scream when you have to. Let it out." She fought self-punishment and guilt. "You would have thrown yourself under a steamroller to save Theo. You didn't have a crystal ball. You didn't kill her by picking December twenty-first for her return. Her life was in the hands of others. They failed to protect her. The terrorists killed her. Not you. Now, go have a cup of tea and play with the animals. Go pat Fergie." And she fought hopelessness. "You got up today. You got dressed. You made dinner. You read for an hour. That's enormously hard to do. What a victory!"

She never put me under pressure to achieve a goal by a specific time. "There's no such thing as a grief schedule. Everybody's different. You'll do things as you're ready to do them. What, you talked to a friend on the phone today. You went with Dan to a movie. What a victory!"

During our regular phone sessions I told her all about Theo, how much I loved her. "There was only one Theo," Eileen would say in return. "She was irreplaceable." And I'd tell her another story about Theo because I remembered everything. In the spring of '89, a whiff of lilacs brought a flashback of nineteen years of spring memories. I gasped and had to hold on to the sink counter to keep from falling down. I called Eileen. When I watched a Pan Am 103 documentary one winter's day, I could feel the warm wind that swirled at JFK on that September evening when Theo left for London. The wind was so real that Dan had to make me a glass of warm milk, and I sat shaking for

an hour. I talked to Eileen about this. I'd talk about so
many things: my life, my childhood, Eileen's dog, my dog,
the cat she had that died and how much she had mourned
the animal, my cats, the dreams where I'd find Theo. The
dreams where I couldn't find her. The time I dreamed she
was all in black playing Sandy in *Grease*, but the song was
hideously slow and distorted, as if played at the wrong
speed. I woke up drenched in sweat.

Ours were and are real conversations, each of us cutting
in, going back and forth. My experiences, my insights.
Eileen's observations, her insights. "With most people grief
settles into one or another dominant emotion over time.
You run the gamut," she said. "Grief is a roller-coaster ride.
It will get easier in time. No rose garden, but you'll be able
to do what you can't do now. You'll have lunch with your
friends again, I promise."

It was Eileen who encouraged me to bake bread, to
enjoy the soothing comfort of kneading dough. To keep
up those long walks. To grab the vacuum cleaner, do the
housework, boring mechanical housework. Beats staying
in bed, structures the day, and keeps you moving. To be-
ware of surprises. From Eileen I learned the benefits of
watching familiar movies and reading familiar books over
and over again. I still do that. It's P. G. Wodehouse, Jane
Austen, Arthur Conan Doyle, and Shakespeare. Wodehouse because he makes me laugh and sets me down in a
make-believe world I wish I could live in. Sherlock
Holmes because he is what justice should be and his world
is thrilling, far better than the real one. The Divine Jane I
had always loved. And I turned to Shakespeare's
tragedies because they are everything that psychobabble
is not.

Eileen did not make false promises. In time the constant
falling apart became less frequent, became what I call mini
breakdowns. I still have them. But they are much rarer.
Though Pan Am 103 never goes away, the days are not
black all the time. All sense of well-being is gone, real happiness disappeared with Theo's death. But I have my
distractions and escapes. I can see friends, keep up a con-

versation, enjoy good food, enjoy a martini, read a good book. It's not much of a life, but it's something, and it has its moments.

All the king's horses and all the king's men weren't able to do much for Humpty Dumpty, but Eileen took the "me" that lay in fragments after the Pan Am 103 bomb blast and helped glue those fragments back into a whole human being. If only there were more like her.

DAN: By spring we were trying to crawl out of depths of despair in a typical way for us. We decided to get another animal. Our cat Max's breeder offered us a new kitten, a beautiful little brown-patch female. We named her Hope—for obvious reasons. When we got her home, she took one look at Max and decided that he was the center of the universe. She attached herself to him and paid scant attention to either of us. It is a relationship that has not changed one bit over the past decade. She has good taste, but she is not the best companion.

By summer I felt that we were strong enough to get another dog. Over the years we had owned many different breeds. I was determined to get another Clumber Spaniel. Clumbers aren't easy to get. They're rare, difficult to breed, and popular; there is usually a long waiting list. But a breeder friend in Rhode Island just happened to have two litters at her kennel, and she moved our names to the top of the list. We drove out to Rhode Island in the summer to see the dogs. I sat on the lawn with about a dozen Clumber puppies jumping on me, pulling on my shoestrings and shirt cuffs. It was the first time since that phone call on December twenty-first that I actually felt happy.

We picked up our dog several weeks later. It was a male, nearly all white. We called him Hugo, after the Sherlock Holmes character Hugo Baskerville, but also after Hurricane Hugo, which devastated Savannah in September 1989. The joke was that Hugo the dog did to our living room what Hugo the hurricane had done to

Savannah. For the next several years both Fergie and Hugo accompanied us practically everywhere we went, and that meant we didn't go many places except to dog shows.

Chapter 6

DAN: On February 4, 1989, Paul Hudson arranged for a Manhattan press conference. I drove down alone. Susan really wasn't up to that much activity yet. A friend had to stay with her all day; she couldn't be left alone.

The room in the Grand Hyatt Hotel was packed with media. There were about thirty relatives there. Many had pictures of their dead child or husband pinned to their clothes. Some wore large buttons with the picture of the dead person (a term few used, preferring "loved one" or some other euphemism). We all looked lousy, like we hadn't slept in days.

Paul read a long opening statement about airline security, warnings, and a lot of other things family members had talked to him about. The real guts of the news conference were the brief personal statements by a collection of family members. I talked about the warning of a Pan Am bombing made to the U.S. Embassy in Helsinki on December 5, concluding, "If the warning was a hoax, why is my daughter dead?"

The most moving and symbolically significant testimony came from a woman whose sister had been one of the flight attendants. She talked about going to the airport in Houston to retrieve her sister's body. When she got to the airport, there was a crowd of reporters. They were there to cover the arrival of president-elect George Bush, who had returned to Texas for his annual quail hunt. The president-elect smiled and waved and talked about how he was getting ready to assume the presidency. He was happy, everybody was happy.

Then the woman went to the cargo area. There were no crowds or cameras there. Her sister's coffin, packed inside of a cardboard box, was delivered on a forklift truck. No ceremony, no dignity, no nothin'.

That the bodies of the victims were returned as ordinary cargo in a haphazard fashion was one of the most bitter complaints of many family members. People were called without warning and told to come down to the airport and pick up their "shipment." One woman described how her brother's body was delivered in the livestock area. The family of twenty-year-old Karen Hunt was actually sent the wrong body. Her body had been switched with that of another victim, and the FBI did not straighten out the mistake until just an hour before Karen Hunt's body was scheduled to be buried in the wrong grave.

Susan and I had never attached any great significance to bodies. Dead is dead was our view. Besides, we weren't really strong enough to handle the details of dealing with Pan Am or Scotland. All of that was taken out of our hands by family friend Charles Graves, who spent a grim Christmas and beyond locating dental records for identification and doing all the other morbid but necessary tasks. He even arranged for the return of Theo's body directly to Port Jervis.

When Theo's body finally did arrive in January, someone in town said to me: "That must be a great comfort." It wasn't. We had her cremated, and it was our plan to scatter the ashes on the grounds of the Forestburgh Theater, a summer theater where Theo had worked for several years, located just a few miles down the road from the house where she spent her first five years. In the end we couldn't even bring ourselves to do that. Her ashes just sat in the funeral home. Though it was on the main street of Port Jervis, I tried to avoid passing the place. We should have scattered the ashes at the theater; that would have had some meaning.

Another angry complaint from those at the news conference was that the government wasn't communicating with them at all. People were sending anguished letters to the President, to the secretary of state, to everyone they could think of, and there was no response from Washington. There wasn't even an official letter of condolence. The media was filled with tales of terrorists, but as far as the new Bush administration was concerned, the bombing of Pan Am 103 was something that had happened far away in a foreign land, and wasn't really very significant anyway. They didn't want to get involved.

After the press conference a reporter said to me, "This must have been very hard."

"No," I replied. "Talking is easy, going back home and facing the reality that I'm never going to see Theo again is what's hard."

By mid-February a fledgling group calling itself "Victims of Pan Am 103" was formed at a meeting on Long Island. Paul Hudson was naturally made chairman. Second in importance was Bert Ammerman from New Jersey, who was given the title chairman of the political action committee. Bert was a balding, thick-waisted man with a loud voice and a bluff, outgoing manner. He was almost the complete opposite of Paul. I took an immediate dislike to him. The feeling wasn't entirely rational, but I knew where it came from. Bert was exactly what he looked like, a onetime high school football coach who had been jumped up to the position of assistant principal. It was a type I knew well from Port Jervis, and he was just the sort of person Theo had often complained about. I felt very unhappy that he would, in a sense, be representing Theo, who would have hated him.

Bert's brother Tom had been on Pan Am 103, so he was an authentic member of this small and exclusive club that no one had wanted to be a part of, and no one could quit. Bert was one of the hardy few who had gone over to Lockerbie right after the crash. He was energetic—"proactive" was a favorite word—whereas Susan and I and most other family members were still at the barely functioning stage. He had every right to the position he was given. I still didn't like him.

SUSAN: Being at a Pan Am 103 family group meeting was a mixed blessing. There I was in a room filled with victims, each with a horror story like my own. I was free to cry, whereas with an ordinary group of people I would have been expected to hold myself together, to smile and say the appropriate thing, to wear a mask. Here I didn't have to pretend, and we could all grieve together. I could be with no other group at that time. But so many people in so much pain was overwhelming. And though some tried to be stoic, most of us were ruins of our former selves. Part of the horror of Pan Am 103 was that we had to form a group and wage a fight when we barely had the strength to crawl out of bed.

When I went to my first group meeting, I was so slumped in depression I couldn't focus on any one person in that sea of mourners. But I was too restless to sit still and wandered around. Wandering around, I came face-to-face with others. We'd talk, and I had come to know individuals. At first it was the people who had some connection with Theo whom I noticed. Lynne Fraidowitz lived in New York. Her son Daniel Rosenthal wasn't one of the Syracuse students, but he too was studying in England and had met Theo and Miriam in London. They'd become friends, and at the last minute he decided to fly back with them. So Theo had held a ticket that was a countdown to murder for months, while Daniel had barely swooped up his at flight time.

Nicole Boulanger was a senior at Syracuse who dreamed of starring in musicals on Broadway. She was vibrantly talented and had even gotten her mother, Jeannine, involved in amateur theater. Jeannine had collapsed at the airport on December 21, screaming, "My baby," when the news of the crash was confirmed. The television cameras loved the image and sent it around America. Like Theo, Nicole had her return ticket with her when she left. When I met Jeannine, she was quiet and practically motionless behind a wall of shock. "I feel like I signed Nickie's death warrant when I signed for the ticket," she told me.

Flo Bissett, who had been calm at JFK, wept desperately when I met her again. "Our lives revolved around those kids," she sobbed, meaning hers, Ken, and mine, Theo. The hopes of the Bissetts were pinned on Ken, who was a scholarship student at Cornell. Adopted when he was only four days old, Ken also had a third adoring adult in his orbit, close family friend John Anselmo, who lived with the Bissetts. Flo was a sturdy but very small woman. I hugged her, and it was like holding a bewildered, frightened child trapped in a war zone.

Turhan Ergin had been a drama student with movie-star looks. So thoroughly destroyed was his body, he had to be identified by his fingerprints. Turhan's father, who was a doctor in Connecticut, his mother, Florence, and their three remaining children looked to me to be people who had had a good life and who were deeply attached to each other. Florence told me how hard it was even to drive the car because she missed the way Turhan had draped his arm over the back of the car seat. One night she dreamed that her own arm had been cut off. "I know what it means. I've lost my good right arm; Turhan was my good right arm." When I had first seen Florence at Syracuse, she was an attractive woman. When I met her again, she was neatly dressed and carried herself with dignity, but her face was ravaged. The physical effects of the horror were taking their toll.

I liked Joanne Hartunian. She was a lady in the best sense of the word. Her daughter Lynne had been afraid of flying home, worried about bad weather. "I told her it would be all right, just a little turbulence." Joe, her father, and Joanne had planned a grand homecoming for Lynne after her glorious trip abroad. There was a splendid Christmas present awaiting her, a shiny new car in the garage, just for Lynne. When the news hit, Joanne ran from room to room of her home in upstate New York repeating, "Lynne is gone, Lynne is gone."

When I first met Sal Capasso, he was too stunned to say much. His wife, Betty, was a warm and friendly woman who had been baking cookies when she got the news. They described their son Gregory as a lively kid with a good sense of humor. Gregory had been a student at the State University of New York.

The gifted Kate Hollister had wanted to be a science fiction writer. Her mother, Babette, had learned about Victims of Pan Am 103 from me. The living victims of the disaster were phoning one another and finding each other. Hope Asrelsky, mother of Rachel, who was good at many things, liked music and books. Hope still expected to see Rachel at her elbow when she set the table. Hope, Babette, and I might have gotten to know each other anyway, if we'd met some other way, for we had much in common. But for now, all that counted is that we shared a fragment of Pan Am 103.

The terrorists had done their work well. There were people in the group who had lost their only child, as we had. The Coaker family lost twin brothers. Krisann Coyle lost her twin sister Patricia. The young guy in the army who had to rush to be on time for the flight, he was gone. And the African American Syracuse student whose brother had died in a car crash not long before, she too was gone. A whole family with three little girls was gone. The young man who had treated himself to a trip to England to celebrate overcoming drug addiction, he was dead. There were little children without fathers, for whom terrorists and bombs became as real as toys. When I came home at night from a family meeting, I was exhausted after being buried all day in so much tragedy.

DAN: One hundred and three days after the bombing of Pan Am 103, April 3, 1989, the Victims of Pan Am 103 group organized a memorial vigil in Washington. The aim of the vigil, which was to be held in Lafayette Park, across the street from the White House, was to get publicity and put some pressure on the administration to act on improving airline security, but primarily to get the White House to authorize an independent investigation of the bombing. The official investigation by the United States and Britain seemed to be going around in circles. As always our complaint, the complaint of all the families, was that we weren't being told anything. The group had adopted the motto "The Truth Must Be Known." We all wore Pan Am blue buttons with those words on it.

Susan and I hadn't been to Washington in years. The last time was when Theo was about ten years old. We took her on the standard Lincoln Memorial, Capitol Rotunda, Smithsonian Institution tour. But we also stayed in the Watergate Hotel. We figured it was good for her to know that there was more, and less, to our government than marble statues and framed documents.

Between two and three hundred family members gathered across from the White House, and easily as many media representatives from all over the world. Paul and Bert gave brief speeches, there was some reading of poetry—bad poetry, but deeply felt—and there was what was to become a regular ritual at all Pan Am 103 memorial events, a reading of the names of the 270 victims.

We had each been given a white carnation labeled with the name of one of the victims. One by one we walked up and wove the flowers into a large evergreen wreath. The wreath was then carried across the street to the gates of the White House. A nervous-looking guard opened the gate to accept it, but when he tried to shut the gate again, the crowd of relatives surged forward.

Eleanor Hudson, Paul's wife, was near the front of the crowd. She shouted that there were more flowers to deliver. "Take the flowers," she told the clearly alarmed White House guard. "Take the flowers."

Then she turned to the crowd. "Pass up your flowers! Hurry! Pass up your flowers! They're closing the gate!"

Bouquets and individual flowers that people had carried on buses and in cars to Washington were passed hand to hand up to the White House fence. Eleanor, now quite hysterical, was screaming, "Take the flowers! Take the flowers!" Others in the crowd took up the cry. The gates closed, but there was a shower of flowers, thrown at and over the White House fence.

President Bush had finally agreed to meet with a select group of five family members before the vigil. The meeting was scheduled to run about fifteen minutes, but it went on for nearly an hour. People who attended the meeting told us that the President said little and mostly listened to the requests for action on airline security and an independent investigation of the bombing. At the end of the meeting, he said that he was touched and would consider everything he had been told very carefully. He then went off with Egypt's president, Hosni Mubarak, to throw out the ball for the opening day of the baseball season in Baltimore. A few hours later Secretary of Transportation Samuel Skinner, who was the administration point man on Pan Am 103 matters, issued a press release that flatly rejected virtually every suggestion that had been made at the meeting. So much for careful consideration.

During the day family members also did some lobbying. We were each given the names of two or three senators whose offices we were to visit, to urge their support for an independent investigation. I went to three senatorial offices, and while I didn't get to actually see a living senator, I did talk to a number of sad-faced and sympathetic young aides.

What I remember best about that first visit to the Senate Office Building was how confusing it was. The numbering system on the offices seemed to be designed specifically to mislead the uninitiated. I've decided that a lot of Washington is designed specifically for that purpose.

SUSAN: On the bus trip to Washington I sat behind two women who were friends of a Pan Am 103 victim's family. They chatted about ordinary life, movies they had seen, a child going off to visit Europe. There was nothing wrong with their conversation, but it made me edgy and anxious. It reminded me of how far away ordinary life had become for me in those few months since the bombing. The easy flow of talk, the casual references to travel, the pleasure of looking forward to a dinner out or a shopping trip were unattainable. I remembered Dan's comment, "Theo will always be just yesterday and a lifetime ago." Anything behind the seismic date of December 21 was a lifetime ago.

We entered Washington by the back door, so to speak,

driving through the black slums. There was some grum-
bling about "the awful neighborhood" from aunts and
cousins of some of the victims, but not from wives, hus-
bands, and parents. I felt closer to the people in the black
neighborhood than I did to the white bureaucrats thriving
elsewhere in the city. Official Washington had turned its
back on both of us.

Traffic was slow, and we were late reaching Lafayette
Park. Dan and I were to be the first to read names of the victims. We got off the bus to cries of "hurry, hurry" from families already in the park. I read the names into a microphone,
my voice cracking as I pushed my way through the "A's."

There was an enormous amount of media coverage.
Lights flashed and cameras rolled. A reporter from a local
newspaper had ridden down with us on the bus. He was
happy. His eyes sparkled. This was as close as he'd ever get
to a big story, and he was savoring the excitement. Most of
the media were matter-of-fact, just ordinary people doing
their job. Today us, tomorrow a fire or some other disaster.
Some families were bothered by the media, found the reporters an intrusion who got in the way of the memorial. I
didn't. Reporters were our best friends.

I had no desire to meet with George Bush and was sorry
that we were holding a "vigil" instead of a "demonstration." The choice of "vigil" by the leadership was partly se-
mantic. Vigil sounded softer. But the genuflection to
respectability was an arrow pointing to the future, as was
the battle royal that had gone on among different group
members eager to meet the President. It struck me as an
unseemly battle, considering that the bones of those who
had died were still fresh in their graves and Bush's treatment of us had been pitiless and cold.

I met Rosemary Wolfe again. I liked Rosemary. She
worked in the Washington bureaucracy, and what's more
she understood it, which would prove invaluable. But
working in Washington had not robbed her of her decency,
loyalty, and courage. She'd been at Hunter College in New
York City when the Vietnam War awoke her political in-
stincts, for she was a political animal by nature, and she'd

joined the antiwar movement. As a stepmother she could
have walked away from Pan Am 103, but she would not
allow Miriam, of whom she had been very fond, to be murdered without fighting for justice for her. When it came to
unswerving morality, Rosemary was a ten.

At last I got to meet Kathleen Flynn. We had been talking on the phone since she'd received my note asking
parents to meet at the Syracuse memorial in January.
Kathleen hadn't gone to the memorial because the Flynn
family had moved to McLean, Virginia, with their three remaining children right after the bombing. They had lived in
New Jersey when their son John Patrick—always called
J.P.—died on Pan Am 103. Jack Flynn, a banker and vice
president of Citicorp, had accepted a transfer to the D.C.
area. J.P. had gone to Colgate, had been a good student, a
superb athlete, and a just plain nice person to know. Kids,
teachers, everybody knew and liked J.P. He was the apple
of his father's eye.

Dan and I were cynical, eccentric, and disaffected, even
before the gruesome epiphany wrought by Pan Am 103.
But the Flynns were the all-American dream family until
December 21, 1988. Children of Irish immigrants, they had
made it in America. They were good Catholics who went to
church every Sunday, who flew the American flag proudly
every Fourth of July. They loved sports. They had a big
house, lived well but not extravagantly, and valued education for their children more than acquiring material possessions. They were the stars and stripes in Kelly green.

Kathleen was burning mad over J.P.'s murder and not
afraid to show it. She was smart, had a clear eye for spot-
ting phonies, and was a sharp-tongued natural fighter who
stood up for local causes. She was perhaps a bit of a
throwback to a relative, Mike Quill, a tough, silver-
tongued New York City labor leader of the 1940s and
1950s. Our mutual anger and willingness to face ugly
truths brought Kathleen and I together despite the distance between Port Jervis and Washington, between freelance writing and Citicorp.

At the vigil I kissed a single white rose before putting it

on the wreath in honor of Theo. White roses were her favorite flowers, and often I had given them to her when she
performed onstage. I joined the crowd throwing flowers
over the White House fence. I even visited Congress, an exercise in futility and a complete waste of time.

Georgia Nucci and I walked along the street together
before Dan and I got on the bus to go home. Georgia had
her full share of grief and more, but she was doing her best
to be cheerful. The cherry blossoms were in bloom. "Smell
the blossoms, Susan. Aren't they beautiful?" But I was too
tense and gloomy to notice. Besides, I'd had enough of
flowers and Washington, and of a White House that had
locked its gates against us.

DAN: Meetings of the Victims of Pan Am 103 during the
first half of 1989 were a bizarre mixture of politics and
psychodrama. There was discussion of a highly successful
effort to collect hundreds of thousands of signatures on
petitions asking for an independent investigation of the
bombing. There were descriptions of the group's lobbying
effort to put through an aviation safety bill. At one meeting two representatives from something called the Air
Transport Association spoke to us. One of them described
herself as a former aide to former senator and vice president Hubert Humphrey. She sympathized with our loss,
praised our courage, and asked us to lend our support to
a change in aviation regulations that they were pushing in
Congress. She said our support would be very important,
and for all I know it would have been. The bill sounded
good as she described it, and I thought we should support
it, though honestly, like most of the other people in the
room, I was not at all clear on the details. Fortunately
the vote was postponed, and later we discovered the Air
Transport Association was the lobbying arm of the airlines, including Pan Am. The bill would have been good
for them, not for us. I never found out who had invited
those particular speakers.

At early meetings bulletin boards were covered with

photos of those who had died. Buttons with pictures of the dead became more numerous. People were likely to break out crying at any moment.

I sat in the lobby of the hotel in which one of the meetings was being held while a woman described to me in great detail how she had gone to Lockerbie and found the crater made when her son's body hit the ground, and how she rolled around in it so that she could be in touch with his spirit. She made my flesh creep. I didn't know how to respond, and I wanted to run away.

We weren't in the leadership of the Victims group. I had thought briefly of running for the board of directors, but they held extra meetings and long conference telephone calls and set up elaborate rules and procedures. I hated that sort of thing and withdrew my name.

One of the central beliefs of the Victims of Pan Am 103 was that the tragedy had created a special, almost mystical bond among us. People who had not known one another a few months ago and had nothing in common except the tragedy were suddenly best friends. Some believed that only those of us who had suffered this loss could truly understand one another. Emotional hugging and weeping was a large part of every meeting of Victims of Pan Am 103. The group's newsletter was filled with homey little details about weddings, anniversaries, and even home renovations of different group members. And yet the group was actually cracking up, almost before it was fully organized.

Since we weren't in the leadership, we didn't really know what was going on. Eleanor Hudson, Paul's wife, who called us at odd hours of the day or night and conducted long, rambling monologues, had begun hinting darkly of a "North Jersey cabal" headed by Bert Ammerman that was out to destroy Paul.

One point of contention—there were many—was Paul's charge that Bert was going off on his own and ignoring the rules that had been established for the group's officers. After a hearing in Washington, Bert was approached by a State Department official who offered to arrange a meeting with Lawrence Eagleburger, then deputy secretary of state. During the meeting, Secretary of State James Baker just happened to drop in. We were to learn that these "drop-ins" were a common Washington technique, designed to make those at the meeting feel important without raising the meeting to the level of being official.

After about fifteen minutes Baker promised Bert that his staff would work to take care of the complaints that family members had about the treatment they had received. Bert was delighted. He followed up with a letter to President Bush, which seemed to imply that what we really wanted was a lunch at the White House and a ceremony in the Rose Garden.

The tone of the letter was fawning. This was the President whose administration had behaved so badly that it had never even sent an official letter of condolence, and had dismissed all of our suggestions out of hand. I was disgusted by it and told Bert so at a meeting. He waved my objections aside by saying, "You can catch more flies with honey than with vinegar." "Yeah," I replied. "But we're going to be the flies." The sort of things he was suggesting would reduce us to becoming props in a Washington photo op: "Grieving but smiling families meet concerned but smiling President on White House lawn."

Matters came to a head at a marathon meeting in Fishkill, New York, on April 29. Bert and his supporters were there, but they stayed in the hotel bar rather than attend the formal session. Paul got up and began to detail his complaints against Bert. He talked and talked, becoming more disjointed as he went on. Several times he broke down in tears. This was the man who had found the strength to go to Lockerbie within hours after the disaster. He put the group together at a time when most of us had trouble just getting out of bed. He had been a marvel of activity and self-control. And here he was going to pieces before our eyes.

Some people in the audience began to scream. Others walked out in disgust. I was confused and frightened, for not only was Paul going to pieces at the meeting, the group was falling apart, and I felt that it was vital that we hold together, despite our differences.

I ran over to the bar and begged Bert and his supporters to come into the session and try to patch up their differences. They refused and detailed their complaints about Paul. He was secretive, deceptive, and devious. He would say one thing one day and something quite different the next. Everything became bogged down in tedious legalistic hairsplitting. Conference calls went on for hours but never seemed to resolve anything. These complaints were coming from people other than Bert, people who had no personal ax to grind. I believed them.

I kept shuttling back and forth between the meeting room and the bar, trying to arrange some sort of a compromise. In the end the two sides did get together on electing a new board of directors with a mail vote. Paul and Bert stood together and said nice things about each other.

The group's newsletter reported that the Fishkill meeting was, "difficult, intense, and above all fruitful . . . With great humility, perseverance, and the collective spirit and commitment of the group, those issues were resolved by the evening and we were back on track and stronger than ever."

The statement was nonsense. Nothing had really been resolved, everybody knew it; there was no "bond" and Victims of Pan Am 103 were indeed cracking up.

I remembered what that cynical New York lawyer told us: "Family groups come and go."

SUSAN: I was on Paul's side at Fishkill. I too was disgusted by Bert's letter to Bush and shared Dan's dislike of him. I stood publicly with Paul, denouncing Bert. It was a strange meeting. Spring had brought its set of memories, birthdays, anniversaries. The grief was growing worse for everyone. Somebody on Bert's side yelled at me as I stood in front of the room. I snarled back. "We've all lost," one of the family members said, "and we all belong in this group." The chaos and noise in the room, later the dash to the bar to hold the group together, made an odd contrast with the peaceful facade put on for reporters outside of the meeting room itself.

The brief days of unity were over. In the end we were just a diverse group of people who had been standing in the same place when the universe exploded. No amount of mystical talk about bonding could change that one simple fact.

Chapter 7

DAN: In 1994 Jeff Kreindler, who was public-relations director for Pan Am, told an interviewer that the public usually remembered an airline disaster for about two months. After that the airline's business returned to normal. This didn't happen in the case of Pan Am 103, he said, in large measure because the families just wouldn't let go of the issue.

Jeff Kreindler incidentally was a cousin of our lawyer, Lee Kreindler, though the names were pronounced somewhat differently. "We're not close!" Lee quickly assured us when we called him in a mood of cold suspicion about this.

In late January 1989, Susan and I were invited to appear on the *Larry King Show*. It was the first time we did an extended live interview, and we were still very shaky emotionally and physically. We spent much of our time on the show denouncing Pan Am. Several callers who identified themselves as current or former airline employees criticized us for attacking the airline when the real culprits were the terrorists and not Pan Am itself.

Then a call came in from another victim's family member. He was John Root, a young lawyer whose wife of just four months had been on flight 103. In tones of eloquent fury, he called Pan Am a corporation of murderers. He described Pan Am's executives, by name, as being covered with the blood of his wife and all of the others. It was one of the very few times that Susan and I actually sounded moderate by contrast. When the break came, King's producer walked into the studio and said, "They could sue that guy for what he said."

"They'll never sue," King growled.

SUSAN: I was afraid of being on television, and this would mean a long time in front of the camera. I thought about dressing up for the show to make a good impression. I looked so awful I thought the sight of me would put the audience off. But I didn't have anything special to wear. I had an all-purpose white T-shirt and a green print blouse and skirt, which I'd bought at a discount store the year before. I put them on whenever I had to look respectable. Mine was a blue jeans life, typewriting to dog walking, to bicycle riding, to cooking and washing dishes. For weeks I had been wearing a ratty gray sweater. Barely knew I had it on till Dan begged me to order something colorful out of a catalog. But I didn't even have the energy for that, so I just machine washed the sweater and put on another one in a different shade of gray. Besides, I had lost eleven pounds in the months since Theo died, and though I would gain it all back, and more, at that moment most of my clothes didn't fit.

I did the right thing in not dressing up for television. Instead of playing a role, I was letting the TV audience see me as I was, a war-crimes victim whose life had been wrecked and whose ill-fitting clothes and haggard face proved it. A car was sent to pick us up, and as we were driven to the CNN studios in New York, I rehearsed what I planned to say. Over time I would learn to speak in sound bites, and would make sure the main points were heard. But you can't script an entire interview, and if you know what you're talking about, it's a waste of time to go over it in your head in advance, so I might as well have spent the drive time thinking of something else.

The CNN studio was far from glamorous, which lowered the pressure and made it easier to do the show. There were cameras and a crew, but the nice thing about television is that while millions of people may see you, you can't see them. Larry King was protective and put us at our ease.

Dan did a lot of the talking but I found my voice, propelled as I was by the passion and anger inside me, and I went after Pan Am.

Some family members were made queasy by John Root's rage. But, again, here was someone telling the truth. I came to admire John. He had a brilliant mind, was extremely well educated and had adored his wife. I saw her picture, she was lovely. John once told me about a grief-filled lonely night in which he lay awake, missing her, remembering her "doe eyes."

John wasn't afraid of bold moves and could be counted on to come to demonstrations. He couldn't endure the sanctimonious mealymouthed talk about forgiveness for mass murderers, and he was one of the first family members to focus on the terrorists as the primary villains. "The West has had a loss of nerve, just as in the thirties." I can still see him standing alone at a meeting, throwing those words out as a challenge to everyone in the room.

DAN: The show had been exhausting, but we were pleased and exhilarated with the way it went. While we were being driven back home, Susan shot a fist in the air and shouted, "That was for you, Theo."

The next evening we got a call from Lee Kreindler, the lawyer we had never expected to hear from again. He gave us his highest compliment: "I think you helped the case," he said.

The shadow of flight 103 hung over Pan Am and continued to hurt its already crumbling business. Pan Am was doing everything it could to escape the shadow and somehow put the disaster behind it. Everything, that is, except admit that they had rotten security and needed to improve it. Pan Am launched a public-relations offensive.

In January of 1989, when Pan Am was resolutely refusing to give Paul Hudson, who was trying to form a family group, the names of the plane's passengers, they did give those names and addresses to New York's Cardinal John O'Connor so that he could hold a Mass at St. Patrick's

Cathedral. We were invited but didn't go. The Mass got wide media coverage, and it was dominated by a large and organized contingent of Pan Am employees, in uniform. The image, quite clearly, was meant to make Pan Am look like one of the victims. A similar, though smaller uniformed group showed up at the April memorial in Washington.

One of the most offensive attempts to get out from under the shadow was something called "Ed's Party." It apparently started innocently enough with a thirteen-year-old New Jersey boy named Ed Blaus. He was sorry that the children of Lockerbie had missed their Christmas. He wanted to send them some gifts. His father contacted Pan Am for help, and Pan Am public relations took it from there. Not only did they offer to send Ed and his family on an expense-paid junket to Lockerbie, they organized an extravaganza—a "Christmas in June" in Lockerbie. The airline lined up corporations and government agencies to support the event. Disney was going to send Mickey and Minnie Mouse, NASA would provide a real astronaut, there would be free food and soft drinks at a barbecue, several bands would provide music, the works. Everybody who was anywhere near Lockerbie was invited. "Ed's Party" was to mark the end of sadness in Lockerbie, and a return to normalcy and good times. The scars in the earth caused by the fall of the plane had already been erased. With this celebration the disaster itself would become a distant memory. It would be more than the usual two months, but maybe people would stop identifying Pan Am with disaster and start buying tickets again. Or so the airline hoped.

I called Pan Am about "the party" and was given Jeff Kreindler himself. He swore up and down that the whole thing had been arranged by thirteen-year-old Ed and his family and Pan Am had nothing to do with it, except perhaps provide a bit of transportation.

SUSAN: It was obvious to me when I phoned Ed's parents that they were decent-hearted innocents who could never have planned and organized an elaborate celebration in a country far away by themselves. We had to deny Pan Am a PR victory—but how could we do it? I thought hard. Then I talked to Jeannine Boulanger and to Jane Davis. Jane was a charming Southerner who had lived in the Middle East. Not only had her daughter Shannon died on the plane, but her husband had been killed in an accident in Saudi Arabia earlier that year. Jeannine and Jane were eager to help, as were other families I talked to. I asked the Syracuse parents to complain to the school about the Scottish-born football coach going to Lockerbie for the festivities. I asked Jane and others to contact corporations who had been roped into supporting the party. I told the families to make sure their local newspapers knew what they had done. Grassroots stuff.

I hit the PR people at Disney, called NASA, and told them in no uncertain terms that they were making a big mistake. The American families didn't like this party. We were going to get lots of publicity and think how Disney, how NASA, and all the rest would look helping this disgraceful airline ingratiate itself with the public. When the PR folks heard that, they shied away like frightened horses. When calls from other families came in as well, many corporations pulled out fast. Had this been a battlefront, it would have been a rout. Well, we had cost Pan Am its party favors and treats. The next step was to organize a demonstration.

The copier and the fax were not yet household gadgets. Dan had to go to the local copy shop to make copies of press releases and fax them out. Forget computers and e-mail. We didn't know how to use a computer. We were still writing books on manual typewriters. Dan wasn't able to work as fast as he used to, and I could barely work at all. So money was tight, and the phone bill was an unavoidable monster every month. We eked out the money for copying and faxing, but we couldn't afford a copier or fax machine, or to put in extra phone lines. We did the best we could.

At the next family meeting I literally jumped to my feet, went to the front of the room, my feelings so strong I could hear the intensity in my voice: "Who will join me in protest in front of the Pan Am Building?" I asked. A woman sitting close by brushed her skirt and pulled as far away from me in her seat as she could. I read this gesture as signaling that she was distancing herself from such radical action. She said nothing but there was cold disapproval in her face.

We had enough families to hold the demonstration, so I got in touch with the media. I had learned to write press releases by now, but since Dan had worked on a magazine for years, he whipped one up for us. It was Dan who thought up the slogan: "If you can't warn them, you'd better protect them. If you can't protect them, you'd better warn them," which was taken up by other members of the group.

We sent out press releases in batches. I called newsrooms, assignment desks, and all the reporters I knew, and by now there were a lot of them. I learned about the news cycle and what a daybook is. Dan went to the copy store again for the umpteenth time till all the press releases were sent. I called the media again, to make sure the faxes had arrived. We did this in advance, and again the night before the demonstration. Every reporter in New York must have been aware of our demonstration.

The media was there in force when we gathered at the Pan Am Building on June 3, the day of "Ed's Party" in Lockerbie. Many families had never been in a demonstration before. New Yorkers seemed to find it easier than residents of the suburbs because street protests were an everyday occurrence in the city. Some family members shouted angrily at Pan Am. Some were quiet, some keen, some hesitant. Passersby and onlookers were generally on our side, many averting their eyes before the enormity of the tragedy. We didn't stop Pan Am's party, but we sure rained on their parade.

DAN: I called Lockerbie and talked to one of the town officials. I told him we didn't oppose Lockerbie bringing its period of mourning to an end with an appropriate ceremony, but what was planned was so gaudy and tasteless that it was offensive. And it was strictly a Pan Am public-ity stunt. "You're being used. Don't you see that?" He kept repeating, "It's fur the children. It's fur the children."

On June 3, the party went on. Some five thousand peo-ple from Lockerbie and the surrounding area showed up. There was plenty of free food. But Mickey Mouse wasn't there, neither was an astronaut or many of the other orig-inally advertised attractions. The Scottish-born coach of the Syracuse football team did show up, though the uni-versity had been quite uncomfortable about his making the trip in the face of strong family opposition. He appar-ently could not resist the lure of a trip to the old country.

About one hundred relatives and friends of the victims held a protest in New York in front of the Pan Am Build-ing. Smaller protests were also held in Cleveland, Detroit, Pittsburgh, and Syracuse. Both the party and the protests got equal press coverage.

The American protests opened up a rift between some of the people in Lockerbie and many American families. "The Americans who are protesting don't live here," said Lockerbie resident Agnes Jamieson. "They were not here on the night. We've had all the trauma, and we need some-thing to lift our spirits." A Lockerbie policeman com-plained that the absence of the Disney characters was a crushing disappointment to Lockerbie's children. "A lot of children from Lockerbie will never get to go to Disney-land. This was their only chance to see Mickey and Minnie. Some of the sympathy for the Americans is going to go down the drain."

The gruesome inappropriateness of turning the spot where 270 people died into a Disneyland substitute, even for a day, did not seem to occur to the policeman.

We got an angry letter from a Lockerbie resident, who complained that we didn't understand what she had suf-fered. She said that her house had been destroyed in the disaster. My reply was not gracious. I told her there was a universe of difference between loss of property and loss of a child, and that we would be quite willing to help her buy a new house if she would just return Theo to us.

Poor Lockerbie! It was, by all accounts, a very ordinary and obscure town. "The kind of place you would pass on the motorway and barely notice," was one description. A Scottish reporter who visited us said it reminded him of Port Jervis, which was also the sort of place you could drive by without noticing. For a time Lockerbie and Port Jervis were declared "sister cities." I sent the town a load of kids books that I had written, and these were put on display in the local library.

Lockerbie had never asked for any of this—flaming airplane pieces and bodies falling out of the sky. The town lost eleven of its own in the disaster, and portions of it were set ablaze. Lockerbie was like one of those innocent bystanders who gets shot during the commission of a crime. It wasn't the target of the terrorists. If Pan Am 103 hadn't left Heathrow Airport late, the plane would have exploded over the open ocean, which was probably the terrorists' plan.

After the disaster many Lockerbie residents helped to gather up the surviving personal effects from the crash. They washed the smell of airline fuel out of the clothes and ironed and folded them with care for return to families. Many victims' family members began making pilgrimages to Lockerbie. By all accounts they were treated with extraordinary consideration and kindness by the people of the town. Some family members have come to regard Lockerbie as almost a holy site—they return there regularly, year after year on anniversary dates, to visit the memorial garden or other monuments related to the disaster. A few family members have returned to Lockerbie to have the ashes of the victim scattered or buried there. A few others, where the victim's body was completely destroyed during the bombing, have no other memorial site.

By contrast, Susan and I have never visited Lockerbie, and never had a desire to do so. It was where Theo died, not where she had lived. What meaning did that hold for us? It was like visiting the spot in the road where your child was killed by a drunken driver, except you had to fly across the Atlantic to get there, and we could barely fly anywhere anymore.

Most of the people of Lockerbie didn't want their town to be forever associated with the horror of the night of December 21, 1988. They wanted the damage repaired as quickly as possible, they wanted to put up their Christmas lights again, they wanted to put the whole thing behind them. And who can blame them?

But they weren't very sophisticated. For months after the disaster, the town was full of Pan Am employees making friends and influencing people. When Pan Am public relations came up with the idea of holding a big Disneyland-type bash on the killing ground, the good citizens of Lockerbie took the bait. They didn't realize that they were being made part of an incompetent airline's attempt to refurbish its image.

SUSAN: I was in terrible shape before I went to the next family group meeting. Word had reached me that two councilmen from Lockerbie would be there to smooth things over after the "Ed's party" debacle. I was shaking by the time I got into the meeting room. The two councilmen spoke. One said, "Pan Am made this mess, let Pan Am clean it up." I called them both to account and asked them if Pan Am had flown them to the United States for free. One hemmed and hawed evasively. The other flatly denied the accusation. I didn't believe him and refused to remain at a meeting where Pan Am used the Scots to schmooze the American families. I contemptuously stalked out.

Dan stayed because he wanted to keep track of what was going on. But just before I left the room, I looked around at the other families and I sensed something else. Call it the myth of Brigadoon. Lockerbie had become a shrine. It was holy ground where "a plane full of angels," as one bereaved mother described Pan Am 103, had fallen to earth. Many families had faith in the Scots. They wanted to believe the councilmen.

I spent the rest of the meeting in a small room with Denise Giebler, the only other person who walked out with me. Her son had died on Pan Am 103. She was as agitated as I was and chain-smoked, lighting one cigarette after another as we talked. She had been to Lockerbie, and when one of the visiting councilmen passed, she cornered him and said, "I liked you when I visited Lockerbie. But now I know the jury is still out on you."

But there was no stopping the myth of Lockerbie as Brigadoon.

DAN: It wasn't just actions of angry family members that kept the hostile spotlight on Pan Am. Far more damaging was the news about the airline's reckless indifference to security that just kept coming out.

The worst news for Pan Am was Ulrich F. X. Weber. He was the head of Pan Am security at Frankfurt Airport, one of the busiest and most dangerous airports in Europe, at the time of the Pan Am 103 bombing. Technically Weber worked for Alert Management Systems, a Pan Am subsidiary responsible for security. In reality Alert was a fiction; it was entirely controlled by Pan Am management.

Pan Am claimed that they screened all of their employees carefully. Somehow Weber seems to have slipped through the cracks, and they were giant-size cracks. Before being hired as Pan Am security chief at Frankfurt airport, the 29-year-old Weber had picked up a modest criminal record in Illinois—mostly bad check charges. He had also been fired from one of his previous jobs after being accused of stealing property. He had been given a "less than honorable discharge" from the Illinois National Guard for unexcused absences, and was court-martialed for being absent without leave from the U.S. Army while serving in West Germany.

This was the guy who was hired by Alert Management Systems, Pan Am's security arm, to protect passengers at one of the most dangerous airports in Europe.

Weber's own hiring practices later came under scrutiny. One of the people that Weber hired to screen baggage was

Sabine Feuchs, whose previous job had been as a hair-dresser.

An interviewer asked her how much training she had received after she was hired. Her reply: "None. None whatsoever."

Another employee hired by Weber was Simone Keller. She also had no training and no experience, but after four days Weber promoted her to supervisor.

"Why?" asked the interviewer.

"Mr. Weber told me that I had wonderful blue eyes."

Why was this guy in charge of airline security at Frankfurt? He shouldn't have been able to get a job emptying toilets on an aircraft!

But far and away the most serious charge against Weber was the one made by Oliver Koch, Alert's head of training at Frankfurt. Koch said that shortly after the news of the crash, Weber called him and told him to report into work early the next morning. The office was in chaos. At that point no one knew the bomb had been placed aboard the 747 at Frankfurt, but it was known that the doomed flight had originated there. At 6 A.M. Koch was working at the computer on Weber's desk. A document among the papers piled on the desk caught his eye. It was a security bulletin that had been sent out as a result of the Helsinki warning—that a Pan Am plane from Frankfurt would be bombed before Christmas. This was a document that Koch had never seen before, though it should have been brought to his attention. The warning had never been stamped as received, and that meant it had never been circulated to the security staff.

According to court papers, this exchange took place between Koch and Weber:

Koch said to Weber, "What is this, after Lockerbie?"

"Oh, my God, don't worry, don't worry. It's nothing. Forget it."

Koch was still upset. "How can I forget it? This is a warning of a potential bomb. It's my job."

"Just forget it. Be quiet or you will get into trouble."

Koch told investigators, and later reporters, that Weber

then took the memo and backdated it to make it appear as though he had received it on December 9. He gave copies of the backdated memo to the staff. But that was after the bombing.

Koch said that he had kept a copy of the original unstamped warning and gave it to Beate Franzki, the senior duty officer and Weber's second in command. She insisted that she had never seen it before and that it had never been given to those employees who screened passengers before Lockerbie.

Koch then took the warning and his story to John Ridd, the head of Alert's European operations. Nothing happened to Weber, but Koch was fired. Weber stayed on the payroll for months, desperately trying to beef up his operation to make it look like something other than the sham it had been in the past. Suddenly his budget for hiring new personnel was increased dramatically, in a classic example of shutting the barn door after the horse has escaped.

In June of '89, Lee Kreindler managed to track down Weber and get a highly damaging deposition out of him for use in the civil suit against Pan Am. The following day Pan Am lawyer James Shaughnessy flew to Frankfurt, and Ulrich Weber was fired. The airline maintained that Weber's dismissal was unrelated to Lockerbie or the way he had handled Frankfurt security. To say otherwise would have come back to haunt them in any future trial. Why was Weber suddenly fired? The problem with Ulrich Weber was strictly a financial one, said Pan Am. He had used a company credit card at a Munich bordello. He had used the same card to pay for Christmas presents for his children. A nice, generous fellow.

Virtually every victim's family member hated Pan Am with a passion and was suing them, not so much for money but for revenge. Susan and I felt that Pan Am had taken away what was most precious to us, Theo. Now we were going to take from Pan Am what was most precious to them, their money.

There was one exception. Bruce Smith was a Pan Am pilot whose wife of four years, Ingrid, had died in the

bombing. In February Pan Am's president Thomas Plaskett sent a letter to all family members offering to settle
our claims for $100,000 each. That was $25,000 above the
limit set by the Warsaw Convention, but far below what
most of the lawyers assumed would be the final settlement
on the case. Only Smith and one other family accepted Pan
Am's offer.

Bruce Smith wrote to all the relatives arguing that we
should settle our claims against Pan Am, and then use the
money to set up a reward for the capture of the terrorists.
He especially urged those of us who had not lost "bread-
winners"—who had only lost wives and children—to take
the money and get the "real killers" and stop persecuting
poor old Pan Am.

As far as I know, not a single family member joined
Smith's efforts to set up a reward fund. I sent Smith a long,
and for me, polite letter explaining why I was rejecting his
idea and why I wanted to grind Pan Am into the dust. He
didn't send a response, and I didn't hear from him for
years, until money came up again in quite a different con-
text.

Chapter 8

DAN: The investigation of the Pan Am 103 bombing seemed to get off to a very fast start. We saw television pictures of lines of Scottish police combing the area around the crash site picking up tiny bits of wreckage from the disaster. Within just a few days the authorities had concluded that the plane was actually brought down by a bomb. From examining and testing the wreckage, they were able to find traces of the Czech-made plastic explosive Semtex at the site of the explosion. Fragments indicated that the Semtex had been inside of a Toshiba radio-cassette player similar to the one seized by the German authorities in the Autumn Leaves sweep. A partially burned Toshiba manual with instructions in English and Arabic was found amid the wreckage. Forensics experts were able to determine that a deadly radio-cassette bomb had been packed inside a hard-sided, bronze-colored Samsonite suitcase loaded into baggage container AVE 4041 PA, which had been placed in the left side of the 747's front cargo hold.

Then the investigation seemed to hit a wall. Whose suitcase was it? How was the bomb actually put aboard the plane? The most obvious possibility was that it was carried aboard by one of the passengers.

Early in January of '89, we were visited by two very polite FBI agents, a man and a woman. The man explained to me, with infinite tact, that the visit was strictly routine, but that in the past terrorists used unwitting dupes to get explosives on airplanes. He cited a 1986 case where a Jordanian working for Syrian intelligence had given a bomb-laden suitcase to his pregnant Irish girlfriend to take aboard an El Al jet. The bomb was discovered at the last minute by El Al security. If it hadn't been found, the Irishwoman and a lot of other people would have died.

I was asked if Theo had met any boys while she was in England. Theo met boys wherever she went. In fact, she had found a new boyfriend in England; he was an American student from Harvard. I wasn't the least offended by his question. This was a murder investigation, and I was ready to do anything I could to help. I gave the agent a letter Theo had written to us about the new boyfriend. He read it several times, took some notes, thanked me, and the two agents left. We never heard from them again. Others were not so lucky.

Karen Noonan, a student at Boston college, was returning from a semester of study in Vienna. Checking over baggage records, investigators found a discrepancy between the number of her bags reported on the manifest and the number of bags she actually checked. This "extra bag" looked suspicious. Her sweatpants recovered from the wreckage appeared to have been near where the bomb exploded. Speculation that she might have inadvertently carried the bomb surfaced briefly. But the discrepancy on the number of bags was a mistake, and no trace of explosive was found on the sweatpants. Ironically, Karen Noonan and her classmate Tricia Coyle had attended a party at the marine barracks at the U.S. embassy in Vienna on December 20. There they heard people discussing the Helsinki warning, but they didn't seem to be worried about it and the following day they boarded Pan Am 103.

Passengers Matthew Gannon and Army Major Charles McKee also became the focus of speculation. Their bags had been loaded in the same luggage container that had held the bomb-carrying suitcase. But more suspiciously, they both had intelligence—that is, CIA—connections, and both had worked in Lebanon, where some U.S. hostages were still being held. They were not viewed as the bomb carriers; however, the theory arose that Pan Am 103 had been specifically targeted because Gannon and McKee were on board.

But no family suffered more from hostile speculation than that of Khalid Nazir Jaafar, a twenty-year-old Lebanese American from Dearborn, Michigan. There were media reports that Jaafar was a drug courier or mule, who had been given the suitcase with the bomb in the belief that the suitcase was full of drugs, part of some sort of elaborate conspiracy. There were stories that his family back in Lebanon was deeply involved in the international drug trade. His father, Nazir Jaafar, was bitter, believing that his son had been singled out for blame because he was Lebanese. "Somebody killed my son, and somebody's trying to kill my family. There's a kind of political Mafia behind this story."

To a great extent Nazir Jaafar was right. Khalid had undoubtedly first fallen under suspicion simply because he was an Arab and because he had traveled in Lebanon and Germany before boarding Pan Am 103. But he had carried only a soft-sided duffel bag, not a Samsonite suitcase, onto the plane, and even that had been loaded in the wrong place to have contained the bomb. The continuing hostile speculation about Jaafar was not fueled by an anti-Arab U.S. government or a frenzied, sensationalist U.S. media. It was kept alive by conspiracy theorists, some of whom were being paid, and whose ravings were reported most fully and uncritically by the sensationalist British media.

I met Khalid Jaafar's family for the first time in Washington in August 1999. I told them how sorry I was for the way they and the memory of their son had been treated. They seemed to appreciate what I said. When I left them, they were jostling to get a picture of themselves taken next to Attorney General Janet Reno, who had just entered the room.

SUSAN: The much feared split in the Victims of Pan Am 103 group finally took place at a late June meeting in Haddonfield, New Jersey. The organizers of the meeting were family members who aimed for calm and tranquillity. They encouraged us to tour Haddonfield's historic sites and planned a get-together breakfast the morning after the meeting. But peace did not prevail. This was the meeting at which the two Lockerbie councilmen showed up. Two representatives of the State Department Office of Counterterrorism were also there. I stood with Lynne Fraidowitz at the back of the room and challenged these representatives heatedly. Others did as well. By the end of the meeting, one of them, Frank Moss, visibly relieved the ordeal was over, hurried away. He looked like a man facing a firing squad who had been given a last-minute reprieve.

Some families were irked and embarrassed by our confrontational methods. After I confronted the Lockerbie councilmen, no one made room for Dan and me at lunch, until finally one man rose and asked us to sit down. After the State Department imbroglio, one of the Pan Am 103 mothers haughtily told me to stop making scenes. She added that she would never make a scene. It was not her style. I just stared at her. She sounded like someone rebuking a dinner partner for making a fuss over a plate of cold potatoes served by a slipshod waitress, not someone whose daughter had died in a terrorist bombing. A man who lost his daughter accused Dan and me of "always tearing everything down," then he burst into tears.

Not everyone responded that way, of course. Marina de Larracoecha, who lived both in Spain and New York, lost her sister when Pan Am 103 went down. Her sister was a Pan Am flight attendant. Marina was a Basque and fiercely proud of their fighting spirit. When the Victims of Pan Am 103 leadership told her she must be polite, she phoned me and said sarcastically, "Polite? Someone in my family is murdered, and I'm supposed to be polite!"

We would remain on good terms with many of the Pan Am families on both sides of the "politeness" divide long after the group split. But the Victims of Pan Am 103 had fractured into factions too different to hold together. There were those for whom the high point of the meetings was having lunch and going to the mall together. This wasn't shallow or frivolous on their part. They needed to be with the only people they believed could understand what they were going through. Many friends from the old days were uncomfortable even mentioning the name of the child who was gone, but Pan Am 103 parents could talk freely with one another about their dead kids. In time, some of the families came to meetings solely to see one another, skipping the political part of the meeting altogether. Others came primarily for the group therapy sessions, and complained that there wasn't enough therapy.

That day at Haddonfield there was turmoil over who would head the Victims of Pan Am 103. It all got very complicated, culminating in an acrimonious board meeting. The board narrowly elected Bert Ammerman president. I was afraid that the group would become too chummy with the Bush administration, that there would be too many "polite" meetings where State Department representatives and their ilk would speak unchallenged.

Most of the families, especially those on the East Coast, stayed in the Victims group. Some, because the group was family to them. But I wasn't looking for a family. I was looking for, if I may use that much abused word, comrades. So Dan and I went home early, skipping the breakfast get-together. Later Paul Hudson formed a new group, Families of Pan Am 103—Lockerbie, which we joined quickly, but not enthusiastically.

The last person we spoke to before we left Haddonfield was Aphrodite Tsairis, mother of one of the Syracuse students and Bert's close ally. Still, we liked Aphrodite, and we told her that if she, rather than Bert, had become president we would have stayed in the group. She said that we would all walk our separate paths, but to a common goal. We hugged. In a few short months we would be at one another's throats.

DAN: Sitting on the sidelines waiting for more information was not merely frustrating, it was absolutely maddening.

Information, or what passed for information, was coming out in pieces, most of it contradictory. The bomb was put on the plane in Germany, the bomb was put on in London, the Iranians were responsible, the Syrians were responsible, the CIA was responsible. There was an unidentified body on the plane. Suitcases of heroin and money had been found at the Lockerbie crash scene and spirited away by CIA men dressed as Scottish policemen. A group of Orthodox Jews or South African government officials had been warned off the Pan Am flight. All of this assailed us daily throughout the early months of 1989.

To make matters worse it soon began to look as if portions of the Pan Am 103 investigation were being handled by a bunch of bunglers.

Bomb-maker Marwan Khreesat, originally identified as a member of the Popular Front for the Liberation of Palestine/General Command, and arrested by the Germans in the surveillance operation they called Autumn Leaves, was interviewed by U.S. and British authorities in Jordan. Khreesat claimed to be a Jordanian double agent, feeding information about terrorist groups to Western intelligence. The Germans knew this, and he wasn't supposed to have been arrested in the first place. Khreesat told U.S. authorities that while he had been in West Germany, he made at least five bombs—only one of which the Germans had found. He assumed that the others were still at the apartment where he and PFLP/GC terrorist Hafiz Dalkamouni had been staying. The Americans and the Scots finally prevailed on the Germans to go back and take another look. In the basement of a market that was owned by Dalkamouni's brother-in-law, and where Dalkamouni and Khreesat's belongings had been stored, the BKA (German secret service) found three more bombs: two concealed in stereo tuners and the third in a computer monitor. Incredibly, three fully armed and operational terrorist bombs had sat undetected in an obvious place for nearly six months.

It got worse. In complete defiance of all regulations and common sense, the bombs were put in a car and driven over bumpy roads to the BKA office in Meckenheim. There they were dumped on a desk with no indication of what they really were. A technician got suspicious and X-rayed one of the tuners with a machine normally used to screen mail to government offices. He found out it was a bomb and asked to have it picked up. He was told to put the thing in his car and drive it over to Wiesbaden, where there were some experts on disarming bombs. Miraculously it didn't blow up during the drive, but when two explosives experts tried to disarm it, the bomb did explode, killing one of the men and crippling and blinding the other. After that disaster the second tuner was intentionally blown up, destroying whatever evidence it might have contained. The bomb in the monitor was finally successfully disarmed by an outside explosives expert.

And there was still that fifth bomb that Khreesat had talked about. After their release, Dalkamouni's other associates simply disappeared, because the German authorities made no attempt to track their whereabouts. No one seemed to know, or care, where they had gone. Was it possible that one of them had taken the missing bomb and used it to blow up Pan Am 103?

The famously efficient German police were acting like the Keystone Kops.

The missing bomb turned out to be a dead end.

Very early in the investigation, records revealed that an extra and unaccounted for bag had been loaded on the Frankfurt to London leg of Flight 103. But no one knew where it came from.

In mid-August the German authorities gave Lockerbie investigators a computerized baggage-loading list for the Frankfurt to London leg of Flight 103. A careful examination of the list showed that a bag from Air Malta flight KM 180 was loaded onto Pan Am 103. None of the thirty-nine passengers aboard the Air Malta flight boarded Pan Am. Here was the extra bag. As unaccompanied baggage, it should have been taken off the plane and searched. But since Pan Am had changed the rules, it was X-rayed by Pan Am employee Kurt Maier, who found nothing out of the ordinary, and it was loaded into baggage container AVE 4041 PA.

In 1988, Frankfurt Airport had one of the most sophisticated baggage tracking systems in the world. Four separate computer networks tracked all the incoming and outgoing luggage in this busy airport. Since January of 1989, Lockerbie investigators had been trying to get the baggage records, but the German authorities first said that these records did not exist, then they said the records had been lost, and finally they said that they had been destroyed. Seven months later a copy of the records suddenly turned up.

Here's what had happened. The computer operator who had been on duty on the night of December 21 heard about the disaster on the radio on her way home. When she went to work the following morning, she made a computer printout of every bag that had been loaded on Pan Am 103. It was a good thing she did because the computer automatically purges itself of this information after eight days. Amazingly, for months no German investigator had ever even talked to the computer operator, an obvious witness. On the morning of August 16, 1989, BKA investigators handed over a small parcel containing the computerized list to the Scots. The exact circumstances for the long delay are still unclear, but what is clear is that the Germans had screwed up again, big time. Months had been lost while Lockerbie investigators had gone up blind alleys and hit dead ends. The trail had grown colder and vital information may have been lost forever. Now the investigators began looking at Malta again.

This was not the first time that the island nation of Malta had come up in connection with Pan Am 103. While going through the clothing that had been packed in the bomb bag, forensics experts identified a baby's blue jumpsuit with the label Malta Trading Company. On the first trip to Malta, the Scottish officers found that this type of baby jumpsuit was distributed throughout Europe and could have come from anywhere.

With the discovery of the unaccompanied bag from

Malta investigators took a closer look. This time they were able to trace other items that had been in the bomb bag to a store called Mary's House at 63 Tower Road in Sliema, Malta's fourth largest city.

The owner of the store, Tony Gauci, actually had a clear recollection of the man who had bought many of the items. He was memorable because he was an unusual shopper who seemed to be shopping at random, without paying any attention to size, color, or price. Among the purchases, there was the blue baby jumpsuit, a pair of brown-checked trousers, a wool sweater, an old tweed jacket, and a black umbrella. This careless shopper was described as a well-dressed, clean-shaven man in his forties—who looked and talked like "a Libyan." He made his purchases on November 23, 1988—twenty-nine days before Lockerbie.

What is more, Gauci said that he had seen the unknown shopper at least two additional times since November. Though the full significance was not clear at the time, investigators noted that the Libyan People's Bureau in Malta was located just a few hundred yards up the Tower Road from the shop.

Bits and pieces of the story of the Malta connection began appearing in the press during the fall of 1989. By then we had been battered by so much speculation about how and where the bomb got on the plane that we didn't know what to make of this new information. No one from the U.S. government ever saw fit to brief us on the significance of the discoveries. As they say, we were left "twisting in the wind."

Susan: Living through December 21 a second time was a horror, coming after a year of horrors, each building on the last. The calendar was my enemy. January snows reminded me of beautiful winter days in Forestburgh, spent with my baby. In February our wedding anniversary brought despair instead of celebration. Every holiday, memories surfaced. Theo sitting at the kitchen table in our first Port Jervis house, printing her name on valentines. Theo at

Easter, eight years old, dressed in a granny dress and bunny ears, delivering a basket of eggs to friends from school. Graduation, summer camp, Theo's birthday, the most horrendous day of all to live through. It still is. Lonely Thanksgiving. We still had to get through Christmas. We had yet to survive New Year's. Even October 3, with its often-used abbreviation 10/3, brought pain. It would be worse pain yet if the first anniversary of the bombing went unnoticed by the wide world.

To mark the day, Hope Asrelsky arranged a memorial at her church, St. George's Chapel, Seventeenth Street in Manhattan, to be preceded by a demonstration at the Pan Am Building. Over the years Hope would often hold a one-woman vigil, reading the names of the people who had died on the plane, first in front of the Pan Am Building and later before the United Nations.

Once again I tackled the media, with the help of Bonnie O'Connor. Bonnie's brother John Ahern was only twenty-six when he died on Pan Am 103. The Ahern family was devastated. Despite his youth, John, who had a very good job in England, was already a success story. His father, mother, brothers, and sisters were proud of him and valued his opinion in all things. Bonnie was his big sister, fiercely loyal and persistent, who once told me she dreamed she weaved her way across a football field to rescue him from harm. Bonnie stayed in the Victims of Pan Am 103 after Dan and I left because she and her husband, Ed, were uncomfortable with Paul Hudson; but being in different groups didn't affect our friendship. After the group split, we just went on doing what we did before: pushing hard to keep Pan Am 103 remembered.

Bonnie had a knack for news and was not afraid to contact anyone in the media, punctuating her days with phone calls to the press while she took care of her home and children. Her forte was television, so we divided up the TV networks and independent stations and phoned each and every one directly about the demonstration and memorial planned for December 21.

I was still in a very deep depression, totally exhausted,

but I did what I had to. It was phone and fax and fax and phone once more. Get out of bed, that was the toughest thing. Then phone the press, vacuum the house, phone the press, bake bread, phone the press, ride the exercycle, phone the press. Keep moving. Keep calling. The more I dealt with the media, the more efficient I became. I was becoming familiar with the system and getting to know the people who worked in it.

There were families who argued from the beginning that we needed a PR staff. In the early months of the Victims of Pan Am 103, the media person was a woman named Sherry Price, a friend of Paul and Eleanor Hudson. Sherry was a rape victim who did public relations for a victim's rights' organization. She did everything she could at the time when the families were in terrible shape and difficult to deal with. After the split the Victims groups went on to hire public-relations firms to advise them. There was no whizbang, high-powered slick media blitz in either case, because neither group had a lot of money.

I didn't think we needed professional PR people. We, the families, were the best advocates for our cause. I got through to prominent people in the media I would never have been able to reach if I were merely an employee at a PR firm. When a reporter heard my voice, he was listening to a mother whose only child died in a terrorist attack. When he read a press release, it came directly from us. No intermediaries, no form letters, no phony hype. Alas, we were the genuine article. Yes, reporters are supposed to be objective. But that does not make them totally inhumane.

How much media attention would we get on the first anniversary? We needed more than tabloid articles and television, useful as they were. I had cried to television, and I would cry again. I wasn't faking. I cried all the time. But we had to reinforce Pan Am 103 as a political issue. And for that we needed the paper of record. But how to reach them? God knows I tried, but I had not yet scaled the smooth gray walls of the *New York Times*.

For close to a year I'd shot letters like bullets into the mail, targeting people I thought might help. One of those people was National Book Award–winning novelist Cynthia Ozick. She wrote me back. A young relative of hers was a victim of terrorism. She offered to help me get an Op-Ed piece in the *Times*.

It was very hard to write. I wrote and rewrote, banging out the words on my old Royal typewriter, ripping the sheets of paper out, crumpling them into a ball, and starting over. My head ached and my body was so tense I had to stop and rub my neck every few minutes. When I finished I could not evaluate what I had written. Cynthia Ozick was an artist, I was not. In my writing career I was just somebody trying to earn a living with my pen. But I sent Cynthia the piece, hoping she'd like it. She told me she found my words very powerful, contacted Howard Goldberg, who was the Opinion Page editor of the *Times*, and sent him my article.

There was no guarantee the *Times* would use the piece. I waited aeons to hear. Finally, when I couldn't wait any longer I called Howard Goldberg. I prepared myself for a turndown while I waited on the phone for him to check the status of the piece. When he told me they would run it, I felt triumphant and deeply thankful to Cynthia Ozick, both for her help and her praise. On December 21, 1989, the most important newspaper in the world would acknowledge the political significance of Pan Am 103. And the bureaucrats in Washington would read what I had to say: "Was my daughter's life, and the lives of all the others on Pan Am 103, of no value to our government?"

December 21, 1989, was a bitterly cold day. The families gathered on the steps of the Forty-second Street Library. Dan, Bonnie, and I had done our work well. The media was all over us, jostling each other, pushing microphones in our faces. There were cameras everywhere you looked. Many family members thanked me for the *New York Times* piece. A kilted bagpiper led us from the library to the Pan Am Building. The police escorted us, helping with the traffic. After the demonstration Dan and I took a subway down to the church.

The memorial at the church was done with dignity and

taste. It had meaning because it was created by the families themselves. It was real. We would continue to hold demonstrations and memorials in New York on December 21 for years to come. Many families would participate, but very soon, some families in the Victims group preferred to attend a ceremony in Washington, D.C., put together by Carmella LaSpada of the organization "No Greater Love," which honored victims of terrorism. It was a decent gesture by Carmella, but except when it was politically important to be in Washington, Dan and I went to New York.

There was something passive about going to Washington. The families didn't plan the ceremony. There was no demonstration. It was sit and be taken care of, sit and be told what to do. Government officials and Washington types abounded. A respectable way to mourn, complete with luncheon. No need to fear what the neighbors would think.

Chapter 9

SUSAN: Pan Am 103 hurled me into a shadowy world of psychopaths, liars, greedy con men, media hogs, power chasers, and opportunists. A few even crossed the line into criminal behavior, as was widely reported in the media. There were hangers-on, people barely attached, or not attached at all, to anyone on Pan Am 103, who clung to the fringes of the family groups because they craved the cameras. There were lawyers who would say almost anything to lure a client and do almost anything to get their fees. There were terrorism "experts" pushing their business, think-tank "experts" promoting their theories. And there was Pan Am, looking for a defense in the civil suit and finding an Israeli named Juval Aviv.

Even before December 21, 1988, Aviv had a shady reputation in Washington. In 1984 Aviv collaborated with Canadian journalist George Jonas on a book called *Vengeance, The True Story of an Israeli Counter-Terrorist Team*. In the book Aviv, under the pseudonym Avner, claimed to have been a member of the legendary Israeli Mossad, and leader of an assassination team that tracked down the terrorists who had killed eleven Israeli athletes at the Munich Olympics in 1972. The book had a huge prepublication interest, but as soon as it was issued, the roof fell in. It turned out that, according to Israeli officials, Aviv had never been part of the Mossad and he had never been more than a cabin steward and low-level security guard for the Israeli airline El Al. Aviv swore the whole story was true, but Israeli officials denounced him as a "crook and a fraud." He produced no evidence to back up his account of his adventures.

By 1988 Aviv was running a small down-at-the-heels security agency called Interfor. He sold intelligence information and advice to companies and occasionally was hired as a consultant on terrorism by news organizations, even prestigious shows like *60 Minutes* and *Nightline*. But his reputation was catching up with him, and business was not booming. Interfor had few if any employees besides Aviv himself, and we were told he sometimes rented a suite of offices with a good address for a day just to meet, and hopefully impress, prospective clients. The fringes of the intelligence world are littered with such people.

By the spring of 1989, many families had become so discouraged with the progress of the Pan Am 103 investigation, and so suspicious of it, that there was serious talk of hiring some sort of private investigator. Not one of us knew anything about the world of international intrigue, and were, therefore, obvious targets for anyone who claimed to be an "expert." At that point Juval Aviv appeared on the scene.

In the spring of '89 Paul Hudson, Rosemary Wolfe, and Kathleen Flynn were invited to the Washington office of a lawyer who also had ties to B'nai B'rith, a Jewish organization. Rosemary was under the impression that B'nai B'rith, an advocacy group, had taken up our cause and would help the families get a congressional investigation into the bombing. That was not the case. When the three arrived, the lawyer introduced them to Aviv, who was described as working with a consulting firm in New York. Aviv said he was formerly with the Israeli Intelligence Service, and had a lot of sources in a lot of places, and so had information that would be of use to the Pan Am 103 families.

Aviv didn't get very specific, but claimed that American intelligence knew about the threat to Pan Am 103 and didn't warn anyone because intelligence didn't want to compromise their sources. The key to the bombing, he said, was that two American organizations were part of a drug-smuggling operation that went bad. Aviv was quiet and reserved, and Rosemary believed he genuinely wanted to get his information out. She asked him to accompany the families in future lobbying efforts on the Hill. He said he would, and added that he'd like more contact with the families. Rosemary never saw him again.

Kathleen had a different impression. She was convinced Aviv was trying to sell information to the families. When she found out that the lawyer who arranged the meeting was not simply some idealistic humanitarian, but was actually Aviv's lawyer, she felt disgusted and betrayed. She wanted the family group to keep away from both Aviv and his lawyer. Henceforth, we would all be wary of the motives of people who offered us help.

DAN: The Malta connection was Pan Am's worst nightmare. If the evidence being developed through the second half of 1989 held up, it would indicate that the airline had deliberately and flagrantly ignored FAA regulations prohibiting unaccompanied baggage on a flight. It had allowed a bag to be checked through from Frankfurt to London to New York without matching it to an actual passenger. And because X rays could not detect plastic explosives, security personnel failed to find the bomb in the unaccompanied suitcase that destroyed the aircraft and 270 innocent lives. Any jury in the land would judge such actions as "willful misconduct," the $75,000 cap on damage awards would be thrown out, and the airline would face massive and perhaps crippling financial judgments.

The world of airline lawyers and insurance companies is a small and clubby one. Everyone knows everyone else and, if there are no hard-and-fast rules, there are at least certain understood procedures that are generally followed. One family member who had witnessed an early courtroom meeting between the Pan Am lawyers and the plaintiffs' lawyers complained that they all laughed and joked together like the best of friends.

Most suits resulting from airline disasters are settled before trial. The more "exposure" an airline has—that is, the more likely it is to be found liable—the greater the chance that the case will be settled out of court. Judges also encourage settlements because they don't want court time wasted on long drawn-out civil suits. U.S. District Court judge Thomas C. Platt, who had been assigned the case, certainly wanted to see a settlement. His court docket was already loaded, and this complicated case would overload it. He actively encouraged lawyers from both sides to work something out before a trial.

It's actually misleading to talk about "Pan Am's lawyers." Pan Am, like every other airline, was fully insured for claims resulting from airline disasters. Pan Am's insurance was held by a large syndicate of international insurance companies. The managing agent for the companies was a little-known insurance firm called U.S. Aviation Underwriters, Inc. Little known outside the aviation law community, that is. U.S. Aviation Underwriters was one of the largest and most powerful aviation insurers in the world, and it completely controlled the Pan Am defense, though the name never appeared in court papers or could be mentioned in open court. The chairman and chief executive of this insurance company was a Long Island multimillionaire named John V. Brennan, or "that sonofabitch Brennan," as Kreindler habitually called him.

It was Brennan's company that employed the firm of Windels, Marx, Davis and Ives to represent Pan Am and picked lawyer James Shaughnessy to lead the defense. While Pan Am CEO, the well-tailored Thomas Plaskett, was the front man, it was really Brennan who pulled all the strings. The airline itself might have wanted a quick settlement, for the longer the case dragged out the more bad publicity it got, and the more people stayed away from the struggling carrier. But U.S. Aviation Underwriters didn't have to worry about bad publicity. The public didn't even know they existed. The longer the case dragged on, the longer it would be before the insurers had to pay any claims. And if the issue became confused enough, then they might actually win in court because the concept of "willful misconduct" can be a difficult one for a jury of laypersons to grasp.

Against all expectations, Pan Am's lawyers dug in their heels and simply refused to discuss the possibility of settlement. Kreindler told us, "My eyesight and my hearing aren't as good as they once were. But my sense of smell is as good as ever, and something smells about this case."

Juval Aviv, who had been attempting without any success to peddle his services to family members or to the press, had finally found the right client for his wares. Around June 1989, Aviv went to work for Shaughnessy and the Pan Am legal team. He was paid a reported $100,000 or more, and urged to come up with something fast. Working virtually alone, in less than three months Aviv delivered to his employers a new, complex, shocking, and very convenient solution to the bombing of Pan Am 103. It was contained in the twenty-seven-page "Interfor Report" and handed over to Pan Am's lawyers early in September of 1989.

The report tells an exotic tale that begins with an alliance between three major Middle Eastern terrorist groups for the purpose of establishing a network of arms and drug smuggling. A central figure in this alliance was said to be a Syrian terrorist and drug smuggler named Monzer al-Kassar.

According to the "Interfor Report," al-Kassar had a system of smuggling drugs through the Frankfurt Airport. He would send one of his couriers or "mules" to the airport with a suitcase packed with clothes and other innocent items. After the bag was checked and passed through security, a baggage handler in al-Kassar's employ would switch it with an identical piece of luggage loaded with drugs. At the other end of the flight the mule would pick up the drug-filled suitcase and deliver it to whomever the customer happened to be. According to Aviv, a regular al-Kassar mule was a young Lebanese American named Khalid Jaafar.

The report states that the smuggling operation became known to the CIA, the U.S. Drug Enforcement Agency (DEA), and the German BKA. Instead of shutting the operation down, they tried to keep it under close surveillance and control. Here the plot thickens because, according to

Interfor, the CIA in Frankfurt was a rogue unit that operated without serious oversight from Washington. This group tried to use al-Kassar to obtain the release of U.S. hostages in Lebanon. The Syrian had played a role in getting French hostages out of Lebanon. In return these CIA rogues would see that his profitable drug smuggling would not be interfered with.

By the fall of 1988, the report says, international terrorists were being pushed by Iran to help revenge the downing of the Iran Air Flight 665 by the USS *Vincennes*. Ahmad Jibril of the PFLP/GC wanted to use the al-Kassar operation to put a bomb on a U.S. plane, but was unaware that al-Kassar was under CIA protection.

Al-Kassar did not inform the CIA about a bombing, and they allowed his operation to continue, even though they had many hints that a bombing was planned. A further complication was that another CIA team working in Lebanon to free hostages learned of the existence of the rogue group in Germany. The team prepared to rush back to the United States and expose not only the rogues but also the drug smuggling. The CIA team was headed by Army Major Charles McKee and Matthew Gannon. There were three other members of the team named in the report and three unnamed, but all eight were supposed to have boarded Pan Am 103 at Frankfurt for the trip home. That is why, according to the report, that particular flight was chosen for ultimate destruction.

This story sounds like the plot outline for a trashy spy thriller. And that's just about what it was. Aviv offered absolutely no evidence to back up his remarkable tale, saying only that it was based on information supplied by highly placed but anonymous informants. Aviv even claimed that he had seen a CIA videotape of the bomb being put aboard the plane and promised reporters that he would get them a copy. But he never did. According to published reports, passages in the report were actually plagiarized from an obscure 1984 German book about terrorism.

Overall, Aviv's tale had all the earmarks of a cooked-up conspiracy theory. Indeed, according to published reports,

Aviv had worked as an investigator for the Lyndon LaRouche organization in 1982, a well-known font of conspiracy theories. Just what the relationship was between the Israeli Aviv and the raving anti-Semite LaRouche is unclear, but over the years Susan and I were called several times by people identifying themselves as LaRouche operatives in Germany trying to get us to support Aviv's thesis, and LaRouche publications like *The Middle East Insider* boosted it every chance they got.

In the end not a single shred of this evidence ever made it into court during the Pan Am civil trial. Nor did any of the highly placed informants ever step forward. Yet the Interfor Report proved to be extremely useful to the airline's lawyers, and it has spread a fog of confusion over the Pan Am 103 story, which persists to this day.

Aviv's fantastic tale had several advantages for Pan Am. It completely exonerated the airline from any responsibility for the bombing. No matter how lousy Pan Am security was, if the bomb got on because of criminal activities condoned by an agency of the federal government, then Pan Am was not liable. Less than two weeks after the report was delivered, the Pan Am legal team hit the government with a blizzard of discovery subpoenas, to the CIA, the FBI, the NSA, the President's National Security Council, and the State Department, asking for sensitive information on activities in Frankfurt and elsewhere. These motions would delay the start of the civil trial. Aviv's report predicted that the agencies would seek to quash the subpoenas on national security grounds. Once that happened, it would look like a government cover-up and thereby "support Pan Am's status as victim."

The next step was to somehow leak the report to the public. Like all good conspiracy theories, the Interfor Report was a mixture of fact and fiction. It was not long since the Reagan administration had been rocked by the Iran-Contra scandal, where American arms had been traded for American hostages and money, and the money used to fund a dirty little war in Nicaragua. The Contras, the side the United States was supporting in Nicaragua, had often been linked to drug smuggling. Aviv's report reprised many of the Iran-Contra themes and spoke of the CIA rogues as running an "Oliver North-like" operation. Al-Kassar's name had even come up during the Iran-Contra investigations. Jaafar had already been identified in the press as a possible drug courier and the man who may have brought the bomb on the plane. McKee and Gannon's CIA connections were public knowledge.

The Pan Am 103 investigation seemed to be stalled, and many families were suspicious of the lack of progress. The public at large didn't trust the government anyway, and most people thought that there had been a conspiracy to kill JFK. So even if Aviv's whole story didn't hang together, a lot of people could conclude that there might be a "core of truth to it," and it was sensational enough to be a surefire attention getter.

Aviv told his employers that the families of the victims might be used to advance their agenda. "The passengers' relatives group can mount pressure on Congress if they are tipped," he said. Their recruitment "widens the field to include multiple players with different agendas."

One way to "tip" the families and the general public was to get the report widely known. But how? Aviv, a man with a shady reputation working for a company that was trying to fight off a massive lawsuit, was not going to be taken seriously by the major media. So Pan Am tried an end run.

A copy of the report was slipped to Ohio Representative James A. Traficant, Jr. Traficant is one of Congress's more exotic demagogues: a man in love with conspiracies and personal publicity. He says lots of goofy things, but he is an elected member of Congress and when a congressman—even an oddball like Traficant—talks, the press generally reports what he says. So practically every family member heard about Traficant's November 3, 1989, press conference. He read parts of the report about CIA involvement, though he didn't give the source.

We had been tipped off by a friendly reporter as to the real source of the "Traficant Report," so we were not particularly impressed or upset by what we heard. Besides, I had already written extensively about conspiracy theories, and I was not going to be easily swept up in this one, no matter how much I distrusted the government. Others reacted more strongly and began to suspect that a giant conspiracy of silence involving the U.S. government and the airline was beginning to unravel.

Basking in the attention, Traficant called another press conference five days later. This time he was accompanied by Victor Marchetti, a former CIA official turned critic and conspiracy theorist. Marchetti revealed that he had given the report to Traficant but had no hand in preparing it, and he would not say who had given it to him. "I think the report is basically accurate," he said. "The fact that the CIA denies it convinces me I am right."

Then the report began popping up in lots of places like the *Toronto Star* and some British newspapers. LaRouche's operatives in Germany had faxed a copy of the report to the family of a British victim who then gave it to the press. John Merritt, chief reporter for the London *Observer,* tried to check out some of the details in the report and found them to be either uncheckable or totally bogus. A long *Observer* article was devastating, but it did not kill Aviv's hydra-headed tale.

All along Aviv denied that he had given copies of his report to anyone but the lawyers for Pan Am. But Merritt later testified before a federal magistrate that Aviv had personally given him the report in a meeting at a New York hotel in November. Aviv then claimed that Thomas Plaskett, the chairman of Pan Am, had already given the report to ABC news in London, a claim that Plaskett vigorously denied.

Pan Am's lawyers were still trying to use Aviv's noxious fantasies as the core of their defense. According to Aviv a key to the drug and bomb plot had been corrupt baggage handlers at Frankfurt. The baggage handlers who worked flight 103 were given polygraph tests, and according to the polygraph operator hired by the airline two of them showed indications of lying. Pan Am management then sent the two handlers, Roland O'Neill and Kilins Aslan Tuzcu, on a mysterious mission to London's Heathrow Airport, where they were supposed to pick up a sealed package from a man in a gray suit. Apparently the airline believed that Scotland Yard would be interested in questioning them once they got to London. Scotland Yard wasn't, so the two baggage handlers returned to Frankfurt, where they found out they had been suspended from their jobs. Though they had already been closely interrogated and exonerated by the German police, they were subject to more intense questioning as a result of the Pan Am polygraph report. At this point O'Neill hired an American lawyer who promptly challenged the polygraph results. By now a minor diplomatic furor had erupted, and the German police considered filing kidnapping charges against those who had arranged sending the two handlers to London. An embarrassed Pan Am backed down and reinstated the two men. Still, some Pan Am 103 relatives (we were not among them) wondered whether this series of events wasn't all part of some sort of cover-up, particularly after the polygraph operator was subpoenaed to testify before a grand jury in Washington.

No action was ever taken by the grand jury and nothing concrete ever resulted from this strange episode, except to deepen the fog of suspicion that surrounded the entire Pan Am 103 case. Perhaps that had been the point of the whole thing in the first place.

By June of 1990, Juval Aviv was no longer employed by Pan Am's lawyers, but the mischief that he had created lingered on, and spread.

SUSAN: Sheila Hershow, who worked for ABC's *Primetime*, a weekly news show with a magazine-style format, came to a Victims of Pan Am 103 family meeting and spoke skillfully and movingly to the families. Sheila had met my father-in-law, Milt Cohen, in Chicago when she worked for Cardis Collins, a black congresswoman who later held hearings on Pan Am 103. Milt, whom I admired enormously, devoted his life to causes he believed in, a list of which included civil rights and equal rights. So Dan and I were a natural route to the Victims group for Sheila.

Primetime was new, and it was not doing well. ABC decided to air a major presentation on Pan Am 103 around the first anniversary, which they hoped would increase the ratings and reputation of the show.

Top reporters and media stars Sam Donaldson and Diane Sawyer would appear on camera and, of course, oversee much of the show. The network put time, effort, money, and staff into the project, even taking out full-page newspaper ads around the country to promote it.

Primetime covered evidence of Iran and Syria's involvement in the bombing, vividly exposed Pan Am's shocking lack of security (the celebrated trained German shepherds that were supposed to be bomb-sniffing dogs got national TV attention), and failures of the FAA. It also focused poignantly on particular victims, including Theo.

A large number of family members had been invited to attend the show, which was broadcast live. During a special second hour, we were able to question the various reporters, at least one member of Congress, Senator Frank Lautenberg, and a number of other experts in various fields who had agreed to appear. Both the U.S. government and Pan Am airlines declined invitations to send representatives.

The network's hopes were realized. Thanks to the Pan Am 103 broadcast, *Primetime*'s ratings soared, and the show won several top journalism awards. It's no exaggeration to suggest that the show saved *Primetime*.

One of my therapists told me that after seeing the show, his wife vowed never to fly Pan Am, and he was sure anybody else who watched it would feel the same way. *Primetime*'s investigative journalism scalded the government and the airline, and proved that the Pan Am 103 story had staying power.

Sheila was a find. Not only was she an outstanding off-camera reporter, she taught me a lot about the inner workings of the media. Dan provided ABC with precious pictures and videotapes of Theo, which Sheila vowed to, and did, return in perfect condition. *Primetime* flew Annie Lareau, Theo's friend from Syracuse, to London to show reporters where Theo had lived. There Diane Sawyer interviewed Annie. I did all that I could to help, but I was scared. I knew that watching the show was going to be emotionally costly.

Primetime ran the Pan Am 103 story on November 30, 1989. Sam Donaldson and Diane Sawyer were pros, but they faced a difficult situation. They had a studio audience of freshly wounded victims of an atrocity; as Eileen Leary, my therapist, said to me, "A year is nothing in grief time." Both journalists handled the live portion of the show very gracefully. I had always considered Diane Sawyer a lightweight brains-wise because she came out of the era of the mushy woman reporter, when women got on-camera jobs in television news because of charm and good looks. But when I met and talked to her, I found her very intelligent.

When the part about Theo aired, I gripped Dan's arm. There Theo was on the enormous television screen in the studio, literally larger than life, looking relaxed and happy, a pretty girl in a yellow sweater, enjoying a nice day. I thought of all the nice days that would never happen. Watching, I learned Theo's body landed in a sheep meadow less than a mile from the main wreckage. For no logical reason I'd always pictured her inside the actual plane. There were corpses in the plane, strapped in their seat belts. Not Theo's. What force could whip my Theo a whole mile, and how hard she must have hit the ground. I could hear the crunch of her bones breaking. Nor did the irony escape me, when ABC showed the video of Theo singing and dancing in a high school musical; that kid who had dreamed of stardom was performing for millions of people after she was dead.

The families were tough and eloquent on *Primetime,* none more so than Hope Asrelsky, who said of Rachel and the other young students who had died on the plane, "They were the best and the brightest, and they were destroyed by the least and the worst."

Primetime ran the Pan Am show again a year later. I couldn't watch it. Not twice.

DAN: While the government didn't actually send a current employee to defend their position on the *Primetime* segment, a former State Department counterterrorism expert attended to fill in. I recognized him as one of the regular talking heads on news shows about terrorism. He had been defending the way the State Department handled the task of contacting the families, and John Root nailed him for all of us:

"I couldn't disagree with you more. In fact, I'm very close to calling you a liar. One month ago, I received back the effects—oh, what the hell! You *are* a liar . . ."

After the show was over, family members poured onto the studio floor. I saw the former State Department official pushing his way through the crowd. He was talking to himself, loudly. "I didn't know what this would be like. I'm never going through something like this again."

Chapter 10

DAN: Quitting the Victims of Pan Am 103 group, an organization we had once believed was absolutely necessary for our survival, turned out to be very liberating. We didn't have to attend any of those depressing meetings anymore. We didn't have to get into arguments with people who were offended by our aggressive style. Paul Hudson had formally left the Victims group in August 1989, and formed a second group, Families of Pan Am 103—Lockerbie. We associated ourselves with that group, but loosely. We didn't attend any of their meetings.

We found Paul increasingly difficult to deal with. He would no longer take calls, and would communicate only by fax. We didn't have a fax, and every time we wanted to get in touch with him, I had to drive over to a local copy shop. It was inconvenient and expensive, and Paul generally didn't answer our faxes. Since we had no hand in making policy, and didn't really know what group policies were, we didn't feel bound by them. "Speaking with a single voice" had always been, and still was, a guiding principle for Victims of Pan Am 103. We had clawed our way out of the state of numb dependency that had gripped us in the early months. Now we were speaking with our own voice, and we were going to make it as loud and strident as possible. If other people didn't like it—too bad. We weren't speaking for a group anymore, we were speaking for Theo.

The call for an independent investigation of the bombing had generated a lot of public support, but it floundered in Washington. President Bush wanted nothing to do with it.

Congress showed no more enthusiasm. There was a proposal to establish an independent commission to examine aviation security and the circumstances of the bombing. However, it was to be chaired by Secretary of Transportation Samuel Skinner and the panel would be made up of representatives of the Department of Transportation, the CIA and the airline industry. "It was like a grand jury where a majority of the members would be relatives of the suspects," Paul quite correctly observed.

The President made an end run. On August 4, 1989, just as Congress was leaving for its summer break, President Bush issued an executive order creating the President's Commission on Aviation Security and Terrorism. The commission lacked subpoena power and was barred from examining intelligence operations and anything to do with the criminal investigation into the bombing of Pan Am 103. Both Bert Ammerman and Paul Hudson hailed creation of the commission. We were much less enthusiastic, particularly when we found out who the members would be.

There would be four members from Congress: senators Frank Lautenberg, Democrat of New Jersey, and Alphonse D'Amato, Republican of New York; and representatives James Oberstar, Democrat of Minnesota, and Republican Paul Hammerschmidt of Arkansas. They were all good party men, not congressional powerhouses known for their independence. Worst of all was the chairman, or in this case chairwoman, Ann McLaughlin, a Republican party stalwart, former secretary of labor in the Reagan administration. She was also the wife of John McLaughlin, host of *The McLaughlin Group*—in my opinion still the most idiotic Washington talk show on television.

This looked like a setup for one of those commissions that is established to deal with a difficult problem by diddling around and keeping it out of the news until it all blows over. Typically these commissions take a long time and then quietly issue a report that no one ever reads, or ever should.

This time our cynical view was wrong.

SUSAN: Kathleen Flynn kept telling me that the best imaginable person was under consideration to head the commission. But she wouldn't tell me who it was. She became cagey and secretive whenever I asked her, maybe because she was afraid I'd tip off the press. When she finally announced to me it would be Ann McLaughlin, I was anything but thrilled. I was suspicious of all Reaganites. Kathleen told me I could trust Ann. She and Ann had been good friends since Marymount College days. Why, Ann had been at J.P.'s christening, had stayed with the Flynns, knew the whole family.

As to being a right-wing Republican, Kathleen said Ann was a people person, very real and down-to-earth, a self-made success story, a woman who'd worked hard to get where she was, a woman who'd done it on her own. Didn't I admire women like that? So what if she'd been Reagan's secretary of labor. She wasn't Bush's secretary of labor. She wasn't a Bush Republican. She was strongly patriotic, highly competent and no weakling when it came to recommending military action. She would not sell out the families.

I was still skeptical. Did friendship matter in Washington? People didn't bother to sell their souls there. They just threw them away at the first whiff of power. I began to trust McLaughlin after she received an endorsement from David Evans, a *Chicago Tribune* military affairs reporter whom I respected. A Marine Corps helicopter pilot during the Vietnam War, he had returned from combat an idealist and a reformer who would eventually work for a publication promoting airline security and safety. He told me Ann McLaughlin was a very good choice. That made two favorable opinions.

Kathleen worked closely with Ann and the commission liaison to the families' Washington lawyer Frank Dugan. I kept in touch with Dugan on my own. As for Kathleen, we talked every day and sometimes late at night, not just about the commission but about Theo and J.P. and our daily suffering, but politics and the fight were what bound us together. I watched Kathleen reassure other families about the commission, interest our mutual lawyer Lee Kreindler in it, and express her faith in the media. There is comedy even in tragedy, and I laughed when Kathleen told me that Ann McLaughlin was so busy that Kathleen had turned over her files of articles, notes, etc., to her in one place they were sure to meet, the beauty salon!

McLaughlin's powers were limited. But she and other commission members did the best job possible under the circumstances. They did not betray the families. McLaughlin's integrity taught me a valuable lesson. Honor does not come with an ideological stamp of approval, and even in Washington you will occasionally find a decent human being.

DAN: When the McLaughlin report was delivered in mid-May of 1990, it was far stronger than anything we could possibly have hoped for. It stated forthrightly that the Pan Am 103 disaster had been "preventable." It criticized the FAA, the State Department, and the aviation industry. It pointed out that months after the bombing, Pan Am had still failed to correct many of the obvious flaws in its security system. And it went further. The report went right after the terrorists themselves. "The United States must not be held hostage by a handful of outlaw nations," Ann McLaughlin told a news conference. Perhaps the report's most controversial suggestion was that the United States should consider conducting preemptive strikes against terrorist centers in order to prevent future attacks.

This report wasn't issued quietly late on a Friday afternoon after all the reporters had gone home, either. It was given full publicity treatment. All victims' family members were invited to Washington for the formal presentation of the report. The President was even going to speak, though we heard that he was not thrilled about the report itself. The press was to be barred from his speech.

SUSAN: I thought it would be a somber and telling act if the families would rise when Bush entered the room, then turn their backs on him. I knew it was pointless to even suggest such a thing, but Dan and I remained seated when the President came in, and a few others did as well. Though some family members were eager to shake his hand, over-all applause was cool.

DAN: I found George Bush's brief speech bizarre. He talked about recently meeting families of sailors who had been killed in an explosion aboard the battleship *Iowa* a few months earlier. He said that was hard to do, but he still loved being president. He broke off in the middle of sentences. He leaned awkwardly over the podium, waved his hands a lot, and wandered randomly from topic to topic, barely mentioning Pan Am 103 or terrorism. John Sununu, the President's Chief of Staff, Brent Scowcroft, the national security adviser, and a couple of other aides hovered at the edge of the stage, looking nervous. Bush's speech was so confused and disjointed, I thought he was drunk or on some sort of heavy medication. I was afterward assured that this was a very typical speech for George Bush. I guess he just didn't want to talk about Pan Am 103, so he didn't.

As we were leaving, a puzzled-looking young woman whose husband had died in the disaster said to me, "He pushed all the wrong buttons, didn't he?"

SUSAN: According to Kathleen, Ann McLaughlin had to fight hard to get the Bush administration to give the Pan Am victims' families the sort of flags that are usually given out to the families of soldiers who die in action. Dan and I decided to refuse the flag. We did not do this lightly. The flag is a powerful symbol, and giving flags to the families acknowledged that the bombing was an act of violence against America. We felt that the flag had been disgraced by the government's cowardice and inaction, and we thought that refusing it publicly was a way of making that point. One other Pan Am 103 family member, Eleanor Bright, agreed with us.

If anyone needed proof that a wife's love for her husband could be as potent and long-lasting as a parent's for a child, Eleanor was that proof. Nicholas Bright had had it all, a happy marriage, a cute baby boy, brains, good looks, a Harvard MBA, a successful business career, and a home near Boston. Eleanor was New England to her bones: youthful, thin, athletic, deceptively steely in appearance; a woman who jogged routinely and was a superb rider of horses. Bright was a good name for this couple who planned to have four children and live happily ever after.

The death of her husband crushed Eleanor, shattering her as Theo's death shattered me. Not a day goes by that she does not cry for him still. Because of Eleanor's obvious suffering, sensitivity, and reverence for her husband's memory, the families liked her. She had been elected vice president of the Victims of Pan Am 103 group. When her turn came to meet Ann McLaughlin and receive the flag, she refused it with quiet dignity, but everyone could see she turned it down. A buzz went through the crowd awaiting their turn. A startled woman sitting behind me said, "Oh, she's not taking the flag." Her refusal made an impression on people. It got them thinking about choices.

When it was my turn, I went up to Ann McLaughlin. I found her friendly and told her why I could not accept a flag. She seemed to understand. I thanked her for all she had done. I wouldn't shake George Bush's hand for a million bucks, but I am glad I met Ann McLaughlin.

DAN: The split between the two family groups was never more obvious than on that May day. Members of Bert's group wore the blue "The Truth Must be Known" pins. Members of Paul's group wore the same button decorated with a sprig of Scottish heather and a tartan ribbon. The two groups held rival press conferences, but both praised the report and both received wide and even-handed media coverage.

Susan and I didn't wear any buttons, and we went to both press conferences. On the platform at Paul's press conference were the officers of his organization, most of whom we knew and a fellow we didn't recognize. Kathleen told us who he was. It was the same lawyer who had introduced her to Juval Aviv. Kathleen said, "I'm outta here."

The next day we wrote a letter to Paul formally resigning from his organization. We didn't know what he was doing, or trying to do. We just couldn't trust him anymore.

While the McLaughlin report was hard-hitting, received a tremendous amount of publicity, and contained a wealth of useful recommendations, in the end it suffered the fate of practically every other special commission report that has ever been issued in Washington. It was ignored. The President offered perfunctory thanks to the commission members, and then, for all practical purposes, shoved the report in the bottom drawer and never looked at it again. Many of the shortcomings in airline security that the report exposed are still with us over a decade later.

Fortunately, there haven't been any successful bombings of U.S. airliners during this period, though several have been attempted or planned. But I am reminded of what was said in the original report on Pan Am security in 1987: "The fact that no major disaster has occurred to date is merely providential." It is still quite possible that determined terrorists with a little luck could blow up a plane going from New York to Disneyland at Christmastime.

The political landscape of the Middle East shifted dramatically during the summer of 1990. Iraq's dictator, Saddam Hussein, once considered a reliable if disreputable ally, suddenly decided to annex the small oil-rich sheikdom of Kuwait on Iraq's southern border. Saddam had been led to believe that America would simply let him do it. Instead the Bush administration reacted energetically and rounded up an international coalition of forces, including some from oil-rich monarchies like Saudi Arabia; there was also Syria, a longtime rival of Iraq. Iran, Iraq's deadliest foe in that part of the world, agreed to stand on the sidelines if there was a war.

Though the forces opposed to Iraq were called a coalition, it was really an American operation with token forces from other nations as window dressing. The United States put hundreds of thousands of troops and an unprecedented array of high-tech military equipment into the Arabian Desert and waited for Saddam to withdraw from Kuwait.

SUSAN: We had been trying to get a meeting with William Sessions, the director of the FBI. We finally got one, but as the Iraq crisis deepened we figured it would be postponed or canceled. I called almost daily to check if the meeting was still on. It was. We went to Washington just two days before the bombing of Baghdad began. Everyone knew what was coming and official Washington was on a semiwartime status, with vastly increased antiterrorist security. The FBI building bristled with guards. Visiting it was eerie for Dan and me.

My mother-in-law went bananas when she learned we were going to the main FBI headquarters. I swear she thought the ghost of J. Edgar Hoover would appear to whisk us off to a secret torture chamber hidden in the bowels of the building and lock us in. I couldn't blame her. She knew from personal experience that Hoover's FBI persecuted the left. The new FBI seemed embarrassed about Hoover. The FBI Building was named for him, and there were pictures of him around, but the atmosphere was more bureaucratic than fanatic.

I prepared for the meeting with FBI Director Sessions and his staff by calling a reporter for advice about talking to big shots. How could I trip Sessions up so that he'd actually tell us something significant? The reporter suggested I direct questions to the other agents at the meeting. They would be the people most familiar with the Pan Am investigation, and if they were taken by surprise they just might let something slip. It was a long shot, but worth a try.

With his silver hair and erect posture, Director Sessions looked like an actor cast in the role, rather than a political appointee. Jack and Kathleen Flynn and the Wolfes were there for the meeting. We sat across the table from Sessions, who was flanked on either side by FBI men, one of whom Jack Flynn knew from the old neighborhood in the Bronx where they both grew up. The FBI agents wore suits and ties and had neat haircuts. They deferred to Sessions. The atmosphere was formal, controlled, and hierarchical. I kept winging questions at Sessions' subordinates, but each time I did, Sessions got so mad his eyes actually flashed with anger. So my end-run approach didn't get me anywhere.

Sessions told us he could not comment on an ongoing case. There already was talk of upcoming indictments of the terrorists. We all said we didn't want sealed indictments because then they could just slam Pan Am 103 into a secret file, say they were working hard to get the terrorists without telling us who they were, and let the case go nowhere, all out of public view. We didn't get answers, we got reassurances.

DAN: As we were leaving, I asked Sessions if indictments would really be of any use, whether Pan Am 103 was something for the judicial system at all. After all, this wasn't a drive-by shooting, it was really a military attack on America, and should properly be answered in political or military terms. He thought for a moment and said, "You may very well be right."

Then we stepped out into Washington, which was readying itself to make war in the Middle East over oil and the safety of the Kuwaiti royal family.

We had no objection to attacking Iraq. Saddam was, and is, a monster, and there may be no other way of dealing with his kind. What struck us, and a lot of other family members that we talked to, was the disproportionate nature of the response. George Bush went on television and said that he had been moved to tears over the plight of the poor Kuwaitis. He had displayed only dithering confusion and evasion over the plight of those, mostly Americans, who had died on Pan Am 103. It seemed clear to us that the royal family of Kuwait were people the President of the United States was genuinely concerned about, while Theo Cohen, American citizen, was quite unimportant.

The Gulf War was a walkover for the spectacularly equipped American forces. Casualties were kept very low; in fact, more Americans were killed in the Pan Am 103 bombing than in the entire Gulf War. Of course a decade later, Saddam Hussein is still with us, so the war was not exactly a famous victory for the United States.

Most upsetting to us at this time was the Bush announcement that right after Thanksgiving he was going to pay a visit to Syria's Hafez al-Assad in Damascus, making him the first U.S. president ever to visit the Syrian dictator. At the time Syria was still, as far as we knew, at the top of the list of suspects in the Pan Am bombing. Syria was certainly implicated in other terrorist acts against Americans: for example, the bombing of the marine barracks in Lebanon in 1984. Al-Assad's record of slaughtering domestic opposition easily matched that of Saddam for brutality. The handful of Syrian troops sent to fight Saddam should not have outweighed his record. But George Bush was going to have a nice cozy little chat with the dictator, pose for a few pictures, and generally boost al-Assad's prestige in the world.

We couldn't stand it. We sat down and wrote a furious letter to Bush containing such words as "cynical, amoral, and unforgivable." We noted that he said he had been "moved to tears" by photos of atrocities in Kuwait and offered to send him some of the recently released autopsy photos of Pan Am 103 victims to cry over. We said, "You have dishonored the nation, which you increasingly fail to lead." Then we faxed the letter to the White House. We didn't expect a response. Bush had rarely, if ever, responded to letters from Pan Am 103 families, even friendly or pathetic letters. So we sent copies of our letter around to various journalists we knew. One of them, Chicago columnist Mike Royko, printed the letter in full in his popular syndicated column, and added a few acerbic comments of his own.

That got Bush's attention. A few days after the Royko

column appeared, we received a response from the White House. It came flat, in a large manila envelope with cardboard backing, as though it was something we would want to frame and hang on our wall to proudly show visitors. "Lookie here—a letter from THE PRESIDENT!"

SUSAN: The letter came on one of those mornings when I was too depressed to get dressed and was sitting near the fireplace in my bathrobe. Pat Ianone, who had driven twenty-five miles from her home every day to help in the first month after the bombing, was with me when it arrived. I read it, and after what Bush had put us through, it was such blatant hypocrisy I was tempted to throw it in the fireplace. I burst into bitter tears. Pat tried to console me and said, "Don't think about George Bush, Susan. Think about your friends who love you." But there was no way the kindest of loving friends could erase what George Bush had done, or to put it more accurately, what he hadn't done. And the letter stung. Bush had a tin ear for language, and a tin ear for justice as well.

The cadences of Bush's speech were so evident in the letter, I assumed he had written it himself. He had signed it himself. He wrote "with a heavy heart" and felt our "hurt and tragic personal loss." He defended his meeting with al-Assad, and said he had spoken "frankly" with the dictator about terrorism. He then thanked us for "writing from the heart." All the letter lacked was the phrase "my heartfelt sympathies" to be a perfect masterpiece of clichés. When I read it to Jim Wolfe, he said sarcastically, "Sounds like him all right. Save it. You can always sell it for a few bucks someday if you get really hard up."

We made a copy of Bush's letter and sent it to A. M. Rosenthal at the *New York Times*, who wrote a strong and moving column about it. Well, at least they now knew who we were at the White House, and though we were too unimportant to matter very much to Bush, at least we wouldn't win any popularity contests with him. Good!

DAN: Buried in a *Washington Post* report on the Bush and al-Assad meeting was the information that al-Assad had actually made a Pan Am 103 joke. Al-Assad was known among dictators as the one with a sense of humor. He told Bush that there would be complications for the American President if Ahmed Jibril were ever extradited. Jibril would, no doubt, be let out on bail, would hire a lawyer and, if acquitted, would "ask for a green card."

There was no indication that Bush made any response to this cruel and tasteless statement. Instead of just feeling sick with rage—though that was certainly how we felt—we put out a press release and sent it around to media people we knew. That generated some stories, and syndicated columnist Martin Schram wrote about it. Embarrassing questions about the joke were asked at White House and State Department press briefings. The response was that they could "find no record" of such a comment. It was the classic Watergate-era non denial denial. The White House called one journalist and registered extreme displeasure at what he had written on the subject.

It wasn't much. Just the tiniest chip in the wall of official indifference. But it was lots better than staying respectful and polite and tearing your guts out in private. Once again, we felt we had done some good work.

SUSAN: Avi Weiss was an Orthodox rabbi who was very different from the other religious leaders I had met or heard from. Like many grief therapists, the others held me back. Avi, as he liked to be called, pushed me forward. A deeply moral man, he was a political activist, one of the camp who saw fighting for justice as an integral part of Judaism. He had led many of the civil disobedience protests at Auschwitz. I first learned of Avi from Cynthia Ozick, who suggested I call him to see if he could help.

It was right after the Gulf War. There was going to be a victory parade in New York City with troops or representatives from all of the countries of the coalition against Iraq. One country on that list was Syria. I phoned Avi and

found him eager to help. He spoke movingly about the loss
of 270 souls as a result of the Pan Am bombing, and passionately about his love for Israel. Syria had not been
cleared in the bombing, and I was sickened as I watched al-
Assad receive administration absolution. Avi was not one
to stand quietly while the Bush administration transformed al-Assad the terrorist into al-Assad the statesman.
He had actually gotten hold of a letter from the State Department to New York Mayor David Dinkins suggesting
Syrian participation in the parade.

We sent a letter to Mayor Dinkins objecting to the Syrian presence, and naturally sent copies to all the news
media. A leading Runyon-esque local New York television
reporter, Gabe Pressman, came out to Port Jervis to interview Dan and me. Gabe loved his work, he loved New
York, and it showed. He knew more about New York politics than anybody. I told him it would be a desecration if
Syrians marched in the streets of America's freest and
greatest city, the city of ticker-tape parades for champions.
Gabe Pressman listened, liked what he heard, and gave me
a newsman's appraisal. "We'll make it a story," he said.

We held our demonstration at City Hall. The protesters
were several Pan Am 103 family members, Avi Weiss, and
a contingent from his synagogue. Mayor Dinkins went into
City Hall while we were there, but he moved quickly, and
we didn't have a chance to confront him. We went to the
office of City Council President Andrew Stein, who spoke
out for us. The demonstration got a lot of coverage, and the
idea of Syrians marching in the streets of New York became a New York story and a New York issue. Mayor
Dinkins said "no Syrians." The Syrians said that they had
never intended to go to New York anyway. The State Department said nothing. Parade day came and there were no
Syrians. Not even a Syrian flag.

Avi possessed a silver tongue and was one of the most
persuasive people I ever met. He loved the grand gesture,
high drama, the shot heard around the world, exploded not
from a gun but recorded by a camera. Brave and bold himself, Avi had big ideas for me. Avi wanted me to fly to Dam-

ascus with Alan Dershowitz, who was also his lawyer. It would be a symbolic statement about Pan Am 103 and Syrian terrorism in general. He told me Dershowitz was interested in doing this. What Dershowitz really thought, I never knew. Were we supposed to ask to see al-Assad? What was the point of this? What was Dershowitz supposed to do?

Avi assured me I would be perfectly safe. I would remain in the plane, which would stay at the Damascus International Airport for a few hours, then take off and return to America. I told Avi I wasn't afraid of going to Syria. I had the courage that comes to those who feel they have nothing more to lose. But while big things didn't scare me anymore, little things petrified me. If I lost sleep, I dissolved. Mini breakdowns hadn't stopped. And flying was a nightmare. I wasn't in shape to fly to Syria. Dan, who doesn't put his foot down on many things, was adamantly against my going. He said it was "a crazy idea." He complained to Avi for suggesting it in the first place.

So Avi came up with another idea. The Syrians were supposed to be going to Rome to take part in Middle East peace talks that were being held there. The world media would be on the scene. He and I should go there together and look for an opportunity to do something that would get their attention. Once again I had to say no. I didn't have the physical stamina for that kind of an adventure, and Dan was dead set against it. In the end Avi went with John Root. The two wandered around Rome, the press found them, and they had their moment in the sun. I could but cheer them on from my home. John denounced the Syrians, and a picture of him denouncing them circled the globe. It was worth a thousand words.

Chapter 11

DAN: Our meeting with FBI Director Sessions was the first solid indication we had that the United States and Britain were planning to indict someone for the Pan Am bombing. But during the Gulf War and its immediate aftermath, all speculation was on hold. By the spring of '91, the rumors began to circulate once again, with a new element added—the individuals to be indicted were Libyans.

That last bit of information left us puzzled and deeply suspicious. We certainly knew that Libya and its loony leader, Colonel Moammar Gadhafi, had been among the chief sponsors of terrorism throughout the world. We knew that in 1986 Ronald Reagan had ordered the bombing of Libya's capital, Tripoli, ostensibly in retaliation for a Libyan-sponsored bombing of a nightclub in Germany, which resulted in the death of an American serviceman and a German woman, and the wounding of several others.

The Tripoli raid was probably an attempt to get Gadhafi himself. The bombs missed "the Leader," and a score of other Libyans were killed, apparently including Gadhafi's adopted eighteen-month-old daughter Hana.

But for over two years Libya had never, as far as we knew, been publicly mentioned in all the speculation and theorizing that had surrounded Pan Am 103. By 1991 Syria and Iran, the chief suspects, had either supported the United States in the Gulf War or remained conveniently neutral. Gadhafi, on the other hand, had been an outspoken supporter of Saddam Hussein. Now, suddenly it seemed, he turned up as a chief suspect in the deadliest terrorist attack on American civilians in history. Libya was also a convenient target. It has lots of oil, though not nearly as much as a country like Saudi Arabia. In 1991 Libya had virtually no direct business dealings with the United States. It had a small population, and didn't represent a significant military threat to the United States or American interests. Gadhafi's irrational behavior had often set him at odds with other Middle Eastern leaders. Of the states that sponsored terrorism, Libya was undoubtedly the weakest and most unpopular. So when the-Libyans-did-it rumors began to flow from Washington, suspicion was inevitable.

By the fall of 1991, there was a flood of rumors in the press that indictments in the Pan Am bombing were imminent. But would we know about them? When we had talked to FBI Director Sessions, he had mentioned the possibility of "sealed indictments." The endless peace talks between Israel and its Arab neighbors had reached a temporary high point. We were afraid that significant developments in the bombing investigation would be kept secret to avoid disrupting the talks. The badly split Pan Am families were united on one point. We were all against sealed indictments; we wanted to know, we wanted the world to know, what was going on.

Early in November 1991, Bert Ammerman and five other members of the Victims of Pan Am 103 group traveled to Europe on what was billed as a "final journey." The trip was given extensive coverage on NBC. They visited Lockerbie, London, and other places associated with the bombing. It was clear that both the Victims group and NBC knew the indictments would be handed down very soon.

On November 14, 1991, the indictments were finally made public. A selected number of "prominent" families— we were among them—were to receive special preliminary briefings from an FBI agent and later a phone call from Attorney General-designate William Barr himself. The leaders of the Victims group had better administration contacts, but we had better press contacts. Susan and I knew exactly what was going to happen before any of the other relatives did. When the FBI agent arrived at our

home on the morning of November 14, he found the lawn
full of reporters and cameramen. We had learned the vital
importance of getting our message out first. Often the first
statement was the only one the press carried. In any case,
those who disagreed then had to react—and your message
got out twice.

The FBI agent who visited us was a rather elderly man,
polite and very uncomfortable. I asked him if he would
mind if we invited the press in during our private briefing.
He said he didn't think that would be a good idea, and I
didn't pursue the point. The media could have been there,
because the agent didn't tell us a thing that we, and they,
didn't already know—that two Libyans were going to be
indicted. It was strictly a courtesy call. We did express our
skepticism that Libya alone could be the culprit, and I
asked how it was possible for the Syrian-based terrorists
and the Libyan terrorists to build nearly identical bombs at
the same time and for the same purpose and not be connected. He said, "Maybe they went to the same school." I
tried to conjure up a vision of the graduating class at Terrorist U. What would their school song have been?

SUSAN: An ABC-TV crew was with me at my kitchen
phone when the Attorney General-designate William Barr
called. They closed around me while I gripped the phone
tightly. Making no attempt to hold back my anger, I said
forcefully, "What about Iran and Syria? What about Iran
and Syria?" The Attorney General was polite but sounded
very uncomfortable. He didn't answer my question but
said that the Justice Department was going to hold a meeting with the Pan Am 103 families to discuss the indictment. I figured it would be a big propaganda session. As
we talked, I repeated every word he said for the reporters. Finally Barr caught on to what I was doing,
gasped, and said, "Do you have the media there?" I told
him there was a crew from ABC-TV. He mumbled about
having to get off the phone, and did so quickly. The
woman in charge of the television crew called her office

in New York. "I think I've got what you want," she said. "She [meaning me] was very aggressive."

DAN: In announcing the indictments of the two Libyan suspects, the Bush administration put on quite a show. The Attorney General-designate and other high-ranking officials of the Justice Department, the FBI, and the State Department trooped in front of the cameras to congratulate one another, and to tell each other and the television audience what a great job they had done "solving" the mystery of Pan Am 103. They bragged about how they had painstakingly examined hundreds of thousands of bits of debris combed from over an 845-square-mile area where the wreckage of the Pan Am plane fell to earth, how investigators had interviewed over fourteen thousand potential witnesses in over fifty countries. As part of the investigation, the shattered wreckage of the plane had been virtually reconstructed in a hangar in Scotland. The Pan Am 103 investigation was called the most extensive criminal investigation in history. It had been an impressive and expensive investigation, but no one had yet been convicted or even arrested. To us, all this mutual backslapping seemed premature and excessive.

Compared to most indictment announcements, which are spare, factual, and short, this was an extravaganza. Administration officials knew they had a lot of convincing to do. The Bush administration had been stung by past criticism of their investigation. They also knew that the public at large and the victims' relatives in particular would be skeptical of the sudden appearance of Libya as sole suspect—and the disappearance of Syria, America's newfound ally, from the list of suspects. However, the administration was eager to sell its case. Later in the day, during an unrelated photo op, President Bush dropped a carefully crafted "casual" remark. "The Syrians got a bum rap on this," he said. It was the most memorable public statement President George Bush ever made on the subject of the bombing of Pan Am 103.

As the indictment was being announced in Washington, a similar high-profile presentation was taking place in London, where the British government announced a nearly identical indictment.

Indicted were Abdel Basset Ali al-Megrahi and Lamen Khalifa Fhimah, both described as experienced Libyan intelligence agents who, as a cover, had worked for Libyan Arab Airlines in Malta. According to the indictments, Fhimah had stored explosives in his Malta office during the summer of 1988. He and al-Megrahi prepared the bomb in the fall and placed it inside the brown Samsonite suitcase. Then Fhimah, because his airline job gave him access to practically everywhere in Malta's Luqa airport, obtained Air Malta luggage tags. On December 21 al-Megrahi inserted the deadly suitcase, with an Air Malta tag (indicating that the final destination of the bag was Kennedy Airport, via Pan Am 103), onto Air Malta flight 180 out of Malta's Luqa airport. On the same morning al-Megrahi boarded Libyan Arab Airlines flight 147 to Tripoli. Al-Megrahi's flight back to Libya checked in at the same airport passenger check-in counter as Air Malta 180, and the check-in periods for the two flights overlapped.

The turning point for the case, we learned that day, came in mid-1990 when investigators were able to identify a tiny bit of an electronic circuit board fragment that had been discovered in the shreds of a shirt that had been packed inside the Samsonite suitcase containing the bomb. Forensic examination was able to determine that the fragment came from an electronic timer manufactured by MEBO, initials for the Swiss firm Meister et Bollier Ltd. Historically this company had close connections with Libyan intelligence. Al-Megrahi had actually rented space at MEBO's Zurich office and had traveled there at least twice in December 1988.

The sophisticated timer was one of a limited number of twenty that had been made as a special order for the Libyan government in 1985 and 1986.

Intelligence information linked the Pan Am 103 timer to timers seized from Libyan intelligence agents in Senegal on February 20, 1988.

There was also a link to another terrorist attack that we had known about, but had failed to pay enough attention to. On September 19, 1989, less then nine months after the destruction of Pan Am 103, a French Union des Transports Aeriens plane, UTA flight 772, was blown up over Niger in Africa, and all 171 aboard were killed. A fragment of this limited edition MEBO timer was found in the wreckage.

The United States had many enemies in the Middle East who could legitimately be suspected of wishing to blow up an American airplane. France did not have nearly as many enemies. But during this period France and Libya were engaged in a bitter struggle over the future of Chad, a former French-African colony, where France was still trying to maintain influence. Chad is on Libya's southern border, and Gadhafi had his own very definite ideas about who should be running that country.

A look at a map provided another clue. The island of Malta is just off the Libyan coast. Oil-rich Libya had close commercial and political relations with the tiny island nation and had a great deal of influence in Malta. Libyans were familiar figures there and were constantly shuttling back and forth between the island and their nearby homeland.

Another piece of information we learned that day was of the existence of a Libyan defector, a former intelligence agent named Abdul Majid Giaka, who was in America hiding in the FBI's witness protection program. Majid had also worked at the Malta airport and said that he could place the suspects on the scene at about the time the bomb was loaded onto an Air Malta flight.

The probable reason for the Pan Am bombing, according to U.S. spokesmen, was revenge for the 1986 bombing of Tripoli.

On the day the Libyan indictments were announced, there was no talk of the two suspects somehow having carried out the bombing on their own. "The Libyan government is responsible for this monstrous act," was the unequivocal pronouncement of State Department spokesman Richard Boucher. In short, if they did it then Gadhafi did it.

In London the attitude was the same. Foreign Secretary
Douglas Hurd said: "This was a mass murder which is alleged to involve the organs of the government of a state.
This was a fiendish act of wickedness. It cannot be passed
over or ignored."

Susan and I never doubted that the Libyans were involved. Reporting on the indictments, *Newsweek* quoted
me as saying, "I'm sure that those who have been indicted
are probably guilty as charged."

It wasn't that we had developed a sudden appreciation
of the honesty of U.S. and British government officials. We
believed, and still believe, that the government will fail to
actively pursue, or at least to report, lines of investigation
that might be diplomatically embarrassing. The government might fail to suggest, for example, that our new Syrian friends or the ever dangerous Iranians, with whom we
wanted to make friends, might be involved in the mass
murder of American citizens. Such an investigation could
be allowed to drift aimlessly until the public forgot about
the case. No one was ever definitively identified, and certainly no one was ever punished, for the deadly truck
bombing of an American marine barracks in Lebanon in
1984. In more recent times the investigation of the bombing of the American military housing at Khobar Towers in
Saudi Arabia has languished in obscurity for years, with no
end in sight.

But the Libyan indictments were of a different order. It's
highly unlikely that the government would have fabricated
such detailed evidence in order to frame two innocent individuals, and quite possibly an entire country, for a monstrous crime they had nothing to do with. This wasn't a
carelessly or casually drawn "oops" indictment. It was the
result of a long and painstaking investigation, and if it was
wrong the investigators would have known it. The investigation had not been carried out by a single U.S. agency or even
by the United States alone. Americans were not always the
lead investigators. There had been investigators from
Britain, Scotland, Germany, and other countries. Construct-
ing an elaborate frame-up in such a high-profile case, in-

volving so many disparate individuals from so many different countries, would not only have been extremely difficult, it would have been very dangerous. The chances are nearly 100 percent that someone, somewhere, sometime would have exposed the truth, the house of cards would have collapsed, and the consequences would have been disastrous.

While I was being interviewed by the media at the time of the indictments, I recalled a phrase that appeared in Eric Ambler's 1937 masterpiece of international intrigue *A Coffin for Dimitrios*: "The important thing to know . . . is not who fired the shot, but who paid for the bullet." That quote appeared in a lot of accounts, sometimes attributed to me. Other Pan Am family members picked it up as well. It's right on target, and I wish I could take full credit for it.

While we accepted the idea that Libyans actually built and planted the Pan Am 103 bomb, we were never comfortable with the official "Libya alone" theory, George Bush's "Syria got a bum rap" defense. We strongly believed in the possibility of multiple sponsors of the atrocity, links between the Libyan intelligence service and the Syrian based PFLP/GC, and a possible connection to the mullahs of Iran as well. We weren't alone in these beliefs. A large percentage, probably a majority, of the Pan Am 103 families in America believed as we did. So did most of the journalists who followed the story, and a lot of international terrorism experts.

And so did the guy who was head of the Pan Am 103 investigation for the CIA. He is Vincent Cannistraro, who retired from the agency shortly before the Libyan indictments were announced. Cannistraro is widely suspected of being one of the early sources of leaks about the Libyan indictments.

If your idea of a CIA agent is drawn from reading spy thrillers, as mine was, Vince (Vinnie the Spy, I called him privately) comes as something of a surprise. He is not the image of a man who keeps secrets. He is humorous, affable, chatty, indeed downright garrulous, though after a while you realize that he is saying a lot less than you think he is. He first came to our notice in a front-page article in the

New York Times in which he commented extensively on
Pan Am 103. This was a man we all wanted to talk to. Rosemary Wolfe tracked him down—it wasn't hard. He had a
listed phone number. "I'm in the book," he said.

If a story about the CIA broke, you were likely to see
Vince being interviewed about it on the evening news. I
liked talking to Vince. At one point he grew a mustache,
and he asked me what I thought of it. I'm partial to facial
hair, and I said it looked good. "My mother hates it," he admitted. The next time I saw him on television, the mustache was gone. He once complained, "I just talked to
Susan, and she really depressed me." I told him he was not
the only one to have had that experience.

Cannistraro said he was uncertain about Gadhafi's motives: "You can speculate. He may have had the (1986)
American bombing of Tripoli in the back of his mind as an
additional incentive. But he did it because Jibril asked him
if he could do it, and because he independently concluded
that his operation was compromised by the Western services. Therefore, everything they were planning to do was
known to his enemies, and he couldn't use his own people."

He related a chilling story. The CIA had learned that
soon after the Pan Am 103 attack, Jibril held a champagne
party at his office in Damascus to celebrate. He was jubi-
lant. "The Americans will never, ever find out how I did it,"
he boasted, referring to the fact that none of his PFLP/GC
operatives had been directly involved in carrying out the
bomb plot. "We didn't know what he meant by that at the
time," Cannistraro said. "Now we do."

Cooperation and sharing of information among various
terrorist organizations and sponsors is hardly unknown in
the Middle East. Even an official State Department briefing paper prepared in 1997 admits, "We cannot rule out a
broader conspiracy between Libya and other governments
and terrorist organizations. . . . We believe that Libya—the
primary source of PFLP/GC funding during the 1980s—
was probably aware of Dalkamouni's earlier plans to
bomb aircraft. The activities in the fall of 1988 by those
Libyans directly responsible for the December 1988 Pan

Am bombing indicate that Libya was planning an aircraft bombing at the same time as the PFLP/GC cell was building its bombs in Germany. Tripoli was aware of the PFLP/GC's relationship with Iran, and was itself a close ally of Tehran during the Iran-Iraq war."

The paper goes on to say that the United States still lacked credible evidence of direct collaboration among Iran, Syria, and Libya in the bombing.

Our suspicions may ultimately remain unproved, or turn out to be completely unfounded. But they are not a baseless "conspiracy theory."

SUSAN: The meeting with Pan Am families that the Attorney General had promised took place in Washington on November 20. Dan and I decided not to go to the meeting. Going to Washington was always a big effort for us. We had to board the dogs at a kennel. We had to spend more than we could afford to stay at a hotel. We were tired, depressed, and sickened over the government's convenient amnesia about Iran and Syria. I told Joanne Hartunian I didn't want to go to be lied to, and she said that she and Joe felt the same way. But about 150 other family members and friends did go.

Eleanor Bright was among them. She went armed with a list of questions about Iran and Syria. Deputy Secretary of State Lawrence Eagleburger was there making the Libya-alone case when Eleanor, who is not normally a confrontational person, challenged him. "With all due respect to the evidence," she began, then rattled off seven or eight of the key unanswered questions. And which of the questions did Eagleburger answer? Not one. Instead, he pointed his finger at her intimidatingly and said, "You haven't called my president a liar, but you've come darn close."

That a top American official could say this to an anguished U.S. citizen whose husband had died in a terrorist attack left Eleanor dumbfounded. Not a single other family member in the room spoke up for her. Bert Ammerman actually apologized to Eagleburger for Eleanor's questions! Only after the meeting was safely over, and no powerful government official was around, did several other victims' relatives come up to Eleanor to tell her they agreed with her.

I learned a useful lesson from this, for there's no question that had Dan and I been there we would have stood with Eleanor, told Eagleburger off, and would have walked out of the meeting to let the waiting reporters know exactly what Eagleburger said, and what was said to him. There's no way we would have allowed Bert Ammerman, or anybody else, to apologize for us. We vowed never again to leave a brave and stricken family member alone to face unaided the arrogance and insolence of power. How could we speak out, how could we react, if we weren't on the spot when something happened?

When we heard what had happened, Dan and I made a pact that either one or both of us would go to all political meetings or events held for the families in the future, whatever the cost to our wallets or ourselves. We were meant to be soldiers in the front lines, and we would always have our say. Yes, always.

Chapter 12

DAN: Pan American World Airways tried desperately to escape the shadow of Pan Am 103. They did away with the 103 flight designation. On the first anniversary of the bombing, the airline ran stark full-page ads encouraging prayers for those killed in the bombing and all other victims of terrorism. Later they switched to cheery ads, trying to invoke the romantic, carefree aura of the "old" Pan Am. Nothing worked. Contrary to public-relations expectations, this was one tragedy the public did not forget.

The airline's losses piled up. In 1989 airline CEO Thomas Plaskett told stockholders that reaction to the bombing was the "principal cause" of the loss. I began checking the stock market listings—something I had never done before—just to see what was happening to Pan Am stock. It was already so far down that there really wasn't much room for movement, but every quarter point drop made my heart leap with joy.

In a desperate attempt to survive, Pan Am began dismembering itself by selling off some of its more profitable routes to raise cash. Nothing worked. A jump in airline fuel prices caused by the Gulf War pushed Pan Am to file for Chapter 11 bankruptcy early in 1991. There were brave statements from management that this was a temporary move and Pan Am would emerge stronger than ever. No one believed that. By August 1991, Pan Am sold most of its assets to Delta and was reduced to a Miami-based operation with a few Latin American routes. A lot of Pan Am employees lost their jobs and their pensions, but top executives had negotiated a good settlement deal for them-

selves, and bailed out with golden parachutes. The rewards
of failure!

Even the Delta bailout was a failure. On December 4,
1991, a little shy of the third anniversary of the Pan Am 103
bombing, what was left of Pan Am ceased operations and
prepared to liquidate its remaining assets. Some sixty-four
years after it was founded, what was once America's flag-
ship airline ignominiously went out of business. That night
we bought a bottle of good red wine and celebrated.

Over the years there were a few attempts to revive the
Pan Am name and symbol. The most ambitious was led by
former Pan Am executive Martin Shagru, the man who
had headed the company when the deadly decision not to
open and check unaccompanied luggage was made. A
number of us protested vigorously, but that was hardly
necessary. This ill-conceived venture stumbled along, losing money for a few months before going under. The Pan
Am name still exists on a small charter airline, but it is
doubtful if anyone will be foolish enough to try and revive
it in a major way again.

Through their activities the Pan Am 103 families helped
establish commissions that studied airline security and
get tougher airline security laws and regulations passed.
But commission recommendations are ignored and laws
and regulations are not enforced. The best thing we ever
did to improve security for the flying public was to help
put Pan Am out of business. First, a notoriously incompetent airline was removed from the scene. More significantly their example sent to other airlines the message: if
you let your passengers die, you may face more than a
lawsuit, you may face a corporate death penalty. As Dr.
Johnson once observed about the effect the prospect of
hanging has on a man, it "concentrates his mind wonder-
fully."

The Pan Am Building in Manhattan had long been regarded as a traffic obstruction and an eyesore. But it had
been around long enough to gain respectability and almost
landmark status. Pan Am sold the building, and after 1991
it no longer had any offices there. The building's owners,

the insurance company MetLife, hinted they wanted to change the building's name and replace the big Pan Am symbol with their own. Some airline buffs mounted a campaign to keep the name as a tribute to the aviation pioneer.

SUSAN: I hated seeing the sign on the Pan Am Building when I went to New York. It depressed me so much to look at it that I would avoid looking whenever I could, which wasn't easy because you could see it all the way up and down Park Avenue. The sign said PAN AM in huge glowing letters. The company's blue and white globe logo was on the east and west sides of the building. I wanted to climb up the building a la King Kong and put a giant 103 after the PAN AM. Announce that on the New York skyline, you bastards.

Peanuts characters were used in MetLife ads. I assumed that a company that wanted people to think of it when they saw Snoopy would not want to be associated with one of the worst air disasters in history. Bad for the image. I wrote a letter to MetLife making precisely this point. I told them how I still had the Snoopy pull toy that Theo played with when she was a toddler. I could see her, chubby and funny, waddling around the back of the house in Forestburgh, towing "Noopy" on a string.

This memory alone was enough to drive me to phone MetLife's PR office. Other families did so as well. I asked them what Charlie Brown and Lucy and Linus and the rest of the Peanuts characters had to do with bombs, with planes falling out of the sky. The PR people I talked to hemmed and hawed, but I got the distinct impression that MetLife wanted to get rid of the sign, and that they welcomed our campaign to see it go. Without us, pressure came from one direction only, the pro Pan Am side. But now there was an anti faction weighing in, and what an anti faction, the American victims of terror. Who would dare blame MetLife for publicly deciding in our favor? The sign came down. Pan Am was becoming a pariah. Visits to New York would be easier for me now.

DAN: I had a letter published in the *New York Times* urging that the name be dumped. A short time later the name and the big blue globe symbols came down. We wouldn't have to see them again.

Vindictive? You bet!

As the airline suffered its long slow death, the Pan Am lawyers, really the U.S. Aviation Underwriters lawyers, were busy. In late October 1990 both NBC and ABC News broadcast stories indicating that the U.S. government had complicity in the Pan Am bombing. There were few details, but the stories sounded very similar to the charges made earlier by Juval Aviv. Now the drug connection was being stressed more strongly, and the chief villain was the U.S. Drug Enforcement Agency (DEA).

Since these stories were being presented by respectable journalists, and did not obviously come from someone working for Pan Am, we took them seriously, as did most of the other families. We even went down to Washington to urge Congress to investigate.

We talked to some congressional staff members. They were bright, energetic, and enthusiastic Democrats. They would have loved nothing better than to pin a huge scandal on the Reagan and Bush administrations. They told us they had looked into the stories, and there was nothing—absolutely nothing—to them. As for holding hearings, they said the main source of the story was a known con man who was hiding out in Europe and was being paid by Pan Am. If they tried to hold a hearing on that sort of evidence, they would look stupid. We were convinced by what they said, and since there were no immediate follow-ups, we forgot about the DEA and the drug connection. Then in April 1992, the gaudiest and most sensational version of this tale appeared as a cover story in *Time* magazine: "The Untold Story of Pan Am 103."

The timing of the magazine's story was significant because the long delayed civil trial of Pan Am was finally scheduled to go to court within a week.

I first heard about the story on the car radio on a Sunday night. I was driving the dogs over to the kennel to be boarded because the next morning we were going to drive to Tennessee, where I had a speaking engagement. With the trial coming up, we figured the long drive to and from Tennessee would be an opportunity to get away from things for a while. Now this.

The radio report listed sensational charges but gave few details, and *Time* would not be on the newsstands until Tuesday. I suppose the magazine's circulation department would be dismayed to discover how difficult it is to locate a copy of *Time* in Tennessee. When we finally did find a copy and read the story, we were dumbfounded. It was a rehash of all the old discredited theories from the Pan Am defense. In fact, the magazine admitted that Pan Am lead lawyer James Shaughnessy had provided the "key witness" for the tale—a man named Lester Knox Coleman, who claimed to be a former intelligence agent and employee of the Drug Enforcement Agency. At the present time, however, he was hiding out in Europe after being indicted for passport fraud in Chicago.

According to Coleman, he hadn't at first realized the connection between the Pan Am bombing and some of the controlled drug shipment operations that he had been involved with for the DEA in Cyprus. Then in July 1990, he saw a picture of one of the Pan Am 103 victims and recognized him as a drug-runner and informant. It was a picture of Khalid Jaafar. Of course, Jaafar's picture and speculation about his part in the bombing had been in the news for over a year and a half. Putting two and two together, said Coleman, he went to Pan Am with his tale, and while they didn't pay him as much as he wanted, they did give him generous expenses, which he needed since he was on the run and hard up.

We already knew a lot of the background to the *Time* story and didn't take it seriously. Other families, less well-informed, were deeply upset.

Almost immediately after publication, *Time*'s story began to unravel. Exposés by Chris Byron in *New York Magazine* and Steve Emerson in *The Washington Journalism Review*, and later on *60 Minutes*, demolished it. *Time* has never exactly admitted they were hoaxed, but they never followed up on the story, or provided additional evidence, and no one was anxious to claim credit for it. To their credit, many of the magazine's top journalists knew nothing of the story until it was about to be published, and when they found out they objected strongly and said it should be "spiked." It was too late.

Shaughnessy insisted that he had "nothing whatsoever to do" with the article. Coleman, who was supposed to have become his "key witness," was never called to the stand in the civil trial and no affidavit, declaration, or deposition from him was ever submitted. The story had no impact on the trial.

Unfortunately, millions had already read or at least heard about the *Time* story; even now people recall bits and pieces of it. Worse still, it was to come up again, this time with a different sponsor.

Finally, on April 26, 1992, the much delayed civil trial began in Brooklyn federal court before Judge Thomas Platt. Brooklyn is a long drive from Port Jervis, and we were only able to get down to view a couple of sessions. The courthouse, however, was within easy walking distance of where we had lived for about five years in the 1970s. The jury appeared to be like people who had once been our neighbors. That gave me a feeling of confidence.

By and large trials are boring, and this one was no exception. There was no talk of renegade CIA agents or protected drug shipments. There wasn't even a lot of discussion of terrorists, Libyan or otherwise. There were no *Law and Order* or *Perry Mason* moments where, under a barrage of questions, the witness breaks down and sobs, "Yes, I did it." In fact, a lot of the witnesses weren't even in court. Their testimony was delivered via videotape or depositions, which were read to the jury. Some of the witnesses who did appear did not speak English, and a great deal of time was spent tediously translating questions and then translating the answers.

The most exciting moment of the trial came when a bailiff rushed in and whispered something to Judge Platt.

The judge rose, said threats had been made against the courthouse, and that he would have to suspend the trial temporarily. He advised us not to go out to lunch. We didn't know what was happening. Had there been a terrorist threat? No. Mob boss John Gotti was being tried in the same courthouse. His supporters had been demonstrating outside. They had gotten out of hand, and there was a small riot during which a car was overturned. As senior judge in the building, it was Platt's duty to oversee security.

Though James Shaughnessy had been the insurance company's lead lawyer, they brought Clinton Coddington from California to handle most of the courtroom work. Coddington was energetic, dapper, and extremely affable. He smiled a lot, particularly at the jury, and tried to create an atmosphere of friendly informality. All of the family members in the audience immediately hated him. Coddington had a showy silver cup, and every morning he placed it prominently on the defense table, filled it with water, and ostentatiously sipped from it. At lunchtime family members' conversations were peppered with phrases like "that damn silver cup" and "I hope someone puts poison in that cup." After the trial was over, Eleanor Bright had copies of the cup made up and presented one to each of the plaintiffs' lawyers, and one to Lee Kreindler's secretary, Pat Robinson.

The most dramatic testimony was supplied by witnesses from Air Malta. Air Malta had investigated itself and declared that its security arrangements were top-notch, and it would not have been possible to sneak a bag onto one of their planes. Under cross-examination the witnesses from Malta were forced to admit that their security was far from perfect, and their record keeping was downright sloppy. And they added one more bit of information; while Air Malta flight 180, the flight suspected of carrying the bomb, was being loaded, Libyan Arab Airlines flight 147 was being processed at an adjoining counter in the airport. The two indicted Libyan suspects were supposed to be working for the Libyan airline in Malta. The Libyan Arab Airlines station manager had a pass, a badge, and easy access to Air

Theodora Eugenia Cohen—called Theo by her friends and family—was just twenty years old, and aspired to be an actress, when she was killed in the explosion of Pan Am flight 103.

Theo traveled to Europe in the summer of 1988 before joining Syracuse University's Study Abroad program in London. (Courtesy of Annie Lareau)

Theo with university friends in London, fall of 1988.
(Courtesy of Ira Jaffe)

Rescue workers examine the nose of Pan Am flight 103 in Tundergarth, near the town of Lockerbie, Scotland, after a bomb exploded at 7:02 P.M., December 21, 1988, killing all 259 people onboard. (AP Photo/Martin Cleaver)

Aerial view of the nose section of Pan Am flight 103 the day after the crash. The 747 airliner was dubbed "The Maid of the Sea." It lies in a field at Tundergarth, near a tiny stone church. (AP Photo/Martin Cleaver)

Charred remains of homes and the deep crater caused by the crash. Investigators combed hundreds of square miles, looking for wreckage, bodies, and clues.
(AP Photo/Martin Cleaver)

Destruction to homes in Lockerbie, Scotland. (Gamma Liaison/ George De Keerle)

The crash devastated the small town of Lockerbie, which lost eleven people. (Gamma Liaison/John Paul)

Pan Am spokesman Jeff Kriendler speaks at a press conference at JFK airport, New York, following the crash of Pan Am flight 103. (UPI/Corbis-Bettman/ Mike Alexander)

Ron Boulanger bends over his wife, Jeannine, trying to revive her after she collapsed upon learning about the crash of Pan Am flight 103. (UPI/Corbis-Bettman/ Mike Alexander)

Susan Cohen is consoled by friends, Fran Kitts on her left and Carol Forbes on her right, during the memorial service for her daughter, Theo, held on December 29, 1988, at the First Presbyterian Church, Port Jervis, New York. (*Times Herald Record*, photo by Ricardo Thomas)

On April 3, 1989, family and friends of the victims of Pan Am flight 103 lay flowers during a rally in Lafayette Park, across the street from the White House. (AP Laser Photo/ Doug Mills)

Near the United Nations in New York, on the third anniversary of the tragedy, Florence Bissett holds a photo of her son Ken, who died in the bombing. She is comforted by close family friend John Anselmo.
(AP Laser Photo/Luiz Ribeiro)

Rosemary and Jim Wolfe on a trip to Niagara Falls in August 1988, just months before their daughter Miriam, traveling with her friend Theo Cohen, was killed on Pan Am flight 103.
(Courtesy of Jim and Rosemary Wolfe)

Kathleen Flynn, whose son John Patrick—called J.P.—was a passenger on flight 103, has actively sought recognition and justice for the victims.
(Courtesy of Kathleen Flynn)

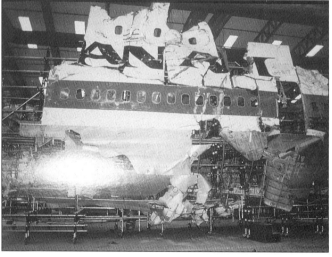

The 747 Boeing aircraft is painstakingly reconstructed from wreckage, large and small, strewn over 845 square miles of landscape. (Gamma Liaison/Spooner)

In December 1991, just shy of the third anniversary of the bombing, Thomas Plaskett, CEO of Pan Am, announces that the company is filing for Chapter 11 bankruptcy. (Gamma Liaison/Bill Swersey)

Lee Kreindler, considered by many to be the dean of aviation law in America, represented many families in the civil suit against Pan Am. (Courtesy of Kreindler and Kreindler)

Unidentified family members of victims of Pan Am 103, outside Brooklyn Federal Court, react to the verdict, which found Pan Am guilty in the civil suit, on July 11, 1992. After the verdict, U.S. District Judge Thomas C. Platt renewed an order barring lawyers in the case from talking to reporters and urged the families not to speak about the case. (AP Photo/Bebeto Matthew)

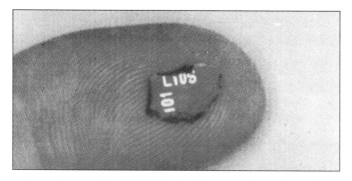

Investigators identified this tiny fragment of an electronic circuit board, which was discovered in the shreds of a shirt packed inside the Samsonite suitcase containing the bomb that brought down flight 103. (Gamma Liaison/Cynthia Johnson)

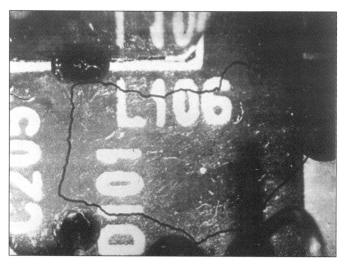

Forensic examination determined that the fragment came from an electronic timer manufactured by a Swiss firm with close connections to Libyan intelligence. A similar fragment of a duplicate timing device was discovered in the wreckage of a French plane that was blown up over Niger in Africa, killing all 171 aboard, on September 19, 1989.
(Gamma Liaison/Cynthia Johnson)

At a press conference on November 14, 1991, Lord Advocate Fraser announces the names of two Libyans accused of bombing Pan Am flight 103. Seated are George Essen (*center*), chief constable of Dumfries, and Stuart Henderson, Lockerbie Air Disaster Inquiry chief. (Reuters/Corbis/Kevin Lamarque)

In New York, two family members await news of the indictment. Helen Englehardt (*left*) holds a photo of her late husband, Tony Hawkins, and Marina Delarracoechea wears a button picturing her sister Nieves, who also died in the bombing. (AP Laser Photo)

Libya refused to
extradite the two men
who were indicted
for the bombing—
Abdel Basset Ali
al-Megrahi *(top)*
and Lamen
Khalifa Fhimah (*bottom*).
(Gamma Liaison/
Brad Markel)

U.N. Secretary-General Kofi Annan (*left*) shakes hands
with Libyan leader Colonel Moammar Gadhafi near Tripoli,
December 5, 1998. Annan departed empty-handed after
failing to secure the two suspects and bring them with
him to the Netherlands. (Reuters/HO/Archive Photos)

Palestinian hard-liners lead a march on December 14, 1998,
at the Yarmouk refugee camp in Damascus, Syria. Second
from the right is Ahmed Jibril of the PFLP-GC (Popular Front
for the Liberation of Palestine/General Command), who is
reguarded by many to have been the mastermind behind the
Pam Am flight 103 bombing. (AP Photo/Saleh Rifai)

President Bill Clinton stands with six-year-old Nick Bright, whose father died in the bombing, during the groundbreaking ceremony for a monument to be erected in Arlington National Cemetery. Nick was chosen by Senator Edward Kennedy to turn the first shovelful of earth. (Gamma Liaison/Brad Markel)

On the tenth anniversary of the bombing, the monument in Arlington National Cemetery is dedicated to the victims of Pan Am flight 103. Just days after he was impeached, President Bill Clinton shakes hands with Daniel Cohen while Hillary Clinton looks on. The monument, a cairn of stones quarried near Lockerbie, contains 270 individually cut blocks of stone, one for each victim.

On May 3, 2000, the long-awaited trial against the two
Libyan suspects, held in Camp Zeist, the Netherlands, begins.
The four Scottish judges are (*left to right*)
Lord Abernethy, Lord Coulsfield, Lord Sutherland (the
presiding judge), and Lord MacLean (the reserve judge).
(AP Photo/Paul O'Driscoll/Pool)

A memorial stone in Lockerbie, Scotland.
(Courtesy of Kathleen Flynn)

A memorial in The Garden of Rememberance at Dryfesdale
Cemetery near Lockerbie marks the site of the Pan Am 103
disaster and keeps the memory of its victims alive.
(Courtesy of Kathleen Flynn)

Malta. That was not the sort of testimony that the Pan Am lawyers had hoped to get from the Air Malta employees.

A couple of Pan Am's witnesses, employees from the Frankfurt Airport, were caught flat-footed in contradictions. They testified one way at the trial, but in previous statements they had said something quite different, something far more damaging to the Pan Am case. Pan Am's lawyers could not have felt very happy when the previous statements were either read or played back to the jury.

The trial dragged on for ten weeks, but by the time it finally staggered to a close, our lawyers and most victims' family members were feeling pretty good about the way it had gone.

Lee Kreindler wanted all his clients to be in court to hear his big closing argument, but Judge Platt tripped him up and wouldn't give him a day's delay so that he could contact us. "Cases aren't decided by the size of the rooting gallery," the judge observed. Afterward Kreindler dutifully sent all of us transcripts of his closing argument on July 6, 1992.

We did rush down to Brooklyn the next day, and arrived just in time to hear Coddington's closing statement.

SUSAN: Coddington's closing statement for the defense of Pan Am left me gasping in disbelief. He read a long, pointless description taken from Dostoyevsky about beating a horse. I had no idea what the man was talking about, or what relevance the story had to the case. You could hear the puzzled families murmuring. They couldn't comprehend why he was reading it any more than I could. I wondered what the jury must be thinking of Coddington's ramble into literature and whether they were asking themselves who this guy Dostoyevsky was who was being quoted here. I watched the jury, hoping to read in their faces that they too thought Coddington's summation was idiotic, and were on our side. I couldn't tell what they were thinking. But they looked like the right kind of people to me, graduates of the school of hard knocks. Some families had complained privately to each other that the jury wasn't well enough educated. But I trusted this Brooklyn jury more than I would a jury full of wealthy people with fancy college degrees who owned airline and insurance stock.

Being in the courtroom was an ordeal, and I wanted to get away from Coddington the troubadour, with his silver cup and his nickel-plated tongue, as fast as I could. I needed air. Everything was made worse because I couldn't talk to the media. I wanted to slam Pan Am and the insurers in the press. I wanted to remind the world again what this case was about, Theo's death, Miriam's death, J.P.'s death, Ken's death, Rachel's death, Kate's death, a family of three little girls' death, and so on. But the judge had slapped a gag order on the case. Kreindler told us to respect it, and we did.

Watching Plaskett in court filled me with disgust. If only I could have been watching him and the other Pan Am executives who violated FAA rules stand trial on criminal charges. Let them spend their personal fortunes on lawyers. Let them worry about whether they would spend time in prison. Now, *that* would do something for airline security. But the Plasketts of this world are usually safe. The law sees to that.

After the trial ended all the families hoped the jury would come back quickly with a verdict against Pan Am. And by quickly I mean within hours. That didn't happen. The jury had questions for the judge, wanted things read back to them, continued deliberating. Awaiting the jury's decision became a form of slow torture in which every minute became an hour, every hour a day. The longer they were out, the more convinced I became that we had lost. I called Pat Robinson, Lee's kind and competent secretary. She did her best to be reassuring but was careful not to offer false hope. Rumors of a deadlocked jury and dire predictions of a Pan Am win soon spread among the families. Kathleen told me she'd seen Kreindler leave the courtroom shaking his head. She thought she heard him say, "Why has everything gone wrong with this case?"

Everyone began second-guessing everyone else. By the morning of the second day, I was sure we'd lost.

On the third day Dan and I were in a bed-and-breakfast on a pretty farm in Pennsylvania. We had gone with friends to try to get away from the stress, since we didn't know how long the jury would be out. I heard the news on the radio that the jury had found Pan Am guilty of "willful misconduct." The tension snapped. But I felt no joy. I felt fear. Within minutes I was a crumpled wreck, lying on the floor crying and trembling. A flashback of memories of Theo poured through my brain. The plane was falling again. I was in it again. It was December 21, 1988, again.

It had all been too much, and I was overwhelmed. Worse, it was a mistake to be away from home with its comforting familiarity; away from the animals, my books, my videotapes, my audiotapes, my crossword puzzles. Kathleen Flynn was away from home too when the verdict came in. She was in the courtroom. When the jury returned, a woman juror looked at her and gave her just a hint of a smile. That made Kathleen sure we'd won even before the verdict was announced.

Judge Platt insisted that the gag order remain in effect, even after the verdict was announced. On the news we saw family members outside of the courtroom waving and smiling at the cameras, but no one would give an interview. They were all very law-abiding. Plaskett and the defense team were handing out press releases announcing their intention to appeal the case, and expressing confidence the verdict would be overturned on appeal.

Eventually I stopped shaking and joined my friends. A sense of relief came over me. That was the most I could muster because, after all, win or lose Theo was gone. But, oh, how much worse I would have felt if Pan Am had won.

DAN: It looked as if the civil case was over—but it wasn't and wouldn't be for years. Naturally Pan Am lawyers announced that they would appeal. That's the standard response. In fact, the vast majority of appeals fail, and in a civil case such an announcement is often just a signal that negotiations on a final settlement will begin. Not in this case. Pan Am filed for an appeal and made no offers. Some of the lawyers estimated that the appeals process would take six to eight months—it took a year and a half.

In the end the appeal was turned down by the three-judge appeals panel on a two to one vote. The one dissenter was the aged Judge Ellsworth Van Graafeiland. He began his dissent by writing, "My name will be an anathema to the hundreds of people who are seeking recoveries . . ." That, I can assure the judge, was an understatement. The rumor was that not merely had the judge dissented, but that he was unconscionably slow in writing his dissent, therefore delaying the inevitable by months. He was right up there with Coddington and his silver cup on our list of least favorite people and things.

End of the line? Not yet. Perhaps encouraged by the vigor of Van Graafeiland's dissent, Pan Am tried another tactic. They appealed to the full judicial panel of the second circuit court of appeals to review the case. That's a rare move, and it succeeds even more rarely. It didn't succeed this time. But it ate up several more months.

And it still wasn't the end of the line because there was the United States Supreme Court. By this time many of us felt we were trapped in Charles Dickens' *Bleak House,* a nightmare novel about the law's delay. The Supreme Court hears only a tiny percentage of the cases that are referred to it. Since this case involved no major constitutional issues, the chance that it would be taken by the Supreme Court was close to zero. But finding that out officially took five more months. On January 23, 1995, the Supreme Court finally ruled that it would not take the case. There was nowhere else that Pan Am could appeal. Over six years had elapsed since Pan Am 103 had been blown out of the sky, and over three years had gone by since a Brooklyn jury found Pan Am guilty of willful misconduct. And still it was not over.

This was just the first half of the case. Pan Am was liable—but liable for how much? Now things really got ugly—as they inevitably do when large sums of money are involved. There are few hard-and-fast rules about financial compensation in cases like this. The general rule of thumb is that the widows of men who are making lots of money get lots of money while the parents of children who were not financially dependent on the children don't. There are lots of other variables: The state of the law at any particular moment—it changes all the time; the state in which the plaintiff happens to live since local damages laws sometimes affect the judgment; the judge before whom the damages trial is heard; and last, and actually least, the jury that hears the case.

Everyone has heard of the multimillion-dollar jury awards in damages cases. But the vast majority of these awards are overturned on appeal. Lawyers for both sides know this is going to happen and generally try to negotiate settlements without going to trial.

Pan Am was still playing hardball, and individual cases started going to trial. Faith Pescatore, widow of a vice president for British Petroleum Company of America, was awarded $14 million. Other widows got multimillion-dollar awards. Even if some of these would not hold up on appeal, the size of the awards jolted Pan Am into beginning serious settlement discussions for what were delicately called the "non-dependency" cases, that is those involving dead kids.

Basically the system works like this. The parents are called in by a "special master" appointed by the court. Also present are the parents' lawyers and representatives of the insurance company. You sit around for an hour or so discussing how much you are to be paid for your child's death. It sounds cold and brutal, and it is. A few parents found the experience so harrowing that they were ready to settle for practically anything just to get it over with.

Cases were being settled, but still progress was slow. Judge Platt was pushing hard to get more settlements. He accused Pan Am of "shocking" foot dragging. "Don't you understand there are widows and people suffering . . . while you guys have been doing this?" In April of 1995, he called together a major meeting of lawyers and clients at the federal courthouse in Uniondale on Long Island.

Kreindler arranged that we would have our meeting with the special master in Uniondale in the morning before the main meeting. While many had found these discussions terrible, this one didn't bother us a bit, because we didn't want to talk about a settlement. We wanted to go to trial. We spent the entire hour yelling at the insurance representative (Lee told us he was basically a good guy who was just doing his job. He wasn't at all that "sonofabitch Brennan." It didn't make any difference; we yelled at him anyway.) We yelled at the special master when he asked us to be reasonable. We were talking about Theo's murder; we had no intention of being reasonable. We dominated the meeting, and for an hour we practically didn't give anyone else a chance to talk. At the end of the hour Kreindler was smiling; he seemed pleased. Now he could go back to the insurers and say, "Better settle now, or you will have to deal with these crazies in court."

In the afternoon about fifty family members, mostly parents, gathered in Platt's courtroom while Kreindler and Coddington made presentations to the judge about the progress of the settlements. In talking about compensation, Coddington said, "If they can show $275,000 worth of lawn mowing or the like, then it is something Your Honor could consider." That remark brought howls of outrage from all of us. Later one of the lawyers speculated that perhaps Coddington wasn't just being insensitive, but was deliberately trying to provoke us. He sure as hell succeeded. Lawn mowing—is that all our children were good for!

At one point Kathleen jumped up and addressed the judge—something a spectator is never supposed to do during a court proceeding. Platt reminded her of this, and she sat down. A few minutes later she jumped up again. The courtroom was charged with emotion.

The meeting didn't seem to accomplish anything, and for a while it looked as if there would be no settlements in the non-dependency cases without at least a few trials to set a sort of standard. We were going to be Kreindler's test case.

We were not his first choice. We had lost our only child, and in the brutal arithmetic of cases like this, that was good, for without other children we would have potentially been more dependent on Theo, and our situation seemed more pathetic, more likely to elicit sympathy from the jury. On the downside was the fact that Theo wanted to be an actress, a notoriously uncertain profession; the defense would have argued that we would more probably have had to support her financially than the other way around. If she had been in business school, she would have been worth more.

As witnesses we wouldn't be the greatest; we were professional writers, rather eccentric and angry loudmouths—not the sort of people a jury would readily identify with. But Lee was stuck with us because none of his other non-dependency clients wanted to go to trial.

We were exhilarated by the prospect. It would be our very personal day in court. We could tell a jury about Theo. For about three weeks we were on standby; a trial could start literally any day.

But it was not to be. The lawyers hammered out what they call a "global settlement." That is, all the nondependency cases were lumped together, and everyone was offered the same amount—$575,000. Kreindler told us that we didn't have to accept the settlement. We had the right to demand a trial. But no matter what the jury award was, in the end we would not get more than $575,000 and probably a lot less. Judge Platt was anxious to get the cases out of the way, and if we insisted on a trial, there was no way of predicting when he might schedule it. Besides, practically all of his other non-dependency clients agreed to settle. We were the last holdouts.

The prospect was bleak. We would be going to court, God knows when, with a reluctant lawyer and an angry judge. We wanted public attention, but since all the other cases would have been settled, who would care about ours?

SUSAN: When I said to my father-in-law, "The law gives to those who have," he laughed. It confirmed his suspicions about capitalism. When Eleanor Bright said, "I believe Pan Am owes me this money for not protecting my husband," I agreed with her. My friends, reading about million-dollar settlements in sexual harassment (and other) cases, happily assumed I would soon be able to buy diamonds and a mansion in Beverly Hills. Sleazy investment brokers, who read our names in the newspapers, called trying to sell us shares in the Brooklyn Bridge. They may as well have saved on their phone bills. By the time the lawyers took their percentage—a percentage we did not begrudge them; this had been a long and difficult case, and they did their jobs well—we were miles away from living in millionaire territory. And when you throw in the income lost from the years that I couldn't work because of the tragedy, we didn't have enough to afford the gas to drive to Easy Street.

I had mixed feelings about settling. It went against the grain to settle. There was the implication of a compromise, of caving in. If we had gone to trial early on, there's a vague possibility we might have been able to affect the judgments for all the parents. At the very least we would have been able to tell the jury about Theo. It would have been an individual trial. We probably wouldn't have gotten any more money in the end, but we would have stood firm and salvaged our pride. Now it was too late to fight. Our lawyer wanted us to settle, and the other families were settling. Telling Theo's story to a jury was not reason enough to drag the case out any farther. So when Dan said, "Susan, we've only got so much energy, and it's only money," I knew he was right. The legal system is the worst bureaucracy of all, and we would get a lot farther shooting arrows at the big, indifferent blimp that was the administration in Washington than we would shooting them at the smooth, impenetrable wall of the court.

Besides, no useful information about the bombing would come out if we went to trial. We would just be fighting over money, and that would be demeaning indeed. However, I resented the law that gives fortunes to young, childless widows, married only a short time, who might remarry and have children, while giving little to parents who spent years caring for children they cherished. I didn't blame the wives; though when I fretted over money worries, paid my phone and fax bills for the Pan Am 103 fight, or thought of the lonely and frightening old age that lay ahead, I couldn't help feeling a twinge of resentment. Many other Pan Am 103 parents felt the same way. I did my best to suppress such feelings, for the wives were suffering too. They didn't make the laws, and every dollar that went to a Pan Am victim was a dollar less for an insurance company that had treated us all with disdain, and added to our miseries. I never felt any resentment about money going to children. To lose your father or mother in a terrorist bombing is to be scarred for life.

There was something else that hurt the parents deeply. The amounts of money were so unequal that the law seemed to be telling us our kids' lives weren't as valuable as the lives of businessmen. This is a society that measures people's worth in money. It was insulting. And the way the court went about distributing the money was terrible. All those beautiful young people, each different, each unique, were rolled up together into a smooth, homogeneous ball, and all the cases were settled together. To the legal system they were all the same. Poor Theo, brutally murdered and then reduced to a number.

The law in its infinite stupidity assumes that the future is merely a replica of the present. Only one's financial status at the time of death counts. No executive will lose his job or make bad investments. No marriage will fail. No student will ever graduate from college and go to work. And no baby will ever be more than a baby. Parents of infants get least of all. As to value awarded simply because a glorious human "soul" has vanished, a good person lost who would make a contribution to society, forget it. The law can't be bothered with sloppy, emotional nonsense like that.

To make matters worse, there are no punitive damages on international flights, and punitive damages help to equalize judgments. So, if you haven't got much money and would like to be destroyed by terrorists when flying on a plane, think of the loved ones you will leave behind and make sure you only take a domestic flight that is targeted by terrorists. That's legal logic for you.

And then, of course, no money is awarded to parents for "loss of companionship." Only "loss of services" counts. How much sense does that make? I would mourn Theo every minute of every day for the rest of my life, and if Dan died and I became sick, what would become of me? I watched my friends help their aged parents. No stranger could or would do as much. Theo would have loved me through cancer, heart attacks, and senility. When the moment came that I couldn't take care of myself any longer, she would take charge.

So, thanks to legal logic the insurers really got away cheap. Only if a plane filled with babies and little kids on their way to EuroDisney were bombed would the insurers have it better. Lesson: When entering a court of law, don't expect justice.

A friend of mine once said, "There's nothing in life that money doesn't make it easier to live with." All I wanted was enough money to have some sense of security, to cushion the shock for the distraught person I had become because of Pan Am 103. Had I been awarded millions, I couldn't have spent a dime of the money in pursuit of pleasure. Enjoy money obtained through Theo's death? The guilt would have killed me.

When the settlement was over, some wealthy parents hid the money, putting it into funds that they wouldn't have to deal with and be reminded of where it had come from. Some parents put their settlement into special accounts for the education of their other children. Some left it to their grandchildren. Some had to live on it. Most of ours went into an annuity fund for me.

The most moving example of what happened to the money is Flo Bissett's. The Bissetts were not rich people. Flo worked three jobs to make sure her son Ken always had the best. Since he could not have the best of life anymore, he would have the best mausoleum in the cemetery. Nothing was too good for Ken.

Nobody bought a beach house or a Mercedes.

Well, here I was, abandoned by the President, pretty well ignored by most of the Congress, and clawed by the courts. Was there a single branch of the U.S. government that hadn't caused me untold agonies? Why? What was my crime? I felt like stepping into a courtroom, facing the judge, and saying, "Yes, Your Honor, I am guilty. Guilty of the crime of maternal love."

Chapter 13

DAN: Right before Christmas, 1989, a year after the bombing, a crew from a local TV station showed up to tape a short feature on us. The reporter was a young woman who had been at our house a number of times before. Since it was the Christmas season, she was looking for a happy ending.

"Are the wounds beginning to heal?" she asked us hopefully.

We both emphatically said no, they were not.

When we watched the local news that evening, the reporter's voice-over at the start of the segment cheerily intoned, "And for the family of Theodora Cohen of Port Jervis the wounds are beginning to heal . . ."

For years, every time there was a major airline disaster, we would get a dozen or so calls from newspapers or radio stations around the country asking if we had any advice to give those who had lost loved ones. We generally answered that we had no advice, because those people were in shock, and when they came out of it, they were going to go through hell. The response from the other end was usually, "Oh, my editor's not going to like that."

I had a long conversation with a woman who was trying to produce a TV docudrama on Pan Am 103. After about forty-five minutes she said to me, "You're so negative! Why are you so negative? That's not what people want to hear." I answered, "My daughter was blown out of the sky at 31,000 feet, and you want me to look for the bluebird?" The docudrama was never made.

We appeared on a show about parents who had lost chil-

dren in high-profile crimes or disasters. The main guest on
the show, which was broadcast live, was the mother of a
young woman who had been killed in a very well-publi-
cized disaster. While being interviewed, the mother smiled
a lot, displayed family pictures, and chatted cheerfully
about her wonderful daughter and the wonderful life they
had together.

Those at home viewing the show would have been impressed with the way this woman was coping with such a
terrible loss.

We were sitting in the green room waiting to go on, and
we were getting a very different view. Sitting directly
across from us, in white-knuckled anxiety, their eyes glued
to the monitor, were three other relatives. They kept shooting glances at one another and saying things like, "How
does she look?" "Why did they ask that question? We told
them not to ask that kind of question." "Does she look like
she's trembling?"

At the break the trio cornered the show's producer and
began yelling at him about the way the interview had been
conducted. The mother, who had been escorted back to the
green room, stood nearby rocking back and forth gently,
with that fixed smile still on her face. She didn't say a word.
It was obvious that she had been drugged to the eyeballs.

The mother never did go back as promised for the
show's final segment.

SUSAN: It was clear to us that we had to leave Port Jervis.
Years were passing, and the house was growing more run-
down. It needed paint. It had become shabby. The backyard was a mess, and who cared? Mail and clutter piled up
on the long dining room table, which had once held holiday dinners and party food. Things were tossed on it now,
and no one bothered to take them away. No one even
knew what was on that table anymore.

Every corner of the house was full of memories. I could
barely bring myself to go into Theo's room. On the wall
was a painting of horses by her Uncle Sol, which came to

her after he died. Every time I saw it I remembered the little girl who came home from horseback riding one winter day and bubbling with excitement over her favorite horse of the summer before said, "Mommy, you should see Dexter. He's so furry." And she held her arms out to show how wide Dexter's winter growth of fur had made him. With pleasure we laughed together over this.

Because Theo never threw anything away, there were lots of remnants of childhood in her room. A doll holding castanets and wearing a bright green dress, bought during a vacation in Puerto Rico. The sweater I'd thrown over Theo's shoulders when we went out in the evenings on that vacation because the warm night seemed cool after the very hot afternoon. How pleasant it was to walk slowly in the tropical night with Dan and Theo beside me.

Buried in a drawer was a little kid's pair of underpants labeled "Bloomie's." The pogo stick she had mastered was in the back of the closet. The stuffed animals in their case on top of the dresser were the hardest objects of all to look at. The sleek black panther. The mouse. The big rabbit. When she was three years old, for some reason I can no longer recall she was allowed to pick out one stuffed toy at K-Mart. She selected a very big rabbit, a solid, substantial choice. It had been in her room ever since. We'd given Theo a brush that Dan's mother had used to untangle his hair when he was a baby. Theo used it to brush her many favorite stuffed bears. She'd line the bears up on her bed and groom them. The bear in the sailor suit would get his hat tilted. The girl bear would have her dress smoothed. There wasn't much she could do with the Chicago Bear, a gift from her grandparents.

There were the nail polish stains that never came out of the purple rug, a hangover from the "I love purple days" when she was twelve. The modestly sexy signed picture of the British actor Anthony Andrews, which I'd cajoled from his agent as a present for her. The poster of Jimmy Dean, exactly like a poster I might have had on my wall when I was a teenager, which she'd bought for herself.

Strands of cheap jewelry hung on small hangers in the

closet and spilled out of jewelry boxes. The one good pair
of earrings she owned, opals, a present from her grand-
mother, was tucked in a desk drawer. The shell necklace
from Disney World. The rope bracelet from Nantucket.
The journalism trophy given to her at day camp when she
was five years old and liked to hang around the camp
newspaper office. The click of the typewriter keys probably
reminded her of her home. Her swimming certificate. The
old Buck and Beaver red camp tote bag.

Mostly it was the room of a teenager. It belonged to the
Theo who lived there before she went to college. The
translucent unicorn decal in the window caught the light,
for Theo's was the best room in the house, the room that
got the most sun. On her desk sat the silly ceramic rabbit I
gave her when she was sixteen, after a summer at Mount
Holyoke's summer theater. There she discovered Chopin.
Record jackets holding musicals were piled on the floor.
There were books too, mostly trashy novels and good
plays. It wasn't till college that she discovered Edith Whar-
ton. A Cole Porter songbook was half stuck under the bed.
A much used Snoopy telephone, which I was convinced
would have to be surgically removed from her hand when
she was in high school, was on her desk.

An angelic white dress and a glittering black dress, more
costumes than clothes, hung on the inside door of the
closet. Clothes to make a grand entrance in. I remember
Theo in black, a long cigarette holder between her fingers,
being very Bette Davis as she played Vera Charles in the
high school production of *Mame*. The two dresses really
got me. I could not go into her room without burying my
face in them and sobbing. Her friend from high school,
Donald Somerville, found a home for the dresses with a
girl he knew who also liked to make grand entrances. I had
nothing to do with that. Such matters were left to Theo's
father. I locked the door of the room and tried to stay out.

The size of the house, once an advantage, now worked
against us. It seemed much bigger than it was. The excess
space made us feel lonelier than ever. We began living in
less and less of it. I locked my office because I couldn't

work anymore. I avoided the attic, where Dan's office was, and never went into the basement. We ate in the kitchen, sat in the den, and kept out of the living room. Not only the house but the town was full of memories. We had to get away.

Into this dismal time came Monty, the new kitten. Monty was a blue tabby. Translation: he was gray and beige. When we introduced him to our other cats, Max and Hope, who were inseparable, Hope looked at Max and the look clearly said, "What's this?" Max, being Max, did exactly the right thing. He accepted Monty without in any way excluding Hope. Still, Hope and Max had each other, and at times Monty was de trop. So Monty, in awe of the grownup cats, became my special friend, sitting in my lap while I ate breakfast, following me around.

If Max was the supercat and Hope the eccentric, Monty remained the perpetual kitten. He didn't spray, and because Dan and I worried about putting a cat under anesthesia, we kept putting off having him neutered. And so today we have what may be the only unneutered, nonspraying male housecat in existence. Monty never got very big, but because he was never neutered his head kept growing, giving him the appearance of a tom kitten or the great pumpkin. He's a sweet, affectionate, jittery, not very adventurous animal who enjoys a quiet life. I am devoted to Monty, for he has eased the pain.

It took a long time to sell the house. Houses weren't selling easily, and ours was big, old, and in mourning. It would take the right people to see the house's potential beauty. In the meantime we could do nothing but wait. The cats wandered throughout the entire house, and I missed them when they vanished into the attic or sat by themselves in the living room. Our Clumbers were downstairs on the first floor at night. Downstairs seemed very far from upstairs, where we slept. I missed them too.

I made up my mind that if and when we ever sold the house, we would look for a smaller place where we could submerge ourselves in the cats and Clumbers and never be too far away from each other. Besides, a large house would have at least one extra bedroom, and an extra bedroom would always seem to be waiting for Theo. At last in the summer of 1992 the right people showed up, an artistic young couple who fell in love with the house and wanted to restore it. Once the house was sold, I had to face up to the reality of leaving. It would be a wrenching experience.

Friends helped. Pat Ianone and Becky Parsons, who had done so much already, helped me pack everything in the huge kitchen, and while they packed they chatted. Ordinary conversation about daily life. I joined in for about twenty minutes before I retreated into silence. Later I realized with a shock that this was the first time I'd been able to be part of an everyday conversation since Pan Am 103.

Liz Hanofee, who'd gone through the clothes sent back to us from Lockerbie, helped pack the living and dining room things. Liz was a marvel. Only Liz would dare to wear white during the packing and get away with it. When I pointed out that nothing in the glass-fronted cabinet was expensive and not to panic if something broke, she said, "Treasures are treasures, whatever they cost." She wrapped everything as if she were handling items in a museum. The special edition bear that Theo and Dan gave me one Christmas. The China Cheshire cat. The glass ape. The crystal ball in its velvet bag that we gave Theo when she was twelve. When girls stayed over for pajama parties, Theo would peer into the glass and read fortunes, or scare everybody with visions of the supernatural. The kids would shriek and giggle wildly, making it hard for me to sleep. But I always fell asleep eventually because I knew Theo was safe at home.

Moving triggered insomnia. To combat it I worked hard. One of my big jobs was dusting and packing books. We had accumulated so many over the years, it took months to sift through them and put them in boxes. Many were being donated to the library because there simply wouldn't be enough room for them where we were going. I hated giving books away. It was like saying good-bye to old friends.

The day the moving van arrived, we put the cats in their

carrying cases and put them in the back of Liz Hanofee's car. Liz would drive them to our new house. We put the Clumbers in our car. Cats and Clumbers could not travel together. Dan was so stressed out, we almost had an accident pulling out of the garage. Once we were out of the driveway, I thought, "I'm leaving the house where Theo lived. I'm leaving the town where she grew up. I may never see this street again. I may never be able to come back here." We were cutting our life in two. I was taking myself away from my baby. I wanted to jump out of the car, go back in the house, bury myself in it, and stay there till I died.

As we got farther from town, I mourned not only Theo but all I was losing. The beautiful hills. The dramatic Delaware River. Forestburgh. The people who stood by me. I cried but I stayed in the car. It really didn't matter where I lived now that Theo was dead. I didn't belong anywhere on the face of the earth.

DAN: In the years following Theo's death we learned to live defensively. We tried to avoid situations that might trigger an emotional reaction we couldn't really handle. We never went to the theater, though we had once loved it. We couldn't listen to any of the music Theo had once sung. The loss of a child not only robs you of your future, it robs you of a large part of your past as well.

You can't protect yourself against everything. Like the time I sat down in a restaurant, ordered a meal, and suddenly heard the music from *The Fantastiks* over the speaker system. That was a show in which Theo had a leading role in the summer of '88, just before she went to England. Memories overwhelmed me. I couldn't stay in the restaurant. I offered a lame excuse, got up, and left.

Or the time I spoke at a school book fair. It was the sort of thing I did regularly. It was part of my job. But this time the local high school drama department gave a brief presentation. Though I had never seen any of these kids before,

I knew them. They could have been Theo's friends. Theo could have been one of them. I fled the scene.

Cars with only one working headlight were also a trigger. For a couple of years Theo worked in summer stock at a theater about fifteen miles from where we lived. Shows, and the cabaret afterward, ran very late, and I always drove down to pick her up. I told her I needed the car so she couldn't have it to drive to work, but really I was afraid to let her drive late at night.

The road was pretty deserted by the time we drove back, but sometimes we would encounter a car with one headlight coming toward us about five miles outside of Port. That happened often enough for us to start looking for "the one-eyed car." Then we began to make up a story about how it was haunting us. We had the same experience the following year, and the one-eyed car became quite a joke between us.

Later, I was driving down a different road at night and saw a car with one headlight coming toward me. Suddenly I could feel—no, I could *see*—Theo in the seat beside me. She was pointing at the one-eyed car. It's a good thing there wasn't much traffic on the road because I swerved so badly I would have hit somebody.

It's the things that you can't guard against, and don't expect, that get you.

When we were packing to move, I knew there would be a lot of potential land mines. Particularly when going through Theo's stuff. So I tried to mentally prepare myself.

In many ways Theo was like Susan. But in one very profound way she was like me. She was a pack rat. She never threw anything out. She would just drop it on the floor, or in a drawer or a box, or kick whatever it was into the back of the closet, until her mother, driven half mad by the mess, straightened up what she could.

Theo's room had remained essentially unchanged since her death, and now it had to be emptied out. Fortunately our friends did most of the hard work. That included opening the boxes of clothes that had been salvaged at Lockerbie for the first and last time. One of the things we found was a Sherlock Holmes–style deerstalker hat that Theo had purchased for me in London. Susan and I are big Sherlock Holmes fans.

We gave most everything away, including her huge collection of stuffed animals. Well, we didn't give everything away. We kept her teddy bear Aloysius. At the age of fourteen Theo had fallen in love with the British actor Anthony Andrews, after seeing him as the sensitive and dissolute aristocrat Sebastian Flyte in the BBC television version of *Brideshead Revisited*. The character carried a teddy bear he called Aloysius. That Christmas we bought Theo a Steiff bear that was immediately named Aloysius. It was her favorite toy for a year or so and the foundation of her teddy bear collection. We couldn't give Aloysius away. And we couldn't give away the stuffed mole she had named Henry, after our literary agent. Heaven knows why. Nor could we part with the Canadian goose she got our first summer on Nantucket, or with—well, lots of other things. Still, there were a couple of trash bags full of lesser animals that were carted away.

I had prepared myself for this, and thought I handled it all very well. Then I was going through a couple of boxes in the attic and I unexpectedly came across a battered copy of *Goodnight Moon*.

As a baby Theo had been a very poor sleeper, and I must have read that book over and over to her a hundred thousand times, or at least it seemed that way, trying to get her to sleep. As she grew older the book disappeared from the shelf, and I doubt Theo even remembered it. But I remembered it, and for a moment I couldn't breathe. I sat down on a box and read it over and over again and cried.

My packing was done for that day.

SUSAN: Cape May, where we moved, is at the very southern tip of New Jersey and belongs more to Philadelphia and Delaware than it does to northern New Jersey or New York. Though not dominated by Washington, it is not unconnected to it. You can get the *Washington Post* as well as

the *New York Times* in the store that sells newspapers. Pan
Am 103 had become more of a Washington story than a
New York story, and by now it was mostly the D.C. media
I had to stay in touch with. We had been to Cape May a
few times, and we liked it. So when the time came to move,
we decided to go there. Cape May county has distinct advantages. The ocean. The bay. A milder climate. A small
town with pretty Victorian bed-and-breakfasts. Good
seafood. A world-class bakery. The best bird-watching in
the hemisphere. And the anonymity of a tourist area.

We bought a modern, ranch-style house north of town.
Appropriately enough for us, it had been built for a veterinarian. Much of the woodlands, marshes, and wetlands surrounding the house were part of a National Wildlife
Refuge. We had nature. We had privacy.

We arrived knowing no one in the county, no one in
Philadelphia, the nearest city, about an hour and forty minutes away. At first I didn't want to meet people. I needed
solitude as much as I needed oxygen. We bought binocu-
lars and learned about birds. The cats took up birding too,
in their own way, spending hours staring out at birds from
the floor-to-ceiling windows. In the springtime when the
windows were open, the house was filled with birdsong
from the woods. With Theo's voice stilled, birdsong was the
only music I could listen to. We took long walks with the
Clumbers on the beach. Fergie didn't like the ocean. It had
been all I could do to lure her into the lake at a state park
near Port Jervis or into the river. But Hugo loved swimming in the bay. He made funny snorting noises, as if he
were humming as he paddled around.

When we were very depressed, we took strolls in Cape
May. The crowds were cheerful, the shops pleasant, and as
long as I could escape back into the quiet of my house when
I needed to, I was okay. When we were ready, we reached out
to people. We started a group for fans of Sherlock Holmes.
We resurrected the Philadelphia branch of the P. G. Wodehouse Society. I started collecting Wodehouse books. We
made new friends. We discovered a restaurant we really liked.

Theo's ashes were finally buried in a historic cemetery

near Cape May. No, that does not mean I have found peace, whatever that is. The loneliness has never left me and will never leave me. The pain is always there. I could leave Cape May in a minute, go somewhere else, and be a stranger there. All I mean is that Cape May is a nice place to live.

DAN: I liked the new house because it had an attached office. It had previously been a small veterinarian's office, so the cats, dogs, and I felt quite at home there. Susan thought a writer's office with tile walls was a bit much.

Until 1990 both of us turned out books on Royal manual typewriters. We loved them and used them until it became nearly impossible to get new typewriter ribbons. I still keep one in the office, just in case the electricity goes out. We switched briefly to an electronic typewriter, and finally to a computer. We also got a fax machine and a copier. We didn't have to run out to the local print shop to fax press releases anymore. We could do it all from home, and our response time has improved considerably.

Chapter 14

DAN: Libya's reaction to the indictments of two of its citizens in the bombing was immediate and predictable. The government emphatically proclaimed its total innocence, and declared that the suspects would never be turned over to the United States or Scotland. The Libyans first said that they would investigate the case on their own and put the suspects on trial if evidence against them was found. In a few weeks they closed down their "investigation" because the United States and Britain would not turn over the evidence they had collected. Gadhafi added his customary bizarre twist by insisting that Pan Am 103 had been brought down by lightning.

Faced with a flat refusal by Libya to turn over the suspects, the Bush administration and Thatcher government felt they had to do something—so they took the case to the United Nations.

We didn't approve of this move. It was, and still is, our view that the Pan Am 103 bombing should have been handled by the United States. It was an American plane that had been bombed, and the majority of those killed were Americans. We weren't even happy with the idea of a trial in Scotland. In fact, we weren't happy with the idea of a trial at all. After Pearl Harbor, did President Roosevelt come before the American people and say that we were urging the Japanese government to turn over the pilots responsible for the bombing for trial?

The United Nations has a well-deserved reputation of being a graveyard for such issues. They are sent to the U.N., which then does nothing for a very long time. The U.N. serves the same function as a special commission in Washington. It gives leaders a respectable cover for ducking a difficult issue—"It's in the hands of the United Nations. The international community must act." But it rarely does, and everybody knows that. The United States never puts anything it considers really important into the U.N. For example, the U.N. was not consulted before Baghdad was bombed in the Gulf War.

Still, an illusion of action must be maintained. In January 1992 the U.N. passed a resolution urging Libya to turn the suspects over to the United States or Scotland. Libya did not. So in April, phase two began. The Security Council was to vote on a resolution imposing sanctions against Libya. The sanctions were to remain in place until Libya turned the suspects over, paid compensation to the victims' families, and cooperated in the investigation of the French UTA bombing. The resolution was to be reviewed every four months to see if Libya had yet complied.

All Pan Am 103 family members were invited to attend the Security Council session at which the matter was to be debated and voted on. But we didn't intend to be passive spectators, window-dressing for yet another proclamation of victory in the war on terrorism. We were determined to get our views out front.

The session was to be held on the afternoon of April 15. We knew that Security Council sessions tend to start late and drag on. There wouldn't be a vote until it was too late to make the evening news or possibly even the morning papers. By the next day the story would be cold, yesterday's news.

We organized a demonstration in the U.N. plaza for 11:00 A.M.—plenty of time to make not only the U.S. news, but also the late TV news and morning newspapers in Europe as well.

Susan worked the phones, calling all the media contacts she had, and there were plenty of them. In the end we may have attracted more reporters and cameramen than family members, but curious onlookers wandered in from the

area, swelling the crowd and making it look quite respectable.

Susan talked to a reporter who was head of the U.N.
correspondents association. He said that U.N. reporters
never leave the building, but he offered to set up a news
conference for us in the correspondents lounge inside
the U.N. building itself. Along with a few other victims'
family members and friends, we were ushered backstage
at the U.N.

I had been to the U.N. before, but always as a tourist.
From that perspective it is an impressive and idealistic-
looking structure. Behind the scenes it appears different,
shabby, even seedy. The walls were gray and the paint was
peeling. The linoleum, or whatever was on the floor, was
loose and cracked. The furniture in the correspondents
lounge was plastic-covered and torn, the sort of stuff you
see left at curbside on trash pickup day.

And who were the people who gathered in the correspondents lounge? Some of them were undoubtedly correspondents; I even recognized a few faces. Others looked
as if they had been in the building since it first opened.
They appeared to have lost any purpose they might once
have had, but like Melville's "Bartleby the Scrivener," they
did not choose to leave. After the press conference some of
them followed me around asking irrelevant questions and
making illegible notes on scraps of paper or imploring me
to make statements into ancient tape recorders.

Still, we all felt pretty good about the demonstration and
the press conference. We trooped over to the U.S. United
Nations Mission, which is right across the street from the
main entrance to the building. Family members had gathered inside for a brief pep talk from Ambassador Thomas
Pickering. And then we were guided back into the U.N.
building and to the visitors gallery in the Security Council
chamber.

As expected, the debate started about two hours late. A
Security Council debate is about as spontaneous as a professional wrestling match, and a lot less exciting. Delegates
do not have the power to make decisions. Everything they

do is dictated by their governments, and the outcome of all votes is known well before a debate starts. In fact, the debates could be dispensed with altogether, and the results would be exactly the same, though they would be arrived at more quickly.

Some family members seemed to actually take this dismal spectacle seriously. They scrambled around to try and find a seat that had a working headset so they could hear simultaneous translations of the speech being delivered. About half of the headsets didn't work. They took copious notes. It was such a waste of time. We knew the sanctions resolution was going to pass. I sat and read a book. Susan didn't want to sit. She left the visitors gallery and pushed through doors that said NO ADMITTANCE into the press offices where the real U.N. reporters worked, and apparently lived.

SUSAN: I'd be damned if I'd play the good citizen and sit through the Security Council delegates' speeches. I had spotted the media area when I came in and was determined to get back there. You can't just walk around on your own at the U.N. They make it very hard for you. The place has its own rules and rituals and does not run like a democracy. But the media area was close by. So I simply ignored the sign that said I couldn't go in. What could they do to me? Just throw me out. In which case I'd wind up like Dan, back in the Security Council gallery reading a book. I could read *Sense and Sensibility* anywhere.

I entered the media area. It was not a glamorous place. Dan was right about the U.N. Once you got past the freshly scrubbed face it put on for visitors, it was very different. Television monitors showed what was going on in the Security Council chamber, and some reporters were watching the monitors while sitting in front of their computers. Others were walking around. There was little privacy and enough chaos to give me cover. I could very well have been just another reporter.

I cased the joint. I noticed that when certain speakers

came on the TV screen, the reporters gave them their full attention, but in between they had nothing to do and could talk to me. No one stopped me. No one minded my being there.

I had the impression that the U.N. was a strange, sealed world all its own, a mix of secrecy and gossip. I assumed that a big part of a U.N. reporter's job was to understand the arcane workings of the organization itself, no easy task, and to try to sniff out from the delegates and other sources what was really going on behind all the diplomatic doubletalk. It would require highly specialized expertise, patience, and the ability to translate diplomatese for the public. Therefore, the best reporters would do their work behind the scenes, and what I was watching now was the pro forma part of the job, covering a debate. This gave me a good opportunity to tackle reporters and express my disdain for what was happening in the Security Council.

I went around introducing myself to reporters from the wire services and major newspapers, even finding my way to the special niche occupied by *The New York Times*. By the time I'd accomplished what I came for, no reporter in the building that day could say that all Pan Am 103 families were shouting a unanimous hurrah for George Bush's sanctions policy. I left with my purse stuffed with phone and fax numbers of reporters. I stayed in touch with several of the more experienced among them for years afterward, getting their take on new developments and giving them what information I could. I could always be counted on for an opinion and a quote.

DAN: Susan talked her way past the guards at the doors to the visitors gallery, who were not supposed to let anybody back in, and told me to come to the press section. I went, eagerly. We met one experienced U.N. correspondent who told me something I never forgot.

"Nobody in this building gives a damn about what happened to your daughter," he said. "The only power you have is the power to embarrass the bastards." It became a sort of motto for me.

The sanctions that the U.N. imposed on Libya have been described as "tough" and "punishing." They were neither. Libya has one cash crop—oil. The country's economy could have been completely shut down if the U.N. had imposed an embargo on Libyan oil. That was never even considered. Instead there were some minor diplomatic penalties, some restrictions on the sale of military equipment, and later on some oil field equipment. But arms and equipment were easily available through the black market. The United States already had much tougher restrictions on Libya in place. Britain had broken diplomatic relations with Libya over a 1984 incident in which a British policewoman, Yvonne Fletcher, was killed by a shot from the Libyan embassy in London during an anti-Gadhafi demonstration.

The most visible and effective U.N. sanction was a ban on commercial airline flights to and from Libya. Even then there were exceptions. For example, Muslim pilgrims from Libya could be flown to Saudi Arabia to visit Mecca for the haj. Libya was certainly not isolated. It was a long, hot, and dusty ride from the Egyptian border to Tripoli, inconvenient but not impossible. A far more pleasant gateway to the outside world was a ferryboat ride to Tripoli from, guess where? The friendly island of Malta.

Visitors to Libya in the years that followed reported that there were no shortages of food or medicine, and that the Libyan people were not suffering the sort of hardships that far stricter sanctions had imposed on Iraq. Even prohibited American goods were readily available in Libyan shops, though they tended to be pricey. Banned technology made its way to Libya with the aid of European and even American businessmen, who found "creative" ways of getting around the restrictions.

While the sanctions may not have been tough, they were inconvenient and embarrassing. After an initial period of sulking, Gadhafi began to look for ways to shake free of them. One tactic has been described as a "charm offensive." It was Gadhafi trying to look like a nice, reasonable fellow who only wanted the best for nearly everyone. But like everything else Gadhafi did, his "charm offensive" had a truly goofy side.

After Bill Clinton was elected president, Gadhafi declared, "Bill Clinton is my friend." He said he would never do anything to hurt his friend Bill. "We consider him the savior of the New World, the United States, and the Western world."

In April 1993 Gadhafi invited Judith Miller, a *New York Times* reporter who was on leave at The Twentieth Century Fund, to interview him in what she called his "untraditional Bedouin tent pitched in the center of the Bab el Aziziya barracks in Tripoli."

In addition to declaring his undying friendship for America's new president, the Leader announced, "Were it not for the problem of Palestine, I would be the first to defend the Jews of the world."

He hinted that he would be willing to help solve the problems between Israel and the Arab states, crack down on Islamic radicals, cut the flow of weapons of mass destruction to the Middle East, and stop supporting every terrorist who showed up in Tripoli asking for weapons or money. In short, after years of vowing that the United States and Israel would be driven from the Middle East, he was making noises like a peacemaker.

But on the subject of Pan Am 103, he was adamant. He would endure any sanctions, but the suspects would not be turned over. In a *New Republic* article with the awful title of "Moammar Dearest," Miller concluded that it would be a good idea for the United States to test Gadhafi's "ostensible desire to no longer be part of the problem, but part of the solution." If the United States would just forget about Pan Am 103, then all sorts of other good things might happen.

Apparently Gadhafi became convinced that the best way to reach Washington was through Israel. In his interview with Miller, he talked about sending 200 Libyans to make a religious pilgrimage to Muslim holy sites in Jerusalem, if Israel would grant them visas. Gadhafi wasn't just talking this time, because in June a group of

192 Libyan pilgrims did arrive in Israel, with at least the tacit blessing of the Israeli government. Moshe Shahai, the Israeli police minister, said that Libya was "an Arab state we have nothing against." The goodwill gesture, if that's what it was, soon fell apart when the Libyan pilgrims began saying that Zionism must be destroyed. They left Israel in haste and confusion, and the incident became a great embarrassment that the Israeli government didn't want to talk about.

This fiasco had been arranged by Yaacov Nimrodi, an Israeli arms dealer who had been involved in the Iran-Contra affair, and another Iran-Contra veteran, Saudi arms dealer Adnan Khashoggi. A key figure in this strange episode was a Libyan Jew named Raffaelo Fellah. Fellah's family and practically every other Jew fled Libya after the 1967 Arab-Israeli War. He became an Italian citizen. In 1993 he was president of the Association of the Jews of Libya, and was negotiating with Gadhafi about compensation for property Libyan Jews had left behind.

Five years later Raffaelo Fellah showed up at our front door in South Jersey. He did not come unannounced. I was called by a man who identified himself (correctly, I was able to ascertain) as a retired official of one of America's largest Jewish organizations. He had known Fellah in Italy and heard that Fellah wanted to talk to us. I was quite puzzled and told the caller that Fellah surely must know that we were the hardest of the hard-liners, and there was nothing he could say to change our minds. But the caller was persistent. He said that Fellah was ready to fly over from Rome immediately if we would just agree to talk to him. More out of curiosity than anything else, we agreed.

SUSAN: I didn't know what Raffaelo Fellah wanted of us when he arrived, and I still didn't know when he left. He was driven to our house by a thin, elderly, somewhat reserved man who was obviously exhausted by the long drive from the airport. This was the person who called and asked us to meet with Fellah in the first place. As to Raffaelo Fellah himself, he was the opposite of his companion. Fellah was fat, gushingly friendly, and wheezed so badly I asked myself if he were physically ill.

He offered me a new scarf as a gift, "to wear in the synagogue." I explained that I didn't go to a synagogue, but it wouldn't make any difference if I did, because under no circumstances would I accept a gift from him. I kept refusing the scarf, and he kept thrusting it at me, until we looked like we were practicing a comic vaudeville routine. Finally, very disappointed, he put the scarf away and sat down. Dan and I hoped we would find out why he'd come to see us, who'd sent him, and if he was talking to other Jewish Pan Am 103 families.

Fellah spoke in generalities, never getting to the point. His English was very limited, and when you add to this that we spoke neither Italian nor Arabic, ours was a very circular, unfocused conversation. I wondered if Fellah's florid, vague, and expansive manner of speaking was a style peculiar to the Middle East, or was it just him?

Fellah told us what a good thing an international trial for the two Libyan suspects would be, how it would help all the unfortunate Jews who have fled Libya get their property back, including himself. Fellah went on to say that an international trial would be a route to the truth about the Pan Am 103 bombing, promote peace in the Middle East, and be good for Jews everywhere. Exactly how he expected Dan and I to help accomplish this goal, he didn't say. He avoided answering our questions, and no matter how hard we tried, we couldn't pin him down.

We, on the other hand, were anything but evasive. We made it perfectly clear that we didn't care whether the Libyan Jews got their property back or not, and we would not be swayed by arguments about the good of world Jewry, the peace process, the New World order, or anything else. What we wanted was justice for Theo. We would not collaborate with Gadhafi by helping him get away with her murder, and that was exactly what we felt an international trial, which he now backed, would do. If it wouldn't, why did Gadhafi want one so much? Not only would we not support such a trial, we would actively fight against it. We believed that the type of trial the Libyans favored would serve only to protect the guilty.

Fellah appeared to listen to us, then started over with world peace and the Jewish stuff again. This went on for some time, but eventually he realized that he may as well have been speaking to a couple of stones. If we couldn't penetrate his flowing style, he couldn't penetrate our resistance. Perhaps if we'd strung him along, he might have become more confiding and specific. But such games were not for us, and besides, we wanted to leave him in no doubt as to where we stood. We told him to take our words straight back to Gadhafi.

To make the long drive back in the summer traffic before dark, the hour came when Fellah and friend had to leave. Ours was not a friendly good-bye. As their car pulled away, I asked myself what the people in the quiet, workaday Cape May County would think if they could have heard the conversation that went on in our house that day.

DAN: Since the U.N. sanctions did nothing to interrupt the flow of money to Libya, Gadhafi had millions to play around with, and he had a long history of buying friends and influencing people. The Libyan dictator once hired Jimmy Carter's disreputable brother, Billy, to help promote Libya's image, much to the embarrassment of the president. After the indictments and sanctions, Gadhafi's "friends" were crawling out of the woodwork.

Here's one way to make a good impression, as described by reporter Bob Greenberger of the *Wall Street Journal*, in a front page article on October 1, 1993. You hire a top Washington consultant, who rounds up a prominent Republican congressman and a former Democratic congressman then whisks them off on an all-expense-paid tour to Libya. "It was first-class all the way—the Concorde to London, a private jet to a seaside resort in Tunisia, and on to Tripoli via Mercedes-Benz limousine.

"In the Libyan capital, they each had a suite with 'three bathrooms, a main salon, a dining room with a table seating ten, a book-lined study [and] a completely equipped kitchen.'"

The players on this luxurious junket were Washington consultant Albert Grasselli, Republican congressman William Dickinson of Alabama, and former Democratic representative John Murphy of New York. Murphy had some experience with this sort of thing and had served twenty months in prison after being caught in the Abscam bribery scandal, in which FBI agents posing as wealthy Arabs successfully attempted to bribe U.S. congressmen.

Grasselli defended himself by insisting that Gadhafi didn't pay the bills. Not quite. The money, he said, came from Hassan Tatanaki, a wealthy Libyan who wanted to improve U.S.-Libyan relations because that would improve his business.

According to the *Journal,* some of the money for the trip was funneled through a Washington Mideast think tank called Council for the National Interest, headed by another former congressman, David Bowen. The CNI made something on the deal as well. After the trip Grasselli, Murphy, and Bowen formed GMB Consultancy, Ltd. Their client was the openhanded Mr. Tatanaki, who wanted to improve the U.S.-Libyan relationship. The partnership didn't last long. The Treasury Department ruled that its activities violated U.S. regulations about dealing with Libya. Grasselli and the two ex-congressmen were fined a few thousand dollars each, but their company was reportedly allowed to keep a $200,000 advance payment from Tatanaki.

Sometimes Gadhafi's attempts to sway private opinion were more direct. It was reported that in September 1992, Gordon Wade, a former Republican chairman in Kentucky, brought Mohammed Bukhari, Libya's finance minister, to see one of the top lawyers for the Bush-Quayle reelection campaign. Bukhari said that Libya wanted to improve relations with the United States and hinted, in a roundabout way, that contributions to the Republican campaign might be offered. It is strictly illegal for any foreign government to contribute to candidates in a U.S. election, and to accept contributions from a country like Libya would have been absolutely suicidal. No money was ever given.

But Bukhari, who was known as "Big Mo" among his American friends, did not give up. Though he had been issued a visa to attend an international financial meeting in Washington, and his travel was limited to Washington, he somehow turned up in Dallas. Big Mo knew a man named Henry Billingsley, who was the son-in-law of a Texas real estate developer and big-time Republican contributor, Trammell Crow.

Bukhari didn't go directly to Dallas; he went to Mexico, where Billingsley picked him up and drove him across the border to attend an annual Texas-style barbecue given by his father-in-law. Here Big Mo mingled with wealthy Republican movers and shakers. Billingsley had been introduced to Bukhari by his old college chum William Bodine, a New York financial adviser who managed investments for some Middle Eastern clients. Libya promised to pay Bodine a very substantial sum for "consulting work," a portion of which was actually deposited in his Swiss bank account. In 1995 Bodine was arrested and later convicted for violating Libyan sanctions restrictions.

All of this was just the tip of the iceberg. According to the magazine *U.S. News and World Report*, "People acting on behalf of the Libyans managed to gain access to top presidential aides. 'There may have been one or more calls made to the President that he referred to me,' says Brent Scowcroft, George Bush's national security adviser. 'The people who came to me were well-known businessmen, whose calls I would return.' Scowcroft would not name those who spoke with him about Libya."

It has never been clear what, if any, influence all of these contacts had. What is clear is that the Libyans, and their wealthy friends, were able to reach the sort of people in Washington who would never return our calls.

But the Libyans knew that if they really wanted to influence U.S. policy on Pan Am 103 the man they would have to get past was Senator Edward Kennedy. Senator Kennedy was known as the leading congressional champion of the Pan Am 103 families, a reputation he deserved. Kennedy was with us right from the start. When the Victims of Pan Am 103 held its first vigil in Washington in April of '89, Kennedy helped make all the arrangements, finding rooms in the Capitol where we could meet and hold press conferences.

Along the way there have been others who helped. Senator Frank Lautenberg, who was on the McLaughlin committee, was with us all the way, and so, in his own peculiar manner, was Al D'Amato. But Kennedy was always the most active, the most constant, and the most effective friend we had in Washington. When we needed help in Washington we always called Kennedy's office. For Susan and I, Ted Kennedy has been "The Man."

SUSAN: Trina Vargo was an aide in Kennedy's office. When Trina met Eleanor Bright in Boston, she saw firsthand what Pan Am 103 had done to living victims left behind. Since I lived in New York, I was in touch with aides to Senators Moynihan and D'Amato. But Eleanor told me I should talk to Trina. So sometime in late 1989 I called her. It was the first of countless calls over a period of years.

Trina was extremely loyal to Kennedy, but she was different from many of the aides I talked to in Washington. Most were opportunists who would push an issue only if it would help their boss. Trina had a conscience. She was genuinely outraged by the Pan Am 103 bombing, and she worried about what would become of the Pan Am 103 families.

It was probably Trina who really brought Pan Am 103 to Kennedy's attention, but it is Kennedy who deserves full marks for making Pan Am 103 one of his major priorities. He didn't have to do it. Far fewer people from Massachusetts died on Pan Am 103 than from New York or New Jersey, and from a strictly political perspective, Kennedy had nothing to gain in taking up the issue. He certainly didn't need it to be reelected.

You may think it should be no big deal for a senator to champion a cause. But when a member of Congress takes the lead on any issue, he pays a price. It will take up his time and the time of his staff. To get anywhere he must stand up to the administration in power, be it Democratic or Republican, and in order to induce other senators to sign on in support of what he wants, he may have to support a favorite issue of theirs. Horse-trading. That's the way Congress works, and it's not all bad. It encourages consensus, stability, and keeps down the number of fist-fights in the Capitol Building.

The Pan Am 103 families were taken under the protection of Senator Kennedy for one reason only. He cared. It says a lot about the senator from Massachusetts that he did not abandon us when the Republicans lost the White House to a Democrat, and he often had to confront a president of his own party.

My first impression of Trina Vargo was that she was both honest and feisty. I liked her. The more I got to know her the more I liked her. In some ways she reminded me of Theo. Like Theo, she was small. I would put my money on Trina having been the runt of the first grade as Theo was, learning to stand up to the big kids in class by becoming one formidable presence. You didn't mess with Theo, and you wouldn't mess with Trina either. If the two could only have met, I think they would have become friends.

Calling Kennedy's office was like calling no other office in Congress. I didn't have to leave pleading phone messages that were ignored. I didn't have to sell a request for help to the aides who called back. And I didn't have to worry about the staff working hard for us.

Trina was intense and tenacious. She dug into the Pan Am 103 issue as if she were a terrier, gripped it with her teeth, and wouldn't let go. Because she was the kind of person who gave herself completely to a cause she believed in, and because she and I were in some ways very much alike, we sometimes fought over tactics ourselves. She was the one person I could turn to in a congressional office who was always on my side. When I broke down on the phone once crying because I'd had a bruising clash with an aide in a different office, Trina was genuinely concerned about my welfare, urged me to take a vacation, to go off and get some rest. When I said I couldn't, she called the aide who'd insulted me and defended me. In a city full of phonies, I'd found one person who was real!

DAN: Ted Kennedy wasn't the sort of guy to be dazzled by promises of big money—so the Libyans tried a different approach. In August 1993 Kennedy was visited by Albert Reichmann, a Canadian businessman whose family owned the gigantic Olympia & York real estate empire, which had two employees on Pan Am 103.

Kennedy assumed that Reichmann, an Orthodox Jew, wanted to talk about Israel, where his family had wide-ranging philanthropic projects. And that's how the conversation started. Then the talk turned to Libya, and Reichmann indicated that a rapprochement with Gadhafi would be good for Israel, and that the Libyans would be willing to pay compensation to the families of the Pan Am 103 victims under the right circumstances.

Kennedy was not merely surprised by the turn the conversation had taken, he was shocked. Kennedy considered this to be totally inappropriate and Reichmann was told that Kennedy was obligated to report any such approaches to the Justice Department. He terminated the conversation and turned Reichmann over to Trina. Trina reported this approach to the Justice Department and later that evening called us—and Mr. Reichmann got his name in the press. He has not been heard from since on this subject.

Chapter 15

SUSAN: A presidential election was coming up, and we had to reach Bill Clinton. If he won, he would have the power to right George Bush's wrongs. The bombing hadn't happened on his watch, and he was a Democrat, so he had no need to defend the policies of the previous administration. I was none too enthusiastic about candidate Clinton, but Bush was such a disaster I just wanted him gone. And, who knows, perhaps Clinton would turn out better than I expected. I was eager to get to Clinton during the campaign, when politicians tend to promise the moon. Then perhaps he would be stuck with Pan Am 103 as an issue if he won. I was afraid that if something wasn't done about the bombing soon, Pan Am 103 would continue to run its sluggish course in the U.N., sinking ever lower as a priority in the years to come, until it ran out of steam entirely and disappeared, forgotten by the public.

But how to get to Clinton? Where could I go for advice? I had more Democratic contacts than Republican ones. But the only Democratic political operative I knew well, though a decent and compassionate man, was not in the Arkansas governor's inner circle. Besides, I noticed a wariness in the political op's voice when he spoke to me now. It was one thing for him to take up the cudgel on our behalf when Bush was in office. But if a Democrat won the White House, it would be time to throw away that cudgel real quick. Disappointing, but never expect anything else from a political op. As Harry Truman said, "If you want a friend in Washington get a dog."

I followed every lead I could think of and at last got

through to Anthony Lake, Clinton's chief foreign policy person, and the likely choice to head the National Security Council (NSC) should Clinton be elected. I wrote Lake a letter in August 1992 and a month later got a reply from Clinton that read, "The United States and the international community must make clear to terrorists that such cowardly attacks on innocent civilians are unacceptable and will not be tolerated. Our failure to respond adequately to the Pan Am 103 bombing jeopardizes the integrity of this commitment. If elected, I will do what is right and necessary to send a message that individuals who engage in and countries which lend support to terrorist activities will pay a high price for doing so."

Clinton went on to say that if the two indicted Libyans were not surrendered for trial, "we would press the U.N. to broaden the sanctions to include an oil embargo" and "I will also assure that all questions regarding Syrian and Iranian involvement in the Pan Am 103 tragedy are addressed and fully answered."

The one candidate I had already talked to was Ross Perot. Perot was genuinely outraged over Pan Am 103, and had said so on television. So one winter day, when we still lived in Port Jervis, I called his office. Then Dan and I took Fergie and Hugo on a walk through the snow at High Point State Park. When we got back, the answering machine light was flashing. I pressed the message button, and there was Ross Perot's voice, right down to the nasal twang, politely offering his help. I was startled and, frankly, pleased. This was how it should be. No political ops. No barriers. No phony baloney. Here at last was a down-to-earth humane response from a powerful political figure. I called him back and asked him to keep talking about Pan Am 103. He said he would and he did, through the whole campaign.

DAN: Just a few days after we got the letter from Clinton, we were scheduled to go down to Kreindler's office where

192192192192

a *60 Minutes* segment was being shot. (*60 Minutes* visited the Pan Am 103 case four times.) We had copies of the letter from the candidate, and I gave one to Mike Wallace. He read it over carefully, took it delicately between his thumb and forefinger, and dropped it on the desk. "It's a politician's promise," he said.

We sent the letter around to media people we knew, but none of them were very interested. The campaign was nearing an end, and most of the reporters agreed with Mike Wallace that Bill Clinton was just making another preelection promise. Oddly, after the election, the letter made headlines in Scotland.

Neither of us had much faith in Clinton, but we detested Bush. We toyed with the idea of supporting Ross Perot, and even went to several meetings of his supporters. They seemed to be nice, decent folk, who were very sympathetic to us, and genuinely wanted some sort of change. The problem was that they didn't seem to know what sort of change they wanted. And they were horribly disorganized. One night we held our meeting in a school parking lot. The meeting had been scheduled for the school itself, but too late the organizers discovered that schools could not be used for political meetings, even after hours. Political meetings couldn't be held anywhere on school property, and we considered ourselves lucky that we weren't thrown out of the parking lot. In the end I think I actually voted for Perot, but without any enthusiasm or hope. Still, I was pleased when Clinton won because I couldn't stand the sight of George Bush anymore.

One thing that the appearance of a new administration did was improve our access in Washington. The Bush administration had spoken almost exclusively to the leaders of the Victims of Pan Am 103 group. They didn't speak often, and President Bush himself had said not one word about the bombing or Libya during the election campaign. He didn't even send a letter. Still, Aphrodite Tsairis, who was then president of the group, urged members to vote for Bush because he had superior contacts "within the terrorist world"—whatever that meant.

The Clinton administration, on the other hand, was ready to talk to anyone.

One of the early acts of the new president was to fire FBI director William Sessions and replace him with Louis Freeh. As it turned out, Susan knew Freeh, and he apparently remembered her.

SUSAN: Back when I tried to find out if the Pan Am executives could be brought up on criminal charges, I wrote or called every prosecutor I could find in the state of New York. Someone directed me to Louis Freeh, who was a federal prosecutor in New York City. I left him a phone message, and he called me back promptly. We spoke on the phone several times. He was very nice, very considerate, and always answered my questions. Then one day I turned on the radio and found out that he was the new director of the FBI. Quickly I called Kathleen Flynn, and we decided to waste no time in requesting a meeting. Freeh remembered me, and we had no trouble getting in to see him.

How different this meeting was from the meeting we'd had with Sessions. The setting was informal. Couches instead of a long table. When Sessions presided we sat at attention. When we spoke with Freeh, we sprawled. He was strong, but thoughtful and considerate, and not in the least bit controlling. The FBI agents who were most involved in the investigation were there, and they spoke freely. We did too. The discussion went on for a very long time. Nobody threw us out. We left when we were ready to leave. I liked Louis Freeh.

DAN: I liked Louis Freeh too, his informality and his straightforward approach. He acted like a cop who had a job to do. I had never been particularly partial to cops, but after dealing with the devious denizens of the State Department for so long, the cops were looking a lot better.

Freeh had only been in office for a very short time and admitted that he wasn't familiar with all aspects of the case against the Libyans. But he said that he had reviewed the evidence the night before our meeting and thought there was a very strong case. It's a case that can be won in "any impartial court in the world," he said. But he was very careful not to rule out the possibility of involvement by countries in addition to Libya in the bombing.

SUSAN: Anthony Lake, now installed as head of the NSC, agreed to meet with us. Unlike the Republicans, he insisted on being absolutely fair to the families by having representatives from each faction at the meeting. Bert Ammerman and a few others from the Victims group refused to come because I was going to be there. They were used to private meetings with Republican officials.

The meeting, held in Lake's office in the Old Executive Office Building, next to the White House, went smoothly until Paul Hudson began talking about money. Paul envisioned receiving enormous sums from the Libyans. He even wanted money to flow into the coffers of Pan Am. This alone was intolerable—that that monstrous airline should receive as much as a dime. Paul argued that having to part with lots and lots of money would be a fitting punishment for terrorist states and would discourage them from future acts of terror. To say I didn't buy this is to put it mildly. I interrupted Paul and told him that we were not there to talk about money. Lake let me have my say, partly because he was a gentleman and partly because he would have had to stuff a sock in my mouth to shut me up.

My tirade, followed by Kathleen's disdainful, "Are you finished?" to Paul, silenced him. But Bruce Smith, the former Pan Am pilot whose wife died in the bombing, continued the pitch for money, and he did it with a melodramatic flair. I hated the very concept of blood money. I wanted Gadhafi to suffer real pain for killing Theo, not the twinge of discomfort parting with some of his easily replaced oil revenues would give him.

There were reporters outside the White House. As we

left, Paul handed them copies of his itemized list of precisely how much the Libyans should pay. I talked to the reporters too about my idea of justice. The word "money" never came up.

DAN: It had long been a dream of many Pan Am 103 families to have a memorial of some sort in Washington. The Lockerbie Trust, set up in Scotland to handle donations that poured in after the bombing, sent 270 pink sandstone blocks—one to represent each victim—for the construction of a memorial cairn, a traditional Scottish monument honoring the dead. The blocks had been quarried just a few miles from Lockerbie.

The blocks were shipped to the United States, and for a long time were stored in a warehouse outside of Philadelphia. The hope was that the memorial could be constructed in Arlington National Cemetery, America's most hallowed burial site. But when the idea was first presented to the authorities that control Arlington, they were dead set against it. Arlington is a military cemetery, and it's rapidly running out of space for graves. Its guardians have long protected it against "outside," that is nonmilitary, monuments, though there are a few, and ultimately Congress and the President have the last word. A number of possible alternate sites were proposed, but those most actively involved in trying to get the monument built always felt that Arlington was the best, the most beautiful, appropriate, and symbolically significant site. While Susan and I were not involved with the monument, we also believed that Arlington was the right place. In uniform or out, those killed on Pan Am 103 were victims of a war—a terrorist war against America—and they should be memorialized in America's national cemetery.

Jane Schultz made the construction of the cairn her special project. Every Pan Am 103 family has a story—Jane and Jack Schultz's story has a particularly terrible irony. Their twenty-year-old son, Thomas, a student at Ohio Wesleyan, died in the explosion of Pan Am 103. Ten years earlier, in 1978, the Schultzes' only other child, Andrew, age eight, found an unexploded grenade in the basement of a house they had just moved into. He picked it up and died from the injuries he received when the grenade went off.

The Schultzes were wealthy people. Jack Schultz had been a top department store executive, and they had connections with the Republican party, particularly with the Bush administration. Jane believed, or at least hoped, that the way could be cleared for the construction of the memorial cairn in Arlington. But George Bush left Washington without doing a thing.

In this respect the new administration was different, more humane, or perhaps just more PR savvy. Anthony Lake said that getting a monument built in Arlington was, "the least we can do." In Congress Senators Kennedy and Lautenberg pushed hard for a resolution designating Arlington as the site for the memorial. With strong backing from the new Clinton administration, a joint resolution was passed unanimously and signed into law by the President.

Ground breaking for the monument was scheduled for December 21, 1993, the fifth anniversary of the bombing.

SUSAN: It quickly became obvious that Clinton had no intention of changing Bush's overall policy on Pan Am 103. There would be no oil embargo, no military action, no stronger sanctions. What's more, instead of "answering all questions regarding Syrian and Iranian involvement in the Pan Am 103 tragedy," as he'd promised in the letter he'd sent us, he was going off to meet Syrian dictator al-Assad in January. Clinton would, however, meet with a small group of Pan Am 103 family members at the White House before the ground-breaking ceremony. Rosemary Wolfe and I would be among them. Afterward, Clinton was scheduled to leave for the ceremony at Arlington, and the families meeting with him would be driven there as well.

The person handling the details for Pan Am 103 in the National Security Council was Dick Canas (pronounced KAHN-yahs). He had worked in narcotics before coming to the NSC and therefore was not a typical State Department type. When I found out the administration planned to rely on the family groups to notify relatives about the cairn ceremony, I complained to Canas. The groups would only notify their own members, and perhaps not all their members. The leaders rarely reached beyond their own inner circle. I believed it was the government's obligation to notify all the families. I managed to persuade Canas that I was right, and he worked hard to insure everyone was told.

The day arrived when the families were to meet the President. Canas later told me that the night before the meeting, he was visited by a small delegation headed by Bert Ammerman, asking that I not be allowed in to see the President, and that they be permitted to take my place. My position, which I'd made clear to the administration many times, is that anyone who had a relative on Pan Am 103 has a right to be included in any meeting. All I asked was that I be included as well. Since the Victims of Pan Am 103 would be well represented at the meeting, and since, after all, I did have a right to be there, the answer from the White House to Ammerman and company was a resounding no.

I could tell when I woke up on the morning of the twenty-first that it was going to be a very long day. To make it even longer, I was scheduled to go on the *Larry King Show* at nine that night. And if that wasn't enough, I had a bad cold. Throw in grief, suffering, and painful memories—I was a mess. I decided to hell with wearing a dress and nylons, and shivering at Arlington for who knew how long, just because I was going to see Bill Clinton. So I put on corduroy pants and a sweater. I never dressed up anyway. Let the President meet the real me. However, when I got to the White House, one of the parents who was there for the meeting was so shocked that I wore pants instead of a dress that she became angrier than I had ever seen her become over the terrorists who murdered her child!

As we stood waiting to go into the Oval Office, Anthony

Lake took me aside and gave me a letter. It was written by Lake himself, on behalf of the President, in response to an angry letter Dan and I had sent to Clinton, accusing him of coddling the terrorist al-Assad. I put the letter into my purse, unread. Next thing I knew I was inside the beautiful Oval Office, with its sweeping views of the White House grounds. The President, wearing a sad face for the occasion, was shaking my hand and photographers were taking our picture. Clinton looked deeply into my eyes, as he did the eyes of each family member who entered the room, with what I would have described in my days as a writer of gothic romances as "an intense blue gaze."

I had no illusions that Clinton would be influenced by anything anyone said at the meeting. We were there for his benefit; he wasn't there for ours. I had two goals. One was to keep Clinton from charming the families into deciding it was okay for him to meet al-Assad. The other was to ask all my questions and make strong responses to Clinton's answers, so that I would be able to tell Larry King that I had confronted the President; here's what he said, and here's what I said.

Rosemary Wolfe opened the meeting, bringing up all the right issues, as I knew she would. Then other family members spoke. When the talk turned to Syria, I interrupted politely but firmly, to keep the focus on what a dangerous terrorist al-Assad was. A couple of times I had to interrupt Clinton. He didn't stop me. I just got more of the blue gaze. By the end of the meeting, I had plenty of ammo for the *Larry King Show*. I figured that by reaching millions of people, as I would from the CNN studios, I had a better chance of influencing Clinton than if I had talked to him face-to-face all day. Still, as the families left, I went up to Clinton and reminded him that despite what might be good for any other country in the world, my daughter was an American, and to the President of the United States, Americans should always come first.

When I got home I read Lake's letter. He must have known I would pass it on to reporters, because I was notorious for giving the media every shred of official paper that came my way. But if that is what he wanted, he almost made a mistake. The letter said Syria would remain on the list of terrorist states until certain conditions were met. Sounded like boilerplate to me, and I almost buried the letter in a big box marked Pan Am 103 that served as a file in our house. Just to be on the safe side, I gave a copy to Tom Lippman at the *Washington Post*. To my surprise, he found it interesting and wrote an article about it. I guess I just didn't know how to interpret Washington boilerplate. I didn't mind being used as a conduit for information so long as it made trouble for terrorists.

DAN: The fifth anniversary at Arlington was the first large gathering of Pan Am 103 families I had attended in several years. The atmosphere was dramatically different from what it had been in the early days. There was less weeping, but also less hugging. Small cliques of friends gathered, but in general we were now a crowd of strangers—people from different backgrounds, often different worlds. We had been thrown together by a horrible tragedy. Now, five years later, we were older, sadder, lonelier, and more bitter, but essentially the same people.

I had never been to Arlington before. I found the cemetery with its rows of neat white grave markers an impressive, even a moving place. But among the families, some of the tensions of the previous five years boiled over.

Chairs had been set up in front of the podium from which President Clinton was to speak. Closest to the podium, a section had been roped off for VIPs like senators, cabinet members, and special guests. Seated in that special area was Eleanor Bright and her six-year-old son, Nick. Nick had been chosen to turn over the first shovelful of earth at the spot where the memorial was to be constructed. The Brights were from Massachusetts, and Nick Bright was Senator Kennedy's choice, a thoroughly appropriate one.

Another family member, a man who lost a daughter, had been trying to get a seat close to the podium. He saw

Eleanor and her son, stood behind them, and began to shout, "What are you doing up there! You don't deserve to be up there!"

Everyone heard him. His wife tried to calm him down. It was a painfully embarrassing moment.

Cars began arriving from the White House. Susan was in one of them. She was ushered into the roped-off section, but didn't feel comfortable there. She drifted back to the press area, where she was always most at home.

We were walking through the crowd together and spotted Bert Ammerman. He seemed to be trying to direct traffic, telling people to go one way or another, though there was no obvious need for crowd control. Susan walked up to him and said sharply, "Bert."

He looked at her, and his face seemed to crumble. "Susan!" he almost shouted. Then he angrily waved his hand and hissed, "Pass on this way now. Don't block the way!"

It wasn't quite a confrontation, but it was close. We didn't see Bert at any public Pan Am 103 event again for years.

I wondered what Theo would have thought of the ceremony. All the flags, the solemnity, the religious overtones. She wouldn't have liked it. And she wouldn't have liked being just a name on a long list of victims.

As we came in, we had each been given a sprig of Scottish heather. Most people pinned the heather to their jackets or coats. I stuck mine rakishly in my hat. Stand out. Be different. It was a gesture Theo would have understood and appreciated.

Over his nearly eight years in office, Bill Clinton has given several speeches about Pan Am 103. The one he gave at the fifth anniversary was the best because it contained this line, "The attack on Pan Am 103 was an attack not only on the individuals from twenty-one different countries who were on board that aircraft. It was, at root, an attack on America."

It certainly was. Unfortunately, that statement coming from Bill Clinton was just another piece of political puffery.

The cairn was built over the next several months. Every cent for the construction and care of the monument was raised by private donation. The dedication ceremony was on November 3, 1994, instead of on December 21. It was hoped that the weather would be better and more people from Scotland would attend. They did, some wearing kilts, which might have been uncomfortable in a Washington winter.

The cairn aggravated tensions within the Victims of Pan Am 103 group. Bert, Aphrodite, and a few others who had led the organization for years resigned. They refused to attend the dedication ceremony. It would be an exaggeration to say that we got on well with the new leadership. Dealing with us is never a day at the beach. But at least there was no overt hostility, and we could appear at the same public events together.

The cairn itself is a rather uninspired, but serviceable monument—a circular tower of stones eleven feet high, with the names of all of those who died engraved around its base. It has become a focal point for Pan Am 103 activities and a place to go on memorial days when there is no place else to go. And it is just where it should be.

What I remember best about the ceremony is Trina Vargo bustling about looking concerned. Her boss, Ted Kennedy, was having serious trouble with his back, and she was worried that he would aggravate the condition while walking up the hill to the memorial site. The job of a loyal aide is to protect your boss any way you can.

The memorial service held at the cairn the following year, 1995, was memorable mainly because there wasn't one. A service had been scheduled, and we went down to Washington to attend. But when we got there, we discovered that Arlington National Cemetery was closed. The U.S. government had been largely shut down due to a budget dispute between the President and Congress, but I couldn't believe the idiots were actually going to close down the national cemetery!

What to do? We could slink sadly and quietly back home, but that was not our style. We grabbed the phone and called every Washington media contact we could find. When we got to the locked gates of Arlington the morning of the twenty-first there was a substantial crowd of reporters and cameramen there to greet us, along with Rosemary and Jim Wolfe and Kathleen and Jack Flynn.

A few minutes later a flock of cars from the White House swept down upon us. In a rage Kathleen had called the White House situation room and demanded entry to Arlington. Sensing a public-relations disaster—grieving parents locked out of memorial service—the White House acted.

SUSAN: I was holding a bouquet of roses and complaining to the cameras that I couldn't get inside the cemetery to put flowers at the base of the cairn in honor of Theo, when Randy Beers, who worked for the National Security Council, drove up in a hurry. Beers knew all about Pan Am 103. He was at the first emergency meeting called by the Reagan administration when the plane was bombed. He was now our NSC contact person, and I talked to him often.

Beers jumped out of the car, nervously grabbed my arm, took me away from the cameras, and walked me around. I respected Beers' intelligence and capacity for hard work. But he was completely the government's man and was always worried about bad publicity, bad from the administration's standpoint, that is. Now he was very worried indeed.

"You're trying to build a news story, Susan," he said. I longed to answer, "I'm not trying, I'm succeeding," but I didn't. The message was clear. The only way the administration could avoid looking heartless was to get us inside that cemetery, which is precisely what Beers did. We were loaded into the cars and driven through the gates and to the cairn.

It was incredibly still inside Arlington that day. Occasionally a car passed slowly or an employee walked along the road. Otherwise, it was completely empty and so seemed less a national monument than simply a place where one could mourn alone. I was overwhelmed by the silence and broke down, crying uncontrollably in front of the cairn. While the tears ran down my face, Randy Beers stood fidgeting beside me, embarrassed and miserable. Bureaucrats, snug in their little rabbit warrens in Washington, almost never have to see the human wreckage created by the government they serve.

DAN: During the first few years of the Clinton administration we went to Washington a lot, for rounds of mostly pointless meetings with various officials. At one point Anthony Lake suddenly called a meeting of about ten Pan Am 103 family members. We gathered in the NSC office in that Gilded Age monstrosity, the Old Executive Office Building, and then were ushered over to the sacred precincts of the White House itself, and installed in the beautiful and historic Roosevelt Room. Randy Beers told Susan that he knew she wasn't impressed by surroundings, "but this is the only room large enough for the meeting that's available." A nonsensical statement, since we had just left a room that was quite large enough for the meeting, and Randy knew that Susan was a great admirer of FDR and Eleanor.

The surroundings were supposed to impress us. Even George Stephanopoulos wandered by. The really impressive thing, however, was what Lake said—the United States was going to push for an embargo on Libyan oil! This was what all of us had been requesting for a long time. An oil embargo was the only thing, short of military action, that could put real pressure on Libya. But it would also require the cooperation of most of the world's industrial nations, and that didn't seem to be in the cards. When I asked what was actually being done to get this embargo, Lake was vague and downright evasive, but he said he needed our cooperation in getting the word out.

That was another nonsense statement. He didn't need us. All he had to do was step into the White House pressroom and tell the assembled reporters that the United

States was going to press for an embargo on Libyan oil, and within a couple of hours the whole world would know. And that may have been what he did, because when we got back home a few hours later, our answering machine was already loaded with messages from reporters asking about the oil embargo.

We answered the questions as honestly as we could, saying that while we favored the embargo we didn't feel that the administration had any realistic plan for getting one. In about a week the oil embargo story faded away. Nothing had been done.

Later we discovered that at this time Libya had been making a serious behind-the-scenes attempt to get a seat on the U.N. Security Council. The oil embargo threat had been part of the pressure to keep them out, not a real policy at all. We had been used. Actually I didn't mind being used. Keeping Libya out of the Security Council was a worthy goal. But we were also misled, and that I resented very much.

SUSAN: Tim Wirth was an ex-senator with movie-star looks, who was put in charge of a motley array of issues at the State Department. For a while Pan Am 103 was one of them. He didn't seem to know or care much about it. I found that out when I was on a television show with him. Wirth's real interests were environmental matters and population control. I cared about the environment too. After all, I had walked in the woods of Forestburgh on snowshoes, and moved to Cape May for the birdsong. But when I went to his office with a small group of family members, it wasn't to talk about birds, it was to talk about bombs.

As we waited in Wirth's outer office, I noticed a big bowl of candy, round chocolates wrapped in foil. Chocoholic that I am, I couldn't resist, and was about to unwrap one when I let out a shriek. Everyone stared at me. It wasn't a piece of chocolate I was holding. It was a foil-wrapped condom! Wirth certainly wasn't kidding about population control, but wasn't leaving condoms on display for visitors carrying things a bit too far? I snitched one though, wrapped in gold. I took it home and put it in the back of a drawer somewhere. A souvenir from our nation's capital.

DAN: Wirth was probably wondering why we were all smiling when we entered his office. It was the last smile he was to see because it was a lousy meeting. Wirth insisted on showing us organizational charts of the State Department, as if that was supposed to mean something to us. We peppered him with hostile questions, which he didn't really try to answer. He began looking at his watch, and finally his secretary came in and announced loudly that he had a lunch appointment with some ambassador. And still we didn't stop. When we finally ran out of questions, he rushed to open the office door and smiled weakly at us as we left. I said, "Mr. Wirth, as far as I'm concerned, you're worthless." Not very clever, but sincere.

SUSAN: In late 1995, a bill reached the Senate floor designed to punish foreign companies investing in Iran. Through a clever political maneuver, Senators Kennedy and D'Amato got Libya added to the bill, which became known as the Iran Libya Sanction Act, ILSA for short. American oil companies were opposed to economic sanctions of any kind, and if ILSA became law, they feared their foreign subsidiaries would be blocked from selling oil-related equipment to Iran and Libya. They argued that ILSA would also invite retaliation from the countries of foreign companies hit with sanctions. The European Union screamed its opposition. "The Europeans are goin' nuts," one of D'Amato's aides gleefully told me.

To put it briefly, a lot of powerful forces hated the bill. So the oil companies fought back, hiring big-name lobbyists and pouring massive sums of money into getting the bill defeated. And that was just for starters. The bill had to get through not only the Senate but also the House, where the chairman of the very powerful Ways and Means Committee was the oil industry's best friend, Texas Congressman Bill Archer. The Clinton administration opposed the bill too. I knew what lay ahead. All out war!

The ILSA war lasted for months. I talked to Trina Vargo all the time. I called congressional offices constantly. The print media, especially business reporters, were very interested in the story. Not a day passed that I wasn't on the phone with reporters, editorial page writers, and columnists. There was a political campaign that year. I went after the two New Jersey senatorial candidates, Robert Toricelli and Dick Zimmer. Both were congressmen on important committees, and I urged them to fight for the bill. They made promises. I monitored them closely to see whether they kept their word.

Several Republican senators took turns quietly putting a hold on the bill. By a curious Senate rule any member can anonymously hold up consideration of legislation. It is possible, however, to find out who the anonymous senator is. One was John Chafee of Rhode Island, a state that lost citizens on Pan Am 103. I phoned the host of a popular Rhode Island radio show. She put me on her show. She put Senator Chafee on. To his surprise she put us on together. It was not a happy moment for Chafee, and after much hemming and hawing he promised to release the bill. He did, and ILSA made it through the Senate.

But there was still the House. Archer played hardball. He did everything he could to emasculate the Libyan part of ILSA before the bill was returned to the Senate. Jewish groups were all over D'Amato to get the bill passed. They didn't care about Libya. Their target was Iran. An aide from D'Amato's office begged me to accept Archer's "compromise." Stubbornly I refused. If Kennedy could hold his ground, I certainly could.

I decided to take on Archer directly. A risky and probably futile tactic, but worth a try. The *Houston Chronicle* did a sympathetic story on me. I was debating whether I should phone Houston and Dallas talk shows when something happened that changed everything overnight. Not something to cheer about. Something terrible that sent me right inside Pan Am 103 again as it fell out of the sky. What happened was that on July 17, 1996, TWA flight 800 blew up in midair off the coast of Long Island.

At first it was assumed that the disaster had been caused by a terrorist bomb. Airline terrorism was back in the news, and Congress capitulated and passed the tough version of ILSA quickly. I even received a call from D'Amato's aide thanking me for refusing to compromise. His boss would have looked terrible backing down on terrorism while an American plane blew up leaving Kennedy Airport, which was practically in the senator's backyard.

I had worked so hard to get ILSA that I demanded to be at the White House when Clinton reluctantly signed the bill into law. So there I was in the Oval Office again, along with several other Pan Am 103 family members. The President smiled at me and said, "Glad to have you with us again." I glared back. I was fully aware that Clinton, the National Security Council, and the State Department would find ways to dilute or dismantle ILSA. Which is exactly what they did. I was there solely as a gesture of defiance. The President gave me a pen. I keep it in a drawer, next to the letter from President Bush.

Senator Kennedy had a *New York Times* article about me and my part in the fight for ILSA placed in the *Congressional Record*. I received a copy of it from the senator's office. It was signed, "To Susan and Dan Cohen. With great admiration for all you do to honor Theo's memory." I framed it and put it up on my office wall.

DAN: I had been lurking outside the Oval Office during the bill signing. Afterward we were all taken over to nearby George Washington University, where the President gave a speech on how important this bill would be in the fight against terrorism. Another politician's promise, for in the months that followed, the provisions of the bill were violated many times, and the sanctions were never invoked, not once.

After his speech President Clinton charged down off the stage to shake hands with members of the audience. I had been placed in the front row, and he may have recognized me from the signing ceremony. He was heading right for me, big smile on his face, big hand outstretched. I didn't like the guy. I didn't want to shake hands with him. I tried to back away, but he was unstoppable. I would have had to knock people over and create a scene to avoid him. So we shook hands, and all I could think was I hope no picture of this appears in the papers.

As far as I know, none did.

The Bush and Clinton administrations were not exactly Tweedledum and Tweedledee on Pan Am 103. They were more like two other Lewis Carroll characters, the Walrus and the Carpenter. Clinton was the Walrus. The Walrus wept for the oysters and said "I deeply sympathize" while the Carpenter said nothing. But as Tweedledee observed, the Walrus ate more oysters than the Carpenter.

Chapter 16

DAN: The demise of Pan Am and the final collapse of the U.S. Aviation Insurance defense did not mean the end of the conspiracy theories they had spawned and sponsored. There was a new defendant in the dock who could make use of them—Libya.

A major publisher planned to publish a book on the Aviv/Coleman drugs and bomb theory of Pan Am 103. But after *Time*'s exposé was itself exposed, those plans were dropped. By the late summer of 1992, Lester Coleman, cited as a key source for the *Time* story, was running out of money and friends. He was living in a Swedish refugee camp in the town of Trolhattan, and telling anyone who would listen that he was claiming political asylum, in flight from CIA assassins who were out to silence him.

He was also trying to sell a book idea of his own, and not having much success at it. At this point the story gets murky. Coleman has always claimed that he received no help from the Libyans. However, he was visited in Sweden by a British solicitor hired by the Libyans to defend the two indicted suspects and the Libyan government. About a year after the meeting Coleman's book, coauthored by a former *New York Times* subeditor and current antique shop owner, Donald Goddard, and called *Trail of the Octopus,* was published in England by Bloomsbury Press.

We first heard of Coleman's book from Dr. Jim Swire, leader of the British Pan Am 103 Victims group. He had met with Goddard and told us that he was impressed by the wealth of information the man seemed to possess. We had never heard of Goddard, and Dr. Swire did not at first mention the name of Lester Coleman.

Jim Swire is an extremely important figure in the story of Pan Am 103. His eldest child, Flora, a medical student, was on Pan Am 103. She would have been twenty-four on December 22, 1988. Swire was a thin, sharp-featured man with a shock of white hair. He reminded me of the British character actor John Laurie, whom I had seen in the old *Avengers* series. For years he has been the chief spokesman for the U.K. Families Flight 103. Indeed it often appears that he is the sole spokesman for the U.K. families.

Swire first came to public notice in the fall of 1990 when he smuggled a fake bomb aboard a British Airways flight bound from Heathrow to JFK to demonstrate that airline security had not improved. Swire constructed his "bomb" inside of a radio-cassette player similar to the one used for the Pan Am 103 bomb. For Semtex he substituted the confectionery paste marzipan. He then carried his "bomb" right through Heathrow security and again through security at JFK, where he transferred to a Boston-bound flight to attend a meeting of the Victims of Pan Am 103.

In the meeting with the American relatives, Swire was persuaded to keep the news of his "stunt" quiet, at least for a while, but when it did become public some six weeks later, he became a celebrity in Britain. Some American relatives objected to Swire's kind of activism, but Susan and I thought it was great.

Though we had never met Jim Swire, we did admire him. Like us, he had been shattered by the loss of his daughter, and his life had been consumed by the Pan Am 103 tragedy. And, like us, he was not one to grieve quietly. He went for media attention with the grand gesture.

Jim Swire was deeply suspicious, as we were, of the "Libya alone is responsible" position adopted by the U.S. and U.K. after the Gulf War. But unlike us, Swire was inclined to believe that Libya had nothing to do with the bombing—that the two suspects had been framed in order to shield Iran and Syria and possibly others, including U.S. intelligence.

After the indictments of the two Libyans were announced, Swire went to Libya and met with Gadhafi. In a highly publicized ceremony, he presented Gadhafi with a picture of his daughter, which was to be placed next to the picture of Gadhafi's adopted daughter who'd been killed in the U.S. raid on Tripoli in 1986 in the memorial dedicated to the Libyans who died in the raid. (Flora Swire's picture is no longer on display in Tripoli.) That was a grand gesture we very definitely did not approve of. Gadhafi has a long and cruel history of exploiting ordinary people for his own propaganda purposes. We thought Jim Swire was being foolish and worse, because those scenes of him presenting Gadhafi with his daughter's picture made great Libyan propaganda. Still we admired Swire for his energy and dedication, and we began exchanging letters and phone calls.

SUSAN: In the beginning I admired Jim Swire a great deal. He seemed a decent person, a real gentleman. Unquestionably he loved his daughter Flora very deeply and suffered terribly over her loss. He had courage, vigor, and unstoppable drive, sterling qualities. And he was effective, always coming up with novel ideas about ways to proceed. I often wished he lived in America, for we needed someone like him here. However, as time passed, and he made more trips to Libya, Swire began to remind me more and more of the British colonel played by Alec Guinness in the movie *The Bridge on the River Kwai.* The colonel was a brave and decent man whose obsession led him to unwittingly serve the enemy cause.

DAN: When I found out that the book project Swire was praising as being informed and useful was really Lester Coleman's, I was appalled. I tried to warn him about Coleman, but he said vaguely that he wanted to "keep an open mind." He did tell me that "Gadhafi would be another Hitler if he had the power." That made me wonder why he was giving a potential Hitler his murdered daughter's picture.

Still I made allowances. Swire was not in the United States and was not fully aware of Coleman's role in Pan Am's defense. And he had not carefully monitored the Pan Am civil trial in which so much evidence implicating Libya had come out. He had loved his daughter, and he would stand up to anything, and endure any hostility, to expose what he truly believed to be the truth about her death. That counted for a lot.

When Coleman's book was published in 1993, we managed to get an advance copy. Reading it over, I found the same mixture of truth, half truth, and outright falsehood that had characterized everything Coleman had said about Pan Am 103—but at greater length. In his foreword to the book, Donald Goddard specifically thanked Pan Am's attorneys "for *declining* to help me with my researches, thereby—I hope—denying room to those government supporters who might otherwise wish to accuse me, as they did in *Time* magazine, of conspiring with the airline to pervert the course of justice." That was a particularly disingenuous claim, since, to my understanding, some of the documents reproduced in the back of the book could only have come from the Pan Am lawyers.

For a brief period *Trail of the Octopus* made Lester Coleman a minor celebrity in that segment of the British and Scottish media that believes that America is behind every evil in the world. Coleman was interviewed and treated quite seriously as a heroic former agent who was trying to expose one of the greatest cover-ups in history, and was living in fear for his life and the life of his family. The gaping holes in his tale were ignored. Here was a gaggle of left-wing journalists promoting a theory that had originally been promoted and nurtured by the conspiracy factory of right-wing fanatic Lyndon LaRouche.

The big prize eluded Coleman—an American publisher. Without U.S. publication, his book was never going to make big bucks. American publishers were apparently afraid that if they published Coleman's book, they would be sued. However, the book did attract enough attention in Britain to warrant a sale to a paperback publisher there. As it happened, I had frequently written books for the American branch of this publisher. When I heard what they were planning to do, I called editors I knew and warned them that if they published Coleman's book, they were going to be sued. They published, and they were sued.

Neither the hardback nor paperback editions of *Trail of the Octopus* had a huge sale, despite the purchase of hundreds of copies by Ibraham Legwell, lawyer for the accused Libyans, for distribution to journalists. The book was available, though not widely available in the United States. It was hawked at meetings by Louis Farrakhan of the Nation of Islam, Libya's favorite American lapdog, and was available through an NOL Web site on the Internet.

Shortly after the book was published, rumors began to circulate that it was going to be made into a movie. The rumors, probably started by Coleman himself, hinted that Oliver Stone was interested. The truth turned out to be less spectacular.

In the fall of '93, we were among a small group of American Pan Am 103 families who were contacted by a woman from California named Andrea Primdahl. She said that she was working with an independent British production company, Hemar Enterprises, Inc. The company was producing a "thorough and chilling documentary on the Lockerbie disaster," and they were looking for American families to interview.

SUSAN: I heard from another American family member that the film was being produced by an American from California named Allan Francovich, who was working in London and was trying to get in touch with the families. I phoned him at once. It took several tries before he called back. Francovich was chatty and friendly. He told me about other documentaries he had made, including one on the civil rights struggle in Mississippi. He said he'd send me videos of them.

He presented himself as a left-wing, anti-Vietnam War baby boomer, a courageous fighter for the truth, ready to expose the secrets of evil governments no matter what. Fancy talk, but when I tried to pin him down about his Pan Am 103 project, he was vague. I didn't know how to interpret this vagueness. Was it some kind of dreamy Hollywood moviemakers' style I was unfamiliar with, or was it something more sinister? I knew about Coleman's book and the movie rumors, and asked Francovich flat out if he was basing his documentary on it. He was cagey, but I was persistent, and finally he said no.

I was suspicious when I hung up, but nothing more. Clearly, Francovich was a braggart, but he wanted the families to endorse his documentary, and perhaps he was just trying to make himself look good for that reason. He didn't sound crazy. I needed to know more about him. When his videos arrived, I watched them and found them very pedestrian. OK, so Francovich wasn't very talented. I could live with that. But I thought that sections of them might be woefully inaccurate, and that had me very worried.

DAN: Any thought of our cooperating with Francovich was shattered in December of '93 when an article in the *Financial Times* of London revealed the real power behind the "independent" production company. Though shielded by a complex screen of shell companies, Hemar Enterprises, the film production company, was owned by Metropole Hotels, which was controlled by a flamboyant British millionaire, "Tiny" Rowland. Rowland had sold a large percentage of his interests to the Libyan Arab Foreign Investment Company (Lafico), shortly after the indictments of the Libyans in the Pan Am bombing. Lafico, in turn, was controlled by Colonel Gadhafi's family. Hemar was set up to produce a film on "Libyan interests." Francovich had been hired to make the film. Cut away all the camouflage, and it was clear that this was to be a Moammar Gadhafi production.

We instantly told Francovich to go to hell, and he never

received a jot of cooperation from any U.S. family. But Jim Swire kept urging us to "keep an open mind" about the film. He told us how, during filming, Francovich had wept at his daughter's grave, had assured Jim that he didn't even know who was paying his salary, and that his investigation was completely independent. To believe this was to carry gullibility beyond the borders of rationality.

What really tore it for us was an interview Swire gave to the British newspaper *The Guardian,* which strongly suggested that those of us who opposed the film were really just interested in collecting money in the civil case against Pan Am, which was still dragging its way through U.S. courts. That we, or any other American family, would seek to cover up the truth about the bombing in order to get money was a vile and unforgivable accusation.

I fired off a furious letter to Swire. I didn't fax it to him because his phone and fax were on the same line, and I would have had to speak to him before he turned the fax machine on. I didn't trust myself to do that. We have not spoken or communicated in any way since then.

Francovich set out trying to sell his yet uncompleted documentary to a TV network. The BBC in England, and PBS and A&E in the United States, quickly turned him down. But he got a bite from Britain's independent Channel 4, an upstart channel with a reputation for running controversial material. Linda Mack was a freelance journalist in London. She had a close friend on Pan Am 103 and became deeply interested in the case. For three years she worked for ABC in London, largely on Pan Am 103 material, and probably knew as much about "alternative scenarios" to the theory that the Libyans placed the bomb, as anyone. She went to Channel 4 and tried to warn them about who they were dealing with and what they were getting into. Channel 4 wasn't listening.

Linda also contacted us. We had met her years earlier at one of the first Victims of Pan Am 103 meetings. We already had a general idea of who and what was behind the Francovich film, but she filled in many details.

The most improbable and exotic of Francovich's associates was Oswald LeWinter, a disgraced English professor from Penn State and a convicted drug smuggler who'd been arrested for impersonating an American army officer. He'd also done time on other unspecified charges. Before being deported in the late 1970s, LeWinter had spent some years in Germany, where he evidently became an associate of the Lyndon LaRouche followers there. He gained a measure of fame by pretending to be a former CIA agent, ready to expose all sorts of agency skulduggery.

He first teamed up with Francovich on a 1990 film, and now they were together again working on the Pan Am 103 project.

One day I got a call from a man with what sounded like a German accent. He would not give his name but said that his brother had been killed by the Libyans and they were "the worst people in the world." He said he was going to help us expose Francovich and company and that he had hospital documents proving that Oswald LeWinter had spent time in a Swiss mental institution.

I didn't know what to make of the strange call, and I phoned Linda. She told me, "You've just been talking to Oswald LeWinter." It seems that calling people using a variety of names and accents was a favorite technique of his. He had recently been calling Pan Am families in the United States, and under different guises trying to dig up dirt on those who opposed the film. Why he'd called us we didn't know. But about two weeks later, a fat envelope, posted in Belgium but without a return address, showed up at our house.

I called journalist Chris Byron of *New York* magazine. He said what appeared to be going on was an attempted scam, and an old one. If the material we received was false, and we talked about it, we would be accused of spreading false rumors. If the envelope contained medical documents, and they were genuine, we would be accused of dealing in stolen hospital records. "Don't even open the envelope," he said. "Send it to the FBI." That's just what we did and we never heard any more about it.

Francovich complained of being persecuted. He said

that there was a CIA team in Europe trying to disrupt his filming. Someone had been tampering with the brakes of his car. His phones had been tapped. He had received death threats from Iran and warned that if he went to Cyprus he would be killed. These stories appeared in the British press.

Soon we were to be listed among his tormentors. I had contacted Channel 4 and exchanged faxes with Peter Moore, who had the title "Commissioning Editor, Documentaries." In a 1994 interview with the British paper *The Guardian,* Moore prided himself on showing "risky, edgy, and zany" films. His defense of Francovich's film was basically, We didn't make it. We can't check it. We just broadcast it. Francovich accused me of carrying out a furious onslaught of faxes and phone calls against the TV channel. It was about five faxes over a period of six weeks. Admittedly, I was outspoken, using such phrases as "a fine bunch of bastards you're playing with," "Drop him like a poisonous snake," and "Whoring for Moammar Gadhafi." It was "risky, edgy, and zany" language that Moore should have loved. He didn't; he just got defensive and pompous.

With Linda Mack taking the lead, we helped to organize a petition against the film. It was signed by a large number of relatives of Pan Am 103 victims, including over forty from the U.K.

Francovich hinted darkly that he was going to expose Linda: "We are fully capable of monitoring her activities. . . ." His solicitor sent us a letter threatening to sue if we did not cease our activities and apologize. We told him to go ahead and sue because getting Francovich into court might be worth the price of admission. We never heard from the solicitor again.

In a letter to us Francovich asserted that he had been in touch with a "high intelligence official" with inside knowledge of the bombing who told him that he had recently talked to Susan and she said, "My God! Don't you ever say that in public because we will lose our case against Pan Am." An obvious implication that we were interested only in getting a big settlement from Pan Am and not in learning the truth. The charge was clearly and demonstrably false—but very nasty.

By the summer of '94, Channel 4 backed away from its commitment to show what was now called *The Maltese Double Cross*. It was also dropped from the London Film Festival. But it wasn't dead. Tam Dalyell, a member of Parliament from the Lockerbie area, a friend of Libya and a promoter of conspiracy theories about Pan Am 103, arranged to have the film screened in the House of Commons in November. It was also shown in Glasgow under the auspices of *The Scotsman*, Scotland's largest newspaper, which had long shown a pro-Libyan bias. My opinion of Scottish politicians and journalists was going downhill fast.

Before the screenings Francovich passed out an information sheet that contained the charge about Susan and the "high intelligence official." This time we considered suing. We contacted a British solicitor who said that with Britain's strict libel laws we could almost certainly win our case, but that it would be expensive. We also realized that Francovich probably didn't have any money and if he did it would be well hidden; we would never be able to recover our expenses. Therefore, we dropped the idea.

The film was also shown on television in France, Australia, and a couple of African countries. Then in May of '95, Channel 4 announced it was going to air *The Maltese Double Cross* after all. It was to be followed by a discussion of the film between Francovich and some of his critics. Though we had been among his most outspoken critics, we were not invited to participate.

A few weeks later I got a video of *The Maltese Double Cross*. It was awful. It was full of lies—I had expected that—and it looked like an amateur production. In it Oswald LeWinter first posed as a former CIA agent and later, in the shadows and out of focus but clearly recognizable, posed as what looked like a reporter. Other scenes showed Lester Coleman weeping in self-pity and people from the Malta airport telling the world how good their security was. Long segments portrayed what looked like a Libyan

travelogue, and plenty of scenes showed Colonel Gadhafi
in various costumes and heroic poses.

It was so bad, so silly, that I wondered if we had wasted
our time trying to stop it. I consoled myself with the thought
that a large percentage of the public believes in alien ab-
ductions on the basis of "documentaries" nearly as bad as
this one.

After the showing of the film on Channel 4, and the poor
reviews it received, even in newspapers that had supported
its basic premise, we never heard about it again. But we
couldn't get rid of Lester Coleman.

Somehow he got hold of our fax number. First he sent us
a notice soliciting money for his defense fund. Then he
called. We hung up on him. The faxes kept coming.

SUSAN: Late on a December night, when I couldn't stop
crying for thinking about Theo, the machine rang and there
was another fax from Lester Coleman. "Holiday Greet-
ings" the cover page said. Coleman had taken to sending
me poetry at the most painful time of year. One of his literary efforts was called "Susan's Rage," a piece of doggerel
that began, "Pay homage to Susan Cohen, a bereaved
mother worth know'n. Lost her only child, you see, over
the village of Lockerbie."

My rage was "misdirected," according to the poet Coleman, who was always eager to assert Libya's innocence
and turn me into a dimwit who had infinite faith in the
government's honesty. He had Susan in the poem say, "The
greatest nation, you see, would never tell a lie to me."

Lester Coleman, a man who deliberately harassed a
grieving mother near the anniversary of her child's death.
I think that says it all.

DAN: A number of the individuals connected with this
tawdry business came to a bad end. Tiny Rowland was
ousted from the leadership of the company he had
founded. Part of the reason appears to have been his close

identification with Gadhafi and the film. He has since died.

In 1997 Allan Francovich dropped dead of a heart attack in the Dallas airport.

In 1998 Oswald LeWinter was arrested in London while trying to sell Mohammed Al Fayed documents proving that his son Dodi and Princess Diana had been murdered. The documents were forgeries.

Then there is Lester Coleman. Coleman was indicted for lying in sworn affidavits he made in the Pan Am 103 case. His British publishers were sued by Michael Hurley, a U.S. Drug Enforcement Agency official in Cyprus whom Coleman had accused of helping to cover up DEA involvement in the bombing. The publishers were not able to produce a shred of evidence to support Coleman's tale, and in July 1996 they agreed to settle for a reported $460,000. They publicly apologized to Hurley, agreed not to sell rights to the book in any foreign country, and to "pulp" all remaining copies. Channel 4, which was also sued, settled later and apologized.

Coleman, abandoned by his sponsors, broke and without hope of making any more money from his story, finally agreed to surrender to U.S. authorities in October 1996. He said he was going home to clear his name and have his day in court. Coleman arrived at an airport in Portugal in a wheelchair, claiming he had been beaten by mysterious assailants. When nobody paid attention, he walked unaided onto the plane to New York. He was jailed on his return, couldn't make bail, and after a few months decided to come clean.

He confessed that he had made the whole story up, and he had done it for money. The final paragraphs of his signed confession read:

"I apologize to the parents of Khalid Nazir Jaafar for my statement that he was involved in drug smuggling and that he may have been used by terrorists to get a bomb on board Pan Am 103.

"I also apologize to the families and friends of the 270 people killed on flight 103 and on the ground in Lockerbie for my role in promoting the story that an agency of the U.S. government was somehow responsible for aiding the terrorists in getting the bomb onto the plane."

Running true to form, just as soon as Coleman was released from prison, he began backtracking, hinting that he never really made the confession, or that it had been forced, and he didn't really mean it.

Somehow he managed to get a job as host of a local talk radio show in Lexington, Kentucky. He challenged me to call his show for a debate. When I did call, he wouldn't speak with me, claiming that there had been no such challenge.

Later, Lester Coleman went back to jail. He was convicted on bad check and forgery charges.

Characters like Francovich, LeWinter, and Coleman are so low, so unabashedly sleazy that they almost provide an element of comic relief in a very grim tale. They are incidental and insignificant. But the respectable people who use them, and help spread their noxious fantasies for their own purposes—the journalists, the politicians, the diplomats, the lawyers, and the businessmen—they are not funny or insignificant at all.

Chapter 17

Dan: One of the core beliefs of Libyan policy is that "everybody's got a price." With billions of dollars in oil profits to play with, the Gadhafi regime has seen this belief confirmed many times—but not always. Shortly after sanctions were imposed on Libya, Colonel Gadhafi offered millions of pounds to help bail out a financially strapped coal mine near Lockerbie. After some initial confusion the miners, who faced the loss of their jobs and were in genuine need, turned down the offer.

In 1992 Libyan officials contacted Henry Kartchner, a wealthy Seattle businessman whose once lucrative agricultural trade with Libya had been killed by the U.S. embargo. The Libyans asked him if he could help ease the situation.

Kartchner hired Washington lawyer M. Val Miller to try to find supporters for a compromise on the Libyan suspects. Miller brought in C. McClain Haddow, a Washington lobbyist who had done jail time after pleading guilty to conflict-of-interest charges while he had been a Reagan administration official.

The pair then set out to contact Pan Am 103 families. They did some research on the families and the first ones they contacted were Glenn and Carole Johnson of Pennsylvania. Their only child, twenty-one-year-old Beth Ann, had been one of the victims. They told the Johnsons that the United States was blocking attempts to reach a solution to the problem. They said that Libya had offered to have the suspects tried, presumably in an international setting, and if they were found guilty, the Libyan government might be willing to pay compensation of at least $1 million to each family. They also said they had discussed the issues at a meeting in Zurich with Libya's vice-minister of foreign affairs.

Arrangements were made for Messrs. Miller and Haddow to meet with a larger group of family members to deliver the same message. What they did not know is that suspicious relatives had arranged to have the meetings secretly taped by NBC. When that was revealed, the contacts came to a screeching halt. "They—Miller and Haddow—were set up and made fools of, so I pulled out," Kartchner told a *Wall Street Journal* reporter.

We had not been contacted, and didn't hear about the deal for $1 million until we saw the tapes on the evening news. No one talked to us about money. But in August of '93, Susan did get a call from a Washington consultant named Robert Greenberg. He said he knew people who had information about Syrian involvement in the bombing. He said that he might be able to set up a meeting with his contacts and possibly a session with intermediaries for Libya as well.

Early on, we had decided that we were not going to try and play secret agent, and we were not going to hold confidential meetings with representatives of any foreign governments. Susan immediately contacted the Justice Department and Lee Kreindler.

The idea that money could somehow equal justice in the Pan Am 103 bombing kept coming up in a variety of ways. The promoters of this view all claimed to be well meaning, and may honestly have believed that they were. But we vehemently disagreed with this approach, on principle, and challenged it at every opportunity.

On July 7, 1992, an Op-Ed piece titled "Compensate Libya's Victims" appeared in the *New York Times*. It was written by Allan Gerson, who was identified as chief counsel to the United States delegation to the United Nations from 1981 to 1985.

Gerson noted that the U.N. resolutions called for Libya to pay "appropriate compensation" to the families of the Pan Am 103 victims. He called for an "impartial international court" to try such terrorism cases, and the establish-

ment of a U.N. claims commission to compensate Libya's
victims. He concluded, "The means for forcing Libya to
pay its victims are at hand. It's a question of political will
in the White House."

Susan, who contacted absolutely everybody who even
mentioned Pan Am 103 in public, tracked Gerson down
and called him.

SUSAN: Gerson told me I was the first family member to
call and wondered why he hadn't heard from other Pan
Am 103 victim's families yet. He ran down a list of important people in Washington he'd been in touch with over the
Libya compensation issue. The only name I recognized was
Abraham Sofaer, because he had been a major figure in
the Reagan-era State Department and a former federal
judge. Gerson and Sofaer were in the same law firm. Dan
commented that Sofaer "is a big fish." Gerson sounded
very confident. He asked me to sign up with him so that we
could get things moving in establishing that international
claims commission. I didn't, of course, but I hung up the
phone feeling curious enough about what Mr. Gerson was
up to to call him a second time. During the second phone
call, he told me he had Bruce Smith in his office at that
very moment. That was all I had to hear. I told him that I
didn't want anything to do with something Bruce Smith
would sign on to, and hung up. Smith was the Pan Am pilot
whose wife had died in the bombing. He had always defended the airline and urged us to accept their settlement
offers.

DAN: During the early months of 1993, Gadhafi and company were looking for a high-profile power broker, a
lawyer, a lobbyist, whatever—someone a cut above the
crowd of lowlifes and ex-felons they had enlisted so far—
to represent their interests in Washington. They must have
gone through the Washington phone book looking for a
champion. Several well-known and well-connected Wash-

ington deal makers, such as lawyer Plato Cacheris, best known to the public today as Monica Lewinsky's lawyer, actually went to Libya for discussions. But they all turned the Libyans down. One Washington insider we knew looked at the list, pointed to one name, and said, "If *he* turned them down, the deal really must have been dirty."

But the Libyans persisted, firm in their belief that if you throw out enough bait you'll eventually catch something. And in April they did. He was Judge Abraham Sofaer. Sofaer was a lot more than Allan Gerson's associate; he had been the State Department's chief lawyer from 1985 to 1990. He had crafted the legal justification for the 1986 trade embargo against Libya and the 1986 bombing of Gadhafi's headquarters in Tripoli. That was the act that allegedly inspired the Pan Am 103 bombing as retaliation. Sofaer was considered brilliant, if arrogant. He was a legal star in Republican circles, a possible Supreme Court candidate. Gadhafi had hooked a big one.

The story of Sofaer's new client broke in the *Wall Street Journal* in July, and we exploded. Susan was on the phone to everybody. She was quoted in the *Legal Times* of Washington as calling Sofaer "a traitor." "There are no words for how evil this is," she said. Rosemary Wolfe called Sofaer's law firm Hughes, Hubbard & Reed, and threatened to picket their Washington offices.

At first Sofaer airily dismissed the criticism. In a *New York Times* interview he said, "I was asked by the government of Libya to look into these cases and advise if there was some way in which it could bring about their resolution. I just can't believe that my government is so perverse as to want this thing to be further escalated where someone may have been able to work on a solution. I don't know what people are so excited about."

A spokesman for Hughes, Hubbard told Rosemary that the families should favor Sofaer's intervention because we would be compensated.

Still, the controversy escalated. The *Washington Post*'s influential columnist Jim Hoagland called the deal "the Washington lawyer's version of the 'Indecent Proposal' Robert

Redford made on screen to Demi Moore." He said Sofaer's firm had already received a retainer of around half a million dollars. In an editorial the *New York Times* called the deal "smelly," and Sofaer became the butt of Jay Leno's jokes.

The heat was intense and within a few days Sofaer withdrew from his Libyan commitment. The retainer was returned. Sofaer was investigated by the D.C. bar, which concluded that he had violated "revolving-door" regulations, using the knowledge and contacts from his government service to aid clients. He was actually publicly admonished by the D.C. bar for violating the "revolving door" rules—the first time that had ever happened. Sofaer appealed his sanction right up to the Supreme Court—but in April of 2000 his appeal was turned down.

Long before that Sofaer had already left Washington for the more hospitable atmosphere of the Hoover Institution in California, a conservative think tank. The old boy network takes care of its own.

Sofaer and his supporters continue to insist that he did nothing wrong—this was just a public-relations "gaffe," and he was "misunderstood."

Writing in *The Jerusalem Report*, Sofaer said he and his firm had never intended to "defend the two criminal defendants if they ever stood trial, and we would not defend the Libyan government in any civil action concerning Pan Am 103."

Actually, if Sofaer had signed on as a Libyan defense attorney, I would not have been nearly so angry. Libya and the two defendants have had American lawyers on their team. Lawyers not only have a right, they have a responsibility to defend unpopular, even disgusting clients.

But Sofaer said he was a "mediator"—helping to solve a difficult problem. Yeah, sure! With a couple of hundred thousand bucks already in his bank account and the promises of much more to come, what kind of a "mediator" would he be? He was hired to use his prestige and contacts to get Libya off the sanctions hook as painlessly as possible.

No, no he says. He wasn't going to help Libya evade its obligations. "Libya accepted the understanding that we

would try only to help it satisfy its obligations . . ." Sofaer
wrote in *The Jerusalem Report*. What, one wonders, are the
"obligations" in a case of mass murder?

Then of course there was "resolving the compensation
issue." Translation—"don't complain, you'll make money."

In the world in which Abraham Sofaer and so many of
his colleagues live and work, money solves everything. He
never seemed able to grasp the simple fact that some of us
don't have a price.

When it all hit the fan, Sofaer didn't have many vocal
defenders. Oddly, one of them was Allan Gerson. Odd because Gerson's client, Bruce Smith, was suing Libya and
that created a conflict of interest within the prestigious
Hughes, Hubbard firm. "A divergence of interests had developed which made it inopportune for me to stay at their
firm," Gerson told the *Legal Times*. But he added that Sofaer's representing Gadhafi was not a bad thing. "Insofar
as Sofaer's representation is aimed, as it appears to be, at
obtaining appropriate compensation, it is a welcome
move."

If our lawyer had ever said anything like that, he would
no longer be our lawyer.

Actually, our lawyer was contacted. In June of 1993, Lee
Kreindler was approached by a U.S. lawyer living in Germany. Earlier, she had met with Libya's ambassador to
Greece and was asked to convey an offer to Kreindler. According to the ambassador, Libya would turn over the indicted officials for trial in some unspecified third country,
and if they were found guilty would pay compensation to
the victims' families. Wisely, Lee declined to become involved in this discussion.

In the realm of lawyerly bad judgment and bad taste, F.
Lee Bailey may take the prize. Bailey represented five Pan
Am 103 victims' families in the civil case against Pan Am.
Some had been attracted by his celebrity. In August of
1993, he went to Tripoli to advise "upper-level" members
of the government about how to proceed in the Pan Am
103 case. Bailey insisted that he was not going to represent
the Libyan suspects, but to tell the Libyans "what the

means of surrender should be." He added, "The families would be in favor of that."

They weren't. In fact, some of his clients were deeply upset. He didn't inform his clients about the trip because the visit didn't become public at first. The trip also became part of an acrimonious multimillion-dollar lawsuit between Bailey and his partner in aviation law, Aaron Broder. Included in court papers was a letter from Broder to Bailey warning of "serious consequences" if he went to Libya, and advising him to "stay away from the entire thing with a ten-foot pole." Broder also noted Bailey's "apparent conflict of interest." Bailey went to Libya anyway, but was not paid the fee he had been promised. F. Lee Bailey was stiffed by Gadhafi!

Allan Gerson, now joined by a young lawyer named Mark Zaid, and their sole client, former Pan Am pilot Bruce Smith, continued to promote the idea of compensation as punishment. It was a simple enough concept. If Libya was forced to pay huge sums of money to victims' families, that would be at least a measure of punishment for the killing of 270 people. In a letter to the *International Herald Tribune,* Bruce Smith wrote, "Sending the bill for all the Pan Am 103 claims would make an impression on Libya and on any other state that might be tempted to use terrorism against America."

The legal strategy behind this plan was a dubious one, particularly in the early 1990s when it was first proposed. American citizens were forbidden by law to sue other countries. Theoretically there may have been some ways of getting around this restriction, but very few seriously believed it was possible.

If Smith and his lawyers wished to waste their time chasing up legal blind alleys, that was their business. But when they actively began trying to pull other victims' families along with them—that was another matter entirely.

Don't get me wrong, neither Susan nor I have taken vows of poverty. I would willingly take every cent Gadhafi has, foreclose on his tent, and sell his fancy dress uniforms to a secondhand costume shop. But there is no chance, absolutely none, that Libya would ever be forced to pay damages that would be truly punitive—that would actually hurt them.

Libya is a very rich country. The Libyans have always signaled through their surrogates that if the conditions and the price were right they would pay us. Sofaer talked of "compensation" for the families and of Libya "satisfying its obligations." In one form or another money has come up in virtually every approach the Libyans have made.

What we feared, what we still fear, is some form of "out-of-court" settlement, in which Libya would pay something—perhaps a great deal—but without admitting responsibility, or admitting responsibility in a vague or ambiguous way. That would be all very nice for the lawyers, who would get a fat percentage of the settlement. Libya too would benefit by being able to claim they had "satisfied their obligations" without actually admitting they killed people. What would we gain? Money, of course. What would we lose? Our souls, that's what. The minute we took Libyan money, we would surrender any moral authority we might possess. As far as we are concerned, the case would be closed. We would be regarded as just another bunch of greedy Americans, interested only in money. And there would be a measure of justification for that label.

In some parts of the world, the concept of "blood money" may be acceptable—a murderer gives money to the relatives of the person whom he killed, and the "debt" is settled. In America it's called a payoff, and it is not acceptable, no matter what kind of a spin, gloss, or interpretation is put on it.

Bruce Smith wrote me a letter complaining about what we were saying about his campaign to get compensation. He asked if we believed we were "morally superior." I answered, yes, we did.

Though Gerson and Zaid had only one client, they proposed a "class action" suit against Libya, and they lobbied hard for it among family members, on Capitol Hill, and with the administration. They even got some favorable court rulings. All of this occurred at a time when we were headed to Washington, where Susan was to testify at another interminable and pointless congressional hearing on terrorism. We wrote a letter that disassociated us, in the strongest possible terms, from any such suit, and made a bunch of copies to pass out to reporters. At the hearing I spotted Gerson and Zaid. They were not happy to see me, but I literally chased them all around the room. They were running and so was I, until I caught them and forced the letter into their hands.

SUSAN: Frank Dugan, the lawyer who had been the families' contact person for the McLaughlin Commission, had continued to hover around the edges of the Pan Am 103 case long after the commission had closed up shop. He pressed me hard to join in the class action suit. He told me that the train was leaving the station, and I'd better get aboard; the amounts of money might be as high as $3 million a victim. He told Rosemary Wolfe the same thing. Right away I started thinking about how to stop the train from getting out of the station. Money is always a story, but there weren't enough hard facts for a print exposé. Still, I managed to get a small item in *Newsweek*'s Periscope section, and I let the business journalists know that I detested the class action suit, and would have no part of it. Ultimately the class action suit was dropped.

DAN: The primary roadblock to suing Libya was the Foreign Sovereign Immunity Act. In October 1996, the act was amended to allow suits against foreign governments in limited cases—Pan Am 103 certainly qualified. This opened a clear legal route for the victims' families to sue Libya individually, and Lee Kreindler filed a civil suit on behalf of his clients. We weren't enthusiastic, but we signed on.

What we assumed, what everyone assumed would happen is this: The Libyans simply would not show up to contest the suit. A default judgment—probably a huge one—would be issued. The Libyans wouldn't pay, and there would be no way to make them pay. That had already happened in suits against Iran and Cuba. But the existence of the judgment itself would create problems for Libya in any future attempts to deal with the United States. Creating problems for Libya seemed like a good idea.

Much to our surprise—much to practically everybody's surprise—lawyers for Libya did show up to contest the case, which is now working its way slowly—very slowly—through the legal system.

Legally these are uncharted waters. No one has the faintest notion of how this case is going to play out. Nor do we know how others involved in this civil suit will respond. This much we can predict with absolute certainty. We will not be part of any confidential or "no fault" out-of-court settlement. If Gadhafi and other high Libyan officials do not confess, then the case of *Cohen* v. *Libya* will go to court in the United States, where all the evidence will be laid out in public.

Susan: The terrorists killed Theo. In a sense they killed me too. If the only way they could get away with murder was by giving me money, how could I take a dime from them? I pictured Colonel Gadhafi gloating, having a good laugh at the families. I imagined him saying to himself, "Have enough money, spend enough money, and you can wear anybody down, buy anybody off in time." Theo's life was more precious than all the diamonds and gold in the world to me. So is her memory. I would never collaborate in the rehabilitation of the evil Colonel Gadhafi. I would never let him get away with pretending that he had nothing to do with this crime. Not for all the oil wells in Libya.

Chapter 18

DAN: Getting the two suspects tried in a "neutral" country, in some sort of "compromise court," was part of the Libyan strategy almost from the start. Libya had first insisted that the suspects be tried in Libya, but that was so clearly unacceptable that it was dropped in favor of the trial in a "third country," that is someplace other than the United States or United Kingdom, the countries that had issued the indictments.

The man who may have originated the idea of the "trial in a third country," and who certainly campaigned for it most actively over the years, is Robert Black, a Scottish lawyer, a professor of Scots law, and a Lockerbie native. Black insists that he has never taken any Libyan money and that his efforts have indeed left him "considerably out of pocket," but he does acknowledge that he was first brought into the picture by a group of businessmen who were anxious to improve relations, and thus business, with Libya.

Black met with Libyan defense lawyers in Tripoli in October 1993, and a short time later proposed what he called his "scheme." He recommended that a trial take place at the International Court of Justice at the Hague in the Netherlands, before an international panel of judges. A senior Scottish judge would preside, and the trial would be conducted in accordance with the criminal laws and procedures of Scotland. The prosecution was to be handled by the lord advocate of Scotland, and the accused would be represented by Scottish lawyers. There was no mention of any U.S. presence in his proposed tribunal, and Black has always dismissed any U.S. involvement in the trial.

Black went to Tripoli to personally present his scheme to top Libyan officials, including Gadhafi himself. The Leader gave a vague and tentative approval.

Over the years variations on this trial-in-a-third-country scheme surfaced. There were suggestions the trial should be held in Sweden, in France, even in Canada. Serious thought was given to holding the trial in Ireland, but the Irish wanted no part of it. When Jesse Jackson went to Libya to interview Gadhafi, the Leader said that he would turn the subjects over to him (Jackson) to be taken to a third country for trial.

We became involved in the international trial scheme in the fall of '96 when we were called by a producer from *60 Minutes*. He said that the show was planning another segment on Pan Am 103. Crews had already been to Libya and interviewed Gadhafi. They had filmed at a conference of international lawyers held in London to discuss a Pan Am 103 trial. The conference incidentally was sponsored by the Libyans. Would we come to New York to be preinterviewed for the show. You bet we would!

At the *60 Minutes* offices, Mike Wallace hit us with a totally unexpected line of questions. Would we support an international trial of Fhimah and al-Megrahi at the Hague to be carried out under U.S. law and prosecuted by U.S. prosecutors? We had never heard this particular version of a compromise court before. It sounded strange and dubious. Our immediate reaction was negative.

Wallace pressed hard. "The trial would fall under U.S. law. Janet Reno could lead the prosecution. It's better than no trial it all. This is a serious offer."

The harder he pressed, the more negative we became. Finally he said he would get a written copy of the proposal to us, and try to set up a panel of American families to discuss it. That was fine with us.

The proposal was prepared by Frank Rubino, a Miami lawyer best known for his unsuccessful defense of onetime Panamanian strongman Manuel Noreaga. We knew that Rubino had served as the American lawyer for the indicted Libyans for several years, though it was not clear what he had actually done. When we read the proposal, we realized that our suspicions had been fully justified. The trial would be presided over by a U.S. judge, but the seven-member judicial panel would be chosen by a vote of the General Assembly of the United Nations and conviction required the unanimous decision of all seven judges. The chance of conviction before such a panel would be zero.

There were other problems. The United States would have to agree not to interrogate or interview the accused. No matter what happened, the suspects could not be prosecuted anywhere else in the world on any charges arising from the bombing of Pan Am 103. And, of course, the accused would not face the death penalty, though it would have been applicable under U.S. law. The proposal looked even worse on paper than it had when Mike Wallace first described it to us. But we were told that it was not "set in stone"; these were just general principles. Details could be negotiated later.

We showed the Rubino proposal to people we knew at the National Security Council and Justice Department. They thought it was just as bad as we did. Proposals like this had been floated before, and they were essentially "bait and switch" operations. Libya would agree in general to a neutral venue for a trial and then negotiate ever more favorable conditions. If the United States pulled out of the negotiations, it would be on the defensive, and would be made to look unreasonable. If the Libyans could get American families behind such a proposal, they would score a major propaganda coup.

There were broader implications. Such an arrangement would set a precedent. International terrorists could dictate where, and under what conditions, they would be tried. By removing the trial to a "compromise court," the United States and Scotland would be acknowledging that certain individuals—Arabs, for example—could not get a fair trial in their own courts. Such precedents might haunt the United States for years to come.

The National Security Council and Justice Department didn't have to worry about us. We were not going to sign on to a Libyan propaganda ploy. Producers from *60 Minutes* contacted the leaders of the Victims of Pan Am 103 and whatever remained of Paul Hudson's group, Families of Pan Am 103—Lockerbie. Both declined to send representatives to the show, and both groups issued strong statements opposing the Rubino proposal. In the end the *60 Minutes* panel consisted of Susan and me, Rosemary Wolfe, Kathleen Flynn, Eleanor Bright, and Stephanie Bernstein.

SUSAN: Stephanie Bernstein's husband, Michael, was a federal prosecutor and Nazi hunter at the Justice Department in Washington when he died on Pan Am 103. He and Stephanie were upstanding and reasonable people, with strong liberal principles and sixties political savvy. They were happy with each other, and loving and responsible parents.

Stephanie had been clear-sighted about Pan Am 103 from the beginning, but with two small children to raise, several years passed before she could devote a lot of time and energy to the Pan Am 103 fight for justice. After the bombing Stephanie continued working as a therapist, eventually remarried, and became president of her synagogue, the same synagogue to which belonged National Security Council head Sandy Berger. Stephanie was able to reshape her life without lying to herself, burying her anger, or hiding the wounds that never heal. Now she was one of the most active Pan Am 103 family members, and we had become friends.

To prepare for appearing on *60 Minutes,* Stephanie went to a media consultant. "You're too nice," the consultant said, critiquing her television style. Stephanie is from Minnesota, where good manners are learned in the nursery. The consultant told her to be very strong and assertive on *60 Minutes.* Niceness would be interpreted as weakness on a show like that, leaving her open to being trapped by Mike Wallace, one of the toughest interviewers around, manipulated by Rubino, or misunderstood by the audience. By the time Stephanie finished her session with the consultant, she was more than ready for Frank Rubino.

The atmosphere in the studio when Mike Wallace and Frank Rubino joined the waiting families was so tense that Eleanor Bright thought she might have to leave. Rubino set about greeting us all individually. When he got to me, because I felt the deepest contempt for him, I refused to shake his hand. He was taken aback. Even Kathleen was unsettled and anxiously asked if the cameras were on. I knew they were. I wanted them on. There was no time to waste in throwing Mr. Rubino off his game and leaving the large *60 Minutes* audience in no doubt as to where this group of Pan Am 103 families stood. Nobody has to work for the interests of the Gadhafis of this world if they don't want to. And that's what I told Rubino. Kathleen made the same point. The families resisted Rubino's overtures so completely that Rosemary later told me she thought he was nearly in tears. I thought he just had a droopy face, but he certainly didn't seem happy with the way things were going.

The confrontation with Rubino was only part of the *60 Minutes* taping. To catch our reactions we were shown a clip from the interview Gadhafi granted to *60 Minutes*. We were shocked at how bizarre The Leader appeared, even for him. He looked like he was on drugs. Gadhafi kept peering in different directions and staring off into space while twirling a porkpie hat. He wore an odd print shirt. None of us could figure out what was on it. Somebody thought it was oil derricks. Somebody else saw palm trees. I thought it was bombs or missiles.

DAN: I'm not sure what the Libyans had hoped to get from *60 Minutes,* but whatever it was they didn't get it. Immediately after the show aired, the chief Libyan lawyer for the two suspects announced that now they would only accept a trial in Libya. The suspects gave a rare interview on television, shown throughout the Middle East, in which they declared that *they* were the true victims in the Pan Am bombing.

But Robert Black's "scheme" would not die. It came back again in yet another incarnation.

Libya's allies were still lobbying hard to get the United States, and particularly the American families, to sign on to the idea. The British relatives—at least their chief spokesman Jim Swire—were already enthusiastic supporters of the compromise. Egypt's ambassador to the United States, Ahmed Maher el Sayed, invited Rosemary and Stephanie to the embassy for a meeting. In the most ingratiating terms, he explained how reasonable Libya was being, how they had already agreed to turn the suspects over for trial—all they wanted was a change of venue.

In 1997 Senator Frank Lautenberg of New Jersey sponsored a bill that would suspend five percent of the U.S. aid to countries that helped Libya violate the U.N. sanctions. Since Egypt received over two billion dollars in U.S. aid every year, this threat really rattled Ambassador el Sayed's cage.

He persuaded Senator Lautenberg to invite some of the relatives among his constituents to meet with him in the senator's office. I was among them. The ambassador delivered his pitch, and I was ready for him. I started out by saying I regarded him as an apologist for the murderers of my daughter, and it went downhill from there. We wound up shouting at each other, and the ambassador threatened to walk out if I didn't stop insulting him. I didn't stop and he didn't walk. Finally he yelled, "What do you want, Gadhafi's head on a plate?" "Yes," I shouted back, "with an apple in his mouth."

The senator and some of his aides sat through this exchange. They said nothing, but I got the impression they were pleased by the way things had gone.

Early in 1998, Trina Vargo announced that she was leaving Senator Kennedy's office. We were devastated. We had lost our most passionate advocate on Capitol Hill. But we were much heartened when we learned that her replacement would be Sharon Waxman, who had been Senator Lautenberg's foreign policy aide. I had met Sharon during my shouting match with the Egyptian ambassador. She was smart, knowledgeable, energetic, and she knew who and what she was dealing with.

SUSAN: I was depressed for weeks after I heard Trina was leaving. I only cheered up when I found out that Sharon Waxman would be Kennedy's new foreign policy aide. I had dealt with Sharon at Lautenberg's office. Sharon was warm, gracious, and sympathetic; very much a lady in the best sense of the word. Hers was not the confrontational style of Trina. But Sharon could be very forceful and quite persistent when it mattered. She knew all about the Pan Am 103 issue, and cared about it deeply.

DAN: The atmosphere around the Pan Am 103 case changed significantly with the 1997 election of Tony Blair in England. Blair was described as one of the "new breed" of world leaders, young, forward-looking, and telegenic. He seemed to have a surgically implanted smile. He wanted to create a "new Britain," a "Cool Britannia," sweep away the old nationalistic prejudices, get with globalization, and devolution (that is, grant more independence to those portions of the United Kingdom, such as Scotland, that had never been entirely happy with being "united" in the first place). And Blair wanted to "get past" some of the problems of the past, like Lockerbie.

A burning desire to see justice done after so many years was not what motivated the Blair government. At the root there was money. There always is. The "Libya trade" was far more significant to Britain's small economy than it was to the huge U.S. economy.

Blair appointed a new lord advocate—roughly the equivalent of the U.S. attorney general—and a new judicial team in Scotland, and the government began serious consideration of the trial-in-a-neutral-country "scheme" as a way around the Lockerbie "problem." A passive and largely disinterested Clinton administration was pulled along.

   In the spring of '98 Tony Blair visited the United States.
Clinton, already engulfed in controversy surrounding his
relationship with Monica Lewinsky, was overjoyed to have
a friendly world leader who would stand next to him and
smile. We wrote to both Clinton and Blair, asking if, in this
tenth year since the bombing, they would issue a joint
statement reminding people of the bombing. Clinton did
make a statement. Blair didn't. For a politician, issuing a
statement against terrorism is about as risky as issuing a
statement against rabies. We wondered if Blair's refusal to
speak out meant something.
   At the U.N. things were heating up. The Libyans mounted
a massive campaign to have sanctions lifted, and to generally portray themselves as victims. The campaign was particularly successful among African states, many of whom
still bear a resentment against the United States, and were
encouraged by Libyan promises of trade and aid. Arab
countries had always pressed for the lifting of sanctions,
and European countries like Italy were beating the drums
for a resumption of full-trade relations with the Gadhafi
regime.
   The Libyans managed to get a full day of General Assembly debate on the subject. The "debate" consisted of a
long list of Libya's friends and supporters delivering
speeches about how much the poor Libyans were suffering. We badgered the State Department and United States
U.N. delegation to sponsor a press conference so family
members could have their say. This press conference was
held in the official U.N. pressroom rather than in the tacky
correspondent's lounge. U.N. Ambassador Bill Richardson
spoke, as did I and George Williams, head of the Victims of
Pan Am 103. The press conference got a lot of publicity,
and it sullied the image of the Libyan love-fest going on in
the General Assembly chamber. Jim Swire turned up at
the U.N. that day. He had refused to come to Washington
to attend any of the cairn ceremonies at Arlington but he
showed up in New York to defend the Libyan position. We
passed each other in the corridor, but did not speak.
   Throughout the early summer there were all sorts of ru-

mors and rumblings that "something dramatic" was going
to happen soon. But nearly ten years of regular rumors and
rumblings had passed. This time, however, something *did*
happen. In late July the *New York Times* broke the story
that the United States and Britain were going to make a
new offer to Libya about a trial for the two suspects.

SUSAN: Early on a hot July morning in 1998, the phone
rang. It was Stephanie Bernstein in tears. She said, "Susan,
the Clinton administration has betrayed us," and told me
there was a story in the *New York Times* that said the
United States had accepted the scheme of a trial in a third
country. A trial either in the United States or Scotland was
supposed to be the indelible, immovable, bottom-line policy of the United States, writ in stone. The Justice Department, the National Security Council, and the State
Department had always told us this. Now Clinton and his
cohorts had caved in to a key Gadhafi demand without so
much as informing or consulting with us. I was furious. I
called the government. I called reporters. There was so
much negative publicity that the State Department and the
National Security Council scheduled a conference call for
the families with Madeleine Albright and Berger.

After they left the Victims of Pan Am 103, Bert Ammerman, Aphrodite Tsairis, and Peter Lowenstein had
formed a splinter group called "The Terrorism Watch
Committee." They were the only families that had joined
Jim Swire earlier in publicly calling for an international
trial. Later Brian Murtagh, chief prosecutor on the Pan
Am 103 case at the Justice Department, told me that Albright had wanted to have a separate conference call, first
with the families who wanted an international trial, then
with a call to the rest of us. I considered this a ploy worthy
of the Bush administration. Apparently the equal treatment for the families policy established by Anthony Lake
had been jettisoned by Madam Secretary. But Murtagh
had insisted on my being included in any conference call,
so the plan for a call to "select families only" was dropped.

Murtagh told me the Justice Department "hates this, hates this," meaning the scheme. I also spoke to Murtagh's boss, Jim Reynolds, about it. Both said the Justice Department had vigorously opposed the change in policy, but had lost to the State Department, and being team players, would not go public about the fight. If there ever was a trial outside the United States or Scotland, the Justice Department would get on board and fully support it.

Not only was Attorney General Janet Reno missing from the first conference call with Albright and Berger, but no one else from Justice was on the call either. (Janet Reno and others from the Justice Department were once again absent during a second conference call among Berger, Albright, and the families that took place the following April.)

As soon as I found out about the first call, I phoned several key reporters. They were extremely interested, and I arranged to talk to them right after it was over. When Albright and Berger got on the phone, I hammered them for caving in to Gadhafi. They claimed they hadn't. They insisted there was no change in the United States policy of not negotiating with terrorists, and they were not going to negotiate with Gadhafi. This was a "onetime, take-it-or-leave-it offer." Albright was cagey, however, about how long the offer would remain on the table.

Those of us who opposed the scheme argued as hard as we could against it. But Albright and Berger hadn't arranged this phone call to listen to us. They were there to sell us the scheme. Berger was gruff, but straightforward. Albright was saccharine. She told us she always thought of Pan Am 103 when she put her grandchildren on a plane, and how sad it was that we poor suffering families were still waiting for justice. She said that all she was doing was trying her best to get us a creditable trial. At the end she actually cooed, "I send you my love."

I could scarcely believe my ears. Pan Am 103 was a monumental crime, and here was the secretary of state of the targeted country handing the monster behind the bombing a huge victory and then resorting to feminine wiles to manipulate the victims of that monster. She wasn't the secretary of state of some tiny country, without any resources to stand up for itself; she was secretary of state of the most powerful nation on earth. You can imagine what I told the reporters. Dan and I also got an Op-Ed piece in the *New York Times* on this shameful cave-in to Gadhafi and the further surrenders likely to come.

DAN: OK, what was wrong with a "Scottish trial," even if it didn't take place in Scotland, and had a panel of judges instead of a jury like every other Scottish criminal trial in history? Lots of things.

First there is the precedent. It would give international terrorists a hand in choosing where, and under what conditions, they would be tried. By agreeing to a "compromise court" in the Netherlands, the United States and United Kingdom opened the door for more compromises. Despite all the brave talk about "calling Gadhafi's bluff," "take it or leave it," "no compromises and no negotiations," the United States and United Kingdom were compromising and negotiating their heads off—though discreetly through surrogates.

Robert Black went to Libya to promote this version of his scheme. He was accompanied by Jim Swire.

The administration was still working hard to sell the trial. In September all family members were invited to Washington for a face-to-face session with Madeleine Albright and Sandy Berger. Susan remained home with the dogs. She was the lucky one. We got the standard "We're doing this for you" routine. There was talk of "creative diplomacy," and we were told that we could not expect "perfect justice." When it came my turn to ask a question, I pointed out that even if the two suspects were found guilty and were given "life sentences," life in Scotland meant twenty or thirty years, and there was a very good chance they would be released early for political reasons. Many IRA terrorists were on the street after only a few years behind bars. There seemed to be no

chance that Gadhafi or other high Libyan officials would
be indicted. I also pointed out that as soon as the suspects were actually turned over, U.N. sanctions would be
lifted. European countries were lining up to do business
with Libya. As a result, Gadhafi would be enriched and
entrenched in power. "Why should I be happy about
this?" Albright just sat there, pop-eyed and silent. Berger
was grumpy. He said this was just an ordinary Scottish
trial, and the United States had no control over what
other countries might do.

Overall, I preferred Berger's boorish bad temper to Albright's grandmotherly concern. He didn't like me for
challenging his authority, and I thought he was a liar. At
least the lines were clear.

There was a great desire to get the suspects turned over
before December 21, 1998—the tenth anniversary of the
bombing. But Gadhafi was playing hardball, and the negotiations—or should I say nonnegotiations—dragged on
and on. Finally, early in December, U.N. Secretary General Kofi Annan flew to Libya. The expectation was that
Annan would actually bring Fhimah and al-Megrahi out
with him. There was a U.N. plane fueled and waiting on
the runway in Italy to take the suspects from Tripoli to
the Netherlands.

But once in Libya, the secretary general was treated
like an office boy. He was shuttled from place to place,
and made to cool his heels for days before the Leader
would even see him. He departed empty-handed. Libya
said that Annan had not come to pick up the suspects at
all but to pay homage to Gadhafi, and offer sympathy for
his injury. Gadhafi had broken his leg or hip in some sort
of accident and was hobbling about on a crutch. Some
world leaders, such as Egypt's Hosni Mubarak, had
rushed to Tripoli to hold the sick man's hand and mur-
mur words of comfort.

The tenth anniversary of the bombing loomed with "the
nonnegotiable, limited-time" offer still being negotiated.

Anniversary dates generally do not mean a great deal
to me, but the tenth anniversary of Theo's death was

hard. I ran across a quote from Mark Twain. He was on a speaking tour in England when he received a cablegram that Susy, his twenty-four-year-old daughter, had died suddenly and unexpectedly. Ten years later, he wrote in his autobiography:

> It is one of the mysteries of our nature that a man, all unprepared, can receive a thunder-stroke like that and live. There is but one reasonable explanation of it. The intellect is stunned by the shock and but gropingly gathers the meaning of the words. The power to realize their full import is mercifully wanting. The mind has a dumb sense of vast loss—that is all. It will take mind and memory months and possibly years to gather together the details and thus learn and know the whole extent of the loss. A man's house burns down. The smoking wreckage represents only a ruined home that was dear through years of use and pleasant associations. By and by, as the days and weeks go on, first he misses this, then that, then the other thing. And when he casts about for it, he finds that it was in that house. Always it is an *essential*—there was but one of its kind. It cannot be replaced.

Ten years later I could testify that Twain had it absolutely right.

SUSAN: A full decade had passed since Pan Am 103 was bombed, and the tenth anniversary was very painful for all the families. At the cairn in Arlington, the atmosphere was somber and muted. I listened to the President's worthless speech, but I bypassed the line waiting to shake hands with him. I had seen Clinton close-up on two occasions and twice was enough for me.

There was one elected official at the cairn ceremony I did want to meet. That was Senator Kennedy. Even though he had attended other Pan Am 103 ceremonies, somehow I'd never actually met him. I dealt with him only through his congressional aides. So while others spoke to Clinton, I introduced myself to Kennedy and thanked him warmly for all he had done.

DAN: Susan wasn't going to shake Clinton's hand, but I got into the receiving line after his speech. Right in front of me was Stephanie Bernstein and her teenage daughter Sarah. Sarah told the President that he had given a meaningless speech, and might just as well have stayed home. She then broke down in tears. Clinton said something about the Security Council. His celebrated empathy wasn't working that day.

When it was my turn, I didn't so much shake the President's hand as grab it and hold on so he couldn't get away until I finished speaking. I also told him he had given a lousy speech, and that he had a lousy policy. Five years earlier he had talked about an "attack on America." Now all he could offer was the possibility of a compromise trial of a couple of alleged triggermen.

He looked directly at me—or rather through me. His face was utterly blank and did not so much as twitch. Two days earlier he had been impeached. This was his first real public outing since then. I guess he'd heard worse. Next to him, Hillary Clinton was equally dead-eyed and blank-faced.

During Clinton's speech someone in the audience jumped up and shouted, "Mr. President, bomb Gadhafi now!" A rumor spread that I was the one. It wasn't me. That wasn't my style, but I applauded the move. I wasn't one of those who unfurled an anti-Gadhafi banner either, though I wish I had been.

A deadline had passed. Another year rolled round and the nonnegotiations were stepped up. The big guns were rolled out. Prince Bandar bin Sultan, Saudi Arabia's ambassador to the United States, got into the act. More significantly, so did South African President Nelson Mandela. When I first heard Mandela had become involved, I thought, "Oh, great, how do you argue with an icon?"

Mandela was a longtime friend of Gadhafi's. The Libyan leader had supported Mandela during the years he had been imprisoned and during a period when the United States had supported or at least tolerated the white apartheid regime. Mandela's sympathy for Gadhafi was understandable. But he had also been going around saying that all of the Pan Am 103 victims' families supported some sort of international trial. That was simply untrue, and the feelings of many American families had been well publicized. We wrote a letter to Mandela and sent it through the South African embassy. Susan spoke to a sympathetic young man at the embassy, and explained our position. She was told that the letter would be presented to President Mandela.

We don't know whether Mandela ever saw our letter. He went on talking about how all the families supported the international trial. Perhaps an icon is engaged in such lofty pursuits that he just doesn't have time to think about what happened to a twenty-year-old woman from Port Jervis, New York. But she was my daughter, I think about her all the time, and I bitterly resented having my position falsified. Even an icon owes something to the truth.

On February 17, 1999, U.N. Secretary General Kofi Annan sent a letter and other documents to Moammar Gadhafi. These were written assurances regarding the trial of the two Libyan nationalists who had been indicted for the Pan Am 103 bombing. These written assurances, which were later to become the center of controversy, were one of the final steps in the handover of the suspects.

For almost two years the Libyan government had been conducting another campaign to win over the American relatives of the bombing victims. They sent letters, copies of speeches by Libya's U.N. ambassador, transcripts of a Scottish television show favorable to Libya, etc. It was a remarkably clumsy campaign that antagonized and even frightened people rather than winning them over. There were also ads placed in newspapers like the *Washington Post*. In one of these ads the Libyans appealed for a "French solution" to the "Lockerbie problem." When we criticized the offer made by Britain and the United States in the *New York Times*, we warned of a "French solution."

What is a "French solution?" In March of 1999, there was an in absentia trial of six Libyan officials in connection with the 1989 bombing of a French UTA airliner in Africa, which resulted in 171 deaths. The Libyan government co-operated with the trial by supplying evidence, and all six were convicted. Among them was Abdullah Senussi, Gad-hafi's brother-in-law and head of Libyan intelligence. The Libyans were supposed to put the six convicted terrorists in Libyan jails. Of course they didn't. Senussi was out greeting distinguished foreign visitors, such as former U.S. ambassador Herman Cohen, who was far too polite to mention the fact that his host had just been convicted of mass murder. Senussi is now reputed to be the second most powerful man in Libya.

The Libyans paid the French victims' families compensation. It amounted to about $30,000 per victim. They admitted no responsibility. Indeed, Gadhafi continued to insist that Libya had nothing to do with the bombing, and paid compensation only because the French had asked them to.

Many of the French victims' families were outraged. So was Judge Jean-Louis Bruguiere, who had investigated and brought the original charges against Libya. He recommended that Gadhafi himself be prosecuted for the bombing.

What did the French government do? It expanded commercial relations with Libya, and French president Jacques Chirac sent the Libyan leader a letter welcoming him back into the international community. That is the "French solution," the act of a nation without honor. Gadhafi was counting on the United States and United Kingdom to act in the same spineless fashion.

Fhimah and al-Megrahi were finally turned over to the U.N. on April 5, 1999. Before the final handover we were treated to another conference call with Secretary of State Albright and National Security Council head Berger. Berger thought somebody had cut him off in mid-sentence, got huffy, and hung up. Albright gave us her love and appealed for our support. Susan and I found it all rather nauseating.

The Libyans had gathered a large number of diplomats and officials from a variety of countries to give the suspects a hero's send-off. The U.N., however, persuaded Libya that a public celebration would be in poor taste. After all, these guys had been indicted for mass murder. "Afterward you can have a big party," one diplomat was quoted as saying.

Almost as soon as the plane carrying the suspects touched down in the Netherlands, and they were transferred to Camp Zeist, a former U.S. air base near the Hague where the trial was to be held, phase two began. The U.N. suspended the sanctions against Libya; they would not be formally lifted until after the trial, but for all practical purposes they were gone. Nations lined up to do business in the suddenly more accessible Libyan market. Britain stood at the head of the line.

Britain had suspended diplomatic relations with Libya in 1984 after the shooting of a policewoman during a demonstration in front of the Libyan embassy. The Libyans paid the woman's family compensation, reportedly around $400,000, and accepted responsibility in a general way. Though the shooter, an employee of the Libyan embassy, is known, he has apparently escaped any punishment. That done, the United Kingdom reestablished relations with Libya. Talks between Libya and British businesses had been going on for months. A $10 billion deal with the British aerospace industry to modernize Libyan airlines had already been negotiated.

A British diplomat, Geoffrey Hoon, came to the United States and, at a press conference at the British embassy, said that U.S. victims' families should think about doing what the policewoman's family had done.

In America the move to rehabilitate Libya has been more cautious, with politicians and businessmen behaving like the family man about to enter the whorehouse—they want to do it, but don't want to be seen doing it.

There is talk of a "new" Libya. Have I missed something? Has Gadhafi been deposed? Of course he hasn't. Exactly the same clique is in control of the country that was in control in December 1988 when the Pan Am 103 bombing was planned, approved, and carried out. Are they to be forgiven and rehabilitated because they have not blown up any American planes recently?

American businessmen such as Conoco's CEO, Archie Dunham, are absolutely salivating to get back into partnership with Libya's leaders. Dunham has said that once the trial of the two Libyans is over and a new U.S. president is elected, there will be a "window of opportunity" for getting back into Libya "in a real big way." Apparently the fact that the folks they will be dealing with have a lot of American blood on their hands does not trouble entrepreneurs like Dunham unduly. A very large part of the story of Pan Am 103 is now being told on the business pages.

Speculation and controversy over Kofi Annan's letter to Gadhafi, and the documents that accompanied it, grew after the suspects were handed over. Despite the fact that portions of the letter had been read to us and other family members by people from the State Department, despite the fact that not only the existence of the letter but also key phrases in it had been confirmed to Susan by Fred Eckerd, Kofi Annan's chief spokesman, the U.S. government began to claim that no such letter existed, or that it couldn't be found. Senator Kennedy's office was told by the State Department that there was "no historical memory" of such a letter. Our latest contact person at the N.S.C. speculated that perhaps Kofi Annan had written the letter on his own. Kofi Annan, the loose cannon. It rhymed but didn't make any sense. The letter and accompanying documents had been read, revised, and approved by both the U.S. and British governments. Annan can't make agreements like that on his own.

Finally, under congressional pressure, the secretary of state admitted that, yes, the documents existed. But now they were classified as secret. Secret from who? Gadhafi certainly knew what was in them. They were being kept secret from the American people, that's who. The line was then softened a bit: "Well, we have nothing to hide, we would like to show you the documents, but they are private correspondence between the secretary general and a head of state." Annan himself would have to release the contents, but he wouldn't because that would be undiplomatic.

In Washington, deniability equals truth.

At least some details from these documents are known. The letter promises Gadhafi that the trial would not be used to "undermine the Libyan regime." The suspects would not be questioned by anyone about any other terrorist activities they may have engaged in. If convicted, they would be housed in their own special wing of a Glasgow prison under special conditions. The prison wing would be monitored by, or actually under the partial control of, U.N. representatives. Libyan lawyers would have unlimited access to the prisoners, and Libya would be allowed to establish a consulate near the prison. Whatever happened, these guys would not be doing hard time for mass murder. They would be under no pressure whatever to "flip"—that is, give up their bosses. And they would be watched more closely by representatives of Gadhafi than they would be by Scottish jailers. If they valued their lives and the lives of their families, they would say nothing.

The deal that Gadhafi negotiated ensured that neither he, nor any of his close associates, would be touched. It's the deal he was angling for all along.

In August of 1999 Lord Andrew Hardie, the lord advocate of Scotland, and several other members of the Scottish prosecution team, came to Washington to update U.S. family members on the coming trial. The silver-haired Lord Hardie had been presented to us as the embodiment of Scottish justice. He was not only upright, independent, fearless, and honest—he also cared. We were told how, at a memorial service in Lockerbie, he had "tears in his eyes." The underlying message was: maybe you don't trust us Washington politicians, but you can trust this honest Scotsman.

About two hundred family members gathered for a series of meetings and presentations. We were given souvenir insignia patches and other mementos from the Dumfries and Galloway constabulary—the Scottish police unit that oversees the Lockerbie area. We were given color photos of the rustic Tundergarth church and the Lockerbie memorial. I felt that the myth of Brigadoon was being worked for all it was worth.

Many family members bought the myth, or tried very hard to. But we found a surprising degree of skepticism as well. While one session was going on, I found Hope Asrelsky out in the corridor. When she saw me, she shouted, "Props! That's what they want us to be, just props!"

The two-day session wasn't very informative, but it got tremendous news coverage, due primarily to Susan, who spent several days phoning everybody on her media rolodex.

Then in mid-February 2000, suddenly and without warning, the honest Scotsman was gone. Lord Hardie resigned, giving no reason other than that he had a chance to become a judge. Here was the man who Tony Blair had assigned to help find a way to get past "the Lockerbie problem," the man who had been waved at us like the Scottish flag; less than three months before the biggest case of his career, the biggest case in Scottish legal history, he walked out because he wanted to make a career move. Incredible! The resignation triggered a flood of stories in the Scottish and British press that he had jumped ship because the case was dissolving and he didn't want to be blamed for losing. The resignation also spread confusion and near despair among many U.S. family members, who also believed the case was falling to pieces.

In March the new lord advocate, Colin Boyd, traveled to America to reassure the American families once again. I met him in Washington and found him to be a pleasant fellow. But he added absolutely nothing to my knowledge of the Pan Am 103 case, and offered only the assurances that had been offered by the now departed Lord Hardie—often in the very same words.

And so to the trial—a most unique and improbable trial, held in a specially built court on a former U.S. air base, which was legally and temporarily declared a little piece of Scotland, outside of the Hague. I did not believe the case had fallen to pieces. Those rumors looked suspiciously like they were being spread by the Libyan defense. Not that the case would be an easy win, however. It was over twelve years since Pan Am 103 was blown up over Lockerbie. Over time evidence was lost, witnesses died or disappeared, and memories faded. The case was almost entirely circumstantial, and much of the evidence—government records, for example—remained in Libya, which was unlikely to be fully cooperative. The defense was well funded, and in the past the Libyans showed a willingness to buy whatever and whomever they needed.

Still, the trial seemed likely to produce startling and chilling evidence about how international terrorism operates.

One thing I was quite sure the trial would not produce was justice. Despite pious mumblings about "following the evidence," it is impossible for me to imagine that anyone else, especially any important Libyan official, will ever be brought to trial in this case. Neither the United States nor the United Kingdom has shown the slightest appetite for pursuing this case one step further, and the Scots lack the resources to pursue the case, even if they wanted to. Whatever happened I knew that Gadhafi would walk. No, more than walk. He would be rehabilitated. That process is going on right now. You hear the gurgle of the flowing oil. It easily drowns out the cry for justice.

In late March 2000, the State Department arranged a conference call between Michael Sheehan, head of the counterterrorism office, and twenty or more Pan Am 103 relatives. He told us that the State Department would be sending four representatives to Tripoli to assess security for Americans in Libya, which has been off limits to most American travelers since 1981. He tried to tell us that the trip was routine, and did not represent any change in official policy.

Susan and I were having none of that. This was to be the first official U.S. government trip to Libya in twenty years, and it was being made just a few weeks before the opening

of the trial of two Libyan agents. It was a clear signal to
Gadhafi that he had nothing to fear and his rehabilitation
was well underway.

Somewhat to our surprise, everyone else on the call
backed what we said, sometimes in terms stronger than the
ones we had used. Even Bert Ammerman spoke up and
said that he agreed with some people that he had not
agreed with in many years.

I said to Sheehan, "Mike, you've done something no one
else has been able to do. You brought the families together."

Predictably the Libyans publicized the State Department trip as a huge victory. Early in April, Gadhafi attended a summit conference in Cairo between African and
European Union leaders. He set up a sumptuous tent in
the garden of one of Egyptian President Hosni Mubarak's
guest houses, where he entertained leaders, including Italian Prime Minister Massimo D'Alema and European
Commission President Romano Prodi.

Gadhafi then invited in a crowd of reporters. "The
Americans made a smart move," he said. "They sent a delegation after long years of boycott and the rise of oil
prices." He said that the Clinton administration wanted "a
good initiative towards Libya" so that it would not block
oil production increases.

He also told Arab News Network television that the
Americans had "returned to their senses" after realizing
they were missing chances to do business with Libya.

Gadhafi sounded like a man who knew that everybody
has a price and that he had won!

SUSAN: I knew Gadhafi actually got a small surprise—the
State Department decided to continue the travel restrictions for another year. We considered that a small victory.
The trial would be a terrible ordeal. A "not guilty" or "not
proven" verdict, which is available in Scottish law, would
leave me hopelessly enraged and depressed. I had no
doubt that Libya carried out the bombing, but twelve years

is a long time, and a trial is best when evidence is fresh and witnesses at their sharpest. The Scottish and English press were full of stories about how the case was weak and the prosecution incompetent, but I discounted these as Libyan propaganda. It was in Gadhafi's interest to discredit the trial in the eyes of the public so that even if the accused were found guilty, he could claim they were framed. Even if there were no Libyan propaganda, how could I tell whether the prosecutors were competent or not?

In the end, if the judges handed down a verdict of guilty, what about Gadhafi? If he escaped, and even worse was embraced by a greedy United States government, then there would be no justice at all. Pan Am 103 would no longer be a historic terrorist crime. It would be a historic terrorist victory.

Oh, my poor Theo!

Chapter 19

DAN: Our attendance at the Pan Am 103 trial in the Netherlands was paid for with drug money.

From the moment that a trial of the two Libyan suspects in the Netherlands became a reality, Susan and I spent a lot of time discussing how, or even if, we would attend.

It would be an ordeal—we knew that. Though we had been fairly frequent fliers before December 21, 1988, we had barely flown at all since then. It's not that we were afraid our plane would be blown up or destroyed in some other kind of airline disaster. Aside from some anxiety over whether the dog and cats would be properly cared for, we have absolutely no fear of death in the air.

What makes flying so difficult is the associations. The mere act of going to an airport revives memories of the nightmare at Kennedy Airport on December 21, 1988. Checking luggage and going through security brings up the question: "Why didn't they check the Pan Am 103 luggage like they were supposed to?" On the plane we count the minutes between the takeoff and the explosion over Lockerbie. "What was it like on Pan Am 103?" we think. That's what makes flying so hard.

Some Pan Am 103 family members have not flown at all since the bombing. One woman we knew toyed with the idea of actually taking a boat to the Netherlands.

And then there was the expense. Going to Holland and staying there, even for a short period, would cost us thousands of dollars. It was an expense we could ill afford.

What would we be going for? I had no illusions about "looking the defendants in the eye." Did I expect them to crumble, confess and ask forgiveness when confronted with my steely and righteous gaze? Of course not. Would I experience some sense of "closure," a feeling that at long last "justice" was being done, in seeing them finally led to the dock? No. I regarded the defendants as only the last and least important links in a deadly chain. The big boys back in Libya were in no danger. They were out there in the desert being fawned over by world leaders. If anything, the sight of only the hit men on trial would remind me just how inadequate, indeed how fraudulent, this "justice" would be.

Listening to the evidence would be sheer torture. And how about rubbing shoulders with—or more likely, trying to avoid rubbing shoulders with—the relatives of the defendants and other Libyans we knew would be at the trial. We didn't want to provoke an international incident, so there was a lot of anger that would have to be kept in check. We are not good at hiding anger.

The balance sheet came down heavily for not going. And yet, as we weighed the pros and cons, I think we both knew it was an empty exercise. We were going to have to attend the trial—just simply to be there and to let the world, and ourselves, know that after nearly a dozen years we were still standing and we could still make ourselves heard.

That's where the drug money came in. The Office for Victims of Crime (OVC), part of the Justice Department, has a fund that helps crime victims and their families in a variety of ways, including helping them attend trials in distant locations. The money for the fund comes from fines and penalties paid by Federal criminal offenders—most of the money really comes from the seizure of property and other assets of big-time drug dealers. A great deal of money has passed through the fund since it was first established—billions of dollars. A decision was made to help family members of Pan Am 103 victims attend the trial in the Netherlands. Two family members of each victim would have their travel and hotel expenses paid for one week—you were on your own for meals and bar bills. This was offered not only to U.S. victims' fami-

lies but to Pan Am 103 victims' families from all countries.

That settled matters for us—like it or not, we were going
to the Netherlands.

SUSAN: When I realized the trial would start soon I
wanted to hide out at the South Pole. I didn't want to
watch the farce begin. I knew what the trial would cost me
emotionally and physically. It would take me months to get
over it. But I knew I had to be there. I had come this far. I
was not going to run away now. There would be worldwide
media coverage for the opening of the trial in the Netherlands. And no matter what the personal cost, I meant to be
there and to have my say.

Starting in March, I began checking the calendar every
morning, each day noting that I was 24 hours closer to the
dreaded date of May 3, 2000, when the trial would begin. I
was scared and depressed. Scared of losing. I very much
wanted that guilty verdict. Depressed because, even if we
won, what would that win actually amount to?

From March to May my life was divided into two parts.
Working to reach the media was part one. Trying to survive
the fear, the depression and the hard work was the other.
My stomach, ravaged by the post–Pan Am 103 years of
tension, rage and despair-induced overeating, did flip-flops
if I so much as thought about flying over the ocean—the
ocean that Theo should have crossed safely on Pan Am
103.

The OVC staff went out of their way to be helpful when
I set the ground rules for flying. No leaving from Kennedy
Airport in New York. No changing planes at either Frank-
furt or London. And please send a car to take us to the
Philadelphia airport so a tense and worried Dan would not
have the stress of driving there.

The anxiety was so unbearable that when I picked up
the phone to call reporters my hand shook, and it was a
struggle to pitch my voice below a scream. To fight the
inner panic, I reminded myself that the next phone call I

made could always be to Eileen Leary, my therapist. She was my safety net. If I needed to at any time, I could fall into the soothing strength of her voice. Usually that comforting thought alone was enough to get me through the next media call.

I wanted reporters to interview me. I wanted them to quote me. I wanted my viewpoint writ large. How to do this? The media would be at the trial regardless of whether I contacted them or not. But there were things that the reporters would not know on their own, such as exactly when the American families would be arriving in the Netherlands and where they would be staying. I made it my business to be the person who got the press that information.

The phone and fax hummed, buzzed, rang and beeped hour after hour at our house. I got in touch with assignment desk editors, radio stations, television networks, bookers, wire service reporters, major journalists—not only in the U.S. but in England, Scotland and the rest of Europe as well. And while I was at it I told them exactly what I thought of the "protect Gadhafi trial."

"Most American families will be leaving May 1, flying out of different airports," I told the press, which was only too glad to have this information. For Dan and me, it would be Delta, leaving Philly, changing planes in Atlanta, arriving, as the other families would, at Amsterdam airport on the morning of May 2. I told the reporters which hotel the families would be staying at: the Holiday Inn Royal Parc. I also told the reporters the name of the Dutch town this Holiday Inn was closest to: Soestdunen. Most American reporters didn't know how to pronounce the name of the town or where it was. I had trouble pronouncing it as well. My tongue stumbled over the unfamiliar word. "It's near Camp Zeist. Not the Hague, Zeist," I'd say.

But the idea of the Hague was firmly embedded in many reporters' minds. They knew the Hague, of course, site of the International Court of Justice and scene of a number of high profile trials. But hardly any reporters seemed to have heard of Zeist. It wasn't surprising. The countries relevant to Pan Am 103 over the years had been Syria, Iran,

Libya, Germany, England, Scotland and the United States. Suddenly out of nowhere the Netherlands had been tossed into the mix, with its obscure outpost called Zeist.

I planned compulsively. How long should we stay? Six days. It was all we could stand. What clothes should I wear? Comfortable ones. What books should I bring? A couple of Dashiell Hammett novels. Crossword puzzles by Merl Reagle. And a pharmacopoeia of nonprescription stuff for every imaginable digestive malfunction, as well as a bottle of aspirin for headaches.

We made elaborate preparations for the animals. Our new Clumber (Hugo and Fergie had died), a hermit at heart, would be at the vet's, where she had made a human friend. The cats would stay home. Twice-a-day visits from the cat-sitter should keep them reasonably content. A house key left with friends in Cape May, just in case.

Right before we left I panicked. Since Pan Am 103, Dan and I had not made out a new will. It was something we knew we should do but we could never quite face up to it. So I rushed to my desk and wrote down instructions about where the animals should go in case the plane crashed and we died. I put the instructions in an envelope, sealed the envelope, left it on the kitchen counter and took a deep breath. It was time to go. Then I remembered I hadn't packed the sleeping pills that I'd been taking every night to ward off insomnia. Normally, I took very few sleeping pills, but this wasn't a normal time. I mean, it isn't every day you go see the people accused of blowing up your kid. I carefully packed the pills. This week they'd be manna from heaven.

DAN: Though we had opposed the idea of a trial in the Netherlands, we had never doubted that the two accused Libyans were guilty as charged. To believe otherwise would mean that the United States government and all its competing agencies—the CIA, the FBI, the Justice Department, the State Department and at least two Administrations—would have had to conspire to frame two innocent

Libyans and a blameless country. And we would also have had to believe that official Washington had been able to keep all this a complete secret for over a decade. The more we got to know Washington, the more incredible such an accusation appeared. In Washington even small secrets are hard to keep, and this would be a very big and dangerous secret indeed. Moreover, this conspiracy would also have to involve the British government, the Scottish authorities and the German government, with help from the Swiss and Maltese governments and probably others. Any leak, any mistake, any weak link at all could bring the entire conspiracy crashing down. Yet the only evidence to support such a conspiracy in over a decade had been provided by wholly unreliable witnesses like Lester Coleman.

For the true conspiracy buff, however, the U.S. is not only thoroughly evil, but omnipotent as well. "They think that not a sparrow falls, but the CIA is behind it," Vince Cannistraro told me.

It became clear that the Libyan defense strategy would be to say that someone else planted the bomb. In the run up to the trial, the defense was looking for every scrap of evidence, every rumor of the involvement of others. They hired people, including one former U.S. government counterterrorism expert, to run down every crackpot theory.

Among those the Libyans hired was a British journalist with whom we had often dealt. We had supplied him with information and genuinely liked him. Among a crowd of often disreputable British journalists, this fellow stood out as someone to be trusted, and when I was first told he was working for the Libyans, I didn't believe it. Or didn't want to.

The very next night that journalist called. It was the first time we had spoken in over a year. My informant had made me promise that I wouldn't tell the journalist what I had learned. So we chatted amiably and he began to ask questions about an obscure incident that had taken place just a few months after the bombing. A man named Carpenter had contacted some family members with a story about how he had been in a bar and heard a couple of Iranians talking about blowing up Pan Am 103. Actually he told several different versions of the story and then advanced a scheme in which Pan Am 103 families would meet with families of those who had been on the Iranian plane shot down by the *Vincennes*. It was a crazy idea and nothing ever came of it, and Carpenter just faded away.

Now a decade or more later, I was being quizzed about this almost forgotten incident. I told the journalist I didn't know anything else—which was quite true. I didn't ask him why he called—because I knew. He signed off saying he was going to cover the trial and hoped he would see me there. I thought, "You better hope you don't!"

There was no "presumption of innocence" on our part. We were convinced Fhimah and Megrahi were guilty as hell and we passionately hoped that they would be convicted. "Presumption of innocence" was a phrase that was to come up again and again in the months immediately preceding the trial. It is one of the most widely misunderstood and misused phrases in legal terminology. It is not a right guaranteed by the U.S. Constitution, though most people seem to believe it is. You won't find those words in the Declaration of Independence either. "Presumption of innocence" is a common-law concept that means simply in a trial the state must prove the defendant guilty rather than the defendant having to prove himself innocent. This "presumption of innocence" applies only to the courtroom. Outside the courtroom, there is no legal or ethical prohibition on presuming whatever you damn well please—and most people do. We presumed guilt.

But to be convinced that the suspects were guilty and to be confident that they would be found guilty under the rigors of Scottish law were two entirely different things. As U.S. prosecutor Bryan Murtagh warned us, guilty people often don't get convicted. And if the two Libyans were found not guilty, that would be a devastating verdict. It would hand the Gadhafi regime a huge propaganda victory, and it would mean that nobody, absolutely nobody, would pay anything for the bombing, for the death of 270 innocent people—for Theo's death. Our emotional commitment to the outcome of the trial was growing.

As the countdown to the trial began, a feeling of uncertainty about the outcome began to set in. Two weeks after the suspects were turned over for trial in the Netherlands, *60 Minutes* devoted the majority of an hour to a two-part report on the evidence in the trial by correspondent Ed Bradley.

To us, the report amounted to little more than a brief for the defense led by Prof. Robert Black, the Scottish lawyer who had first proposed the "scheme" of a trial in a third country to Gadhafi back in 1993. He was now promoting himself as the world's leading legal authority on the Lockerbie case, and he was highly critical of the prosecution.

Most of what appeared on *60 Minutes* was old news, such as the interviews with employees of the Malta airport who insisted that their security was so good that no one could have slipped a bomb past them. These same employees had appeared at the civil trial in Brooklyn in 1992, but their testimony had been severely undermined in cross-examination. Somehow *60 Minutes* never mentioned this. Indeed most of the information in the report had already appeared in a 1997 BBC Scotland TV program, which the Libyans had liked so much that they sent transcripts to all the U.S. victims' families they could locate. But seeing the same information on *60 Minutes* gave it greater authority, and the show plunged many family members, particularly those who had not followed the case closely, into depression.

"We're going to lose the case, aren't we?" several people asked me. I tried to reassure them that Black always seemed to take the Libyan side and that *60 Minutes* or not, we were hearing a one-sided story. I don't know whether I reassured anyone. I don't know whether I was really able to reassure myself.

Then came Lord Hardie's resignation, and all the rumors that he was abandoning a sinking ship, getting out before the case was lost and he was blamed for it.

There was a steady stream of stories, most originating in the Scottish press, but quickly making their way to the wire services and into the U.S. media, about the fatal weakness of the case against the Libyans. There were rumors, allegedly originating from a secret source in "the prosecution camp," that the case was so weak that it would not even be brought to trial, or that it would be conceded after a few weeks, when the flaws became apparent.

A whole host of theories were floated, including one that the bomb itself had never been in the luggage container but had actually been attached to the inside of the cargo hold, and thus could not have been put aboard Pan Am 103 in an unaccompanied piece of luggage from Malta. Another theory held that there was a renegade CIA official out there who had information that could blow the case right out of the water, but he had been "gagged" by the government.

Most of the stories centered on three witnesses. The first was Edwin Bollier. Bollier was head of a Swiss electronics firm called MEBO. A fragment of a MEBO timer was found in the charred clothing from the suitcase that had contained the bomb. When first questioned, Bollier identified the fragment as part of a shipment of timers that his company had sold to the Libyan government. The identification was a key moment in the investigation.

Bollier was a strange character, and he quickly began telling a variety of different stories to investigators and reporters. He said that he had also sold these timers to the East German secret police, the Stasi, who could then have passed them on to Palestinian terrorists. He said that he had misidentified the timer, that he was shown only photographs of different timers, that the timers had been altered. He said lots of different things to lots of different people at lots of different times. And then he began working with the Libyan defense team to develop alternate scenarios to the bombing. He was the one who came up with the theory that the bomb had never been inside the cargo container.

The story now spread that Bollier's testimony was worthless or could actually destroy the prosecution case.

The second witness to come under press scrutiny was

Tony Gauchi, one of the owners of the Malta shop Mary's House, where the items of clothing found in the bomb-bearing suitcase had been purchased. Gauchi was supposed to have identified Megrahi as the man who bought the clothing. But now rumors said that Gauchi's memory was bad and that he had actually identified Mohammed Abu Taub—a known Palestinian terrorist who was already in prison in Sweden for terrorist acts in that country—as the man who made the purchase. Taub had been under suspicion for the Pan Am bombing because he had been in Malta in the latter months of 1988 and was said to have purchased clothing there. On a 1988 calendar found in his apartment in Sweden, he was supposed to have circled the date of December 21.

The third and most interesting witness to fall under press scrutiny was Abdul Majid Giaka—usually called Majid—the defector. Majid had been a member of the Libyan intelligence service. Like the defendants Fahima and Megrahi, his cover was a job at Luqa Airport in Malta. He was the individual who was supposed to be able to link Fhimah and Megrahi directly to Libyan intelligence and to the bomb. He had defected, bringing with him what was supposed to be vital evidence about the bombing. Though the details of his testimony were not known, he was generally believed to be one of the most crucial witnesses in the case.

Since the early 1990s, when he defected, Majid had been in the U.S. witness protection program, living somewhere in the United States. There was good reason to believe that his life was in real danger. Shortly after his defection became public knowledge, there were rallies in Libya, where he was denounced and members of his own family stood up and called for his death. He was described as a traitor, a drunk and a madman.

Shortly before the trial began, Majid was interviewed by members of the Libyan defense team. According to reports on that meeting, which had been leaked to the press, Majid insisted on being interviewed in the back of a moving vehicle, and during the interview he wore a dress, heavy makeup and a "Shirley Bassey" wig. This certainly sounded crazy. Bryan Murtagh, chief U.S. prosecutor, assured me that "we have no transvestites on our witness list." The story was an imaginative construction.

Majid was interviewed in the kitchen of an unidentified house. As is standard for interviews of individuals in the witness protection program, those who do the interviewing are put into a van with blocked windows and then driven around, often in circles, for a long time so they are unable to identify where they have ultimately been taken. During the interview, Majid was wearing a loose North African robe, not a dress, and a disguise. Again standard for interviews of this type. The wig idea apparently came from a discussion with judges in the case about how certain witnesses might disguise their identity when testifying. The judge ruled that there would be no "Shirley Bassey" wigs, a reference to a once popular British singing star with a distinctive hairdo.

The stories also claimed that Majid had in some significant way altered his testimony.

The trial had first been scheduled to start in February 2000, and the prosecution submitted a list of over 1000 potential witnesses. The defense then asked for and was granted a delay of 90 days—and the new scheduled date for the trial to start was May 3. That date seemed firm and we made our plans to go to the Netherlands. Then, just three weeks before the trial was scheduled to start, the defense submitted their witness list, which apparently contained some surprise witnesses from Libya. The prosecution then asked for a delay so the witnesses could be examined. The request led to another rush of stories that the prosecution was unprepared and would surely lose.

This time, however, the judges refused to grant a delay, saying in essence that this was going to be a long trial and the prosecution would have plenty of time to examine the witnesses as the trial went along. So the trial of Lamen Khalifa Fhimah and Abdel Bassest Ali al-Megrahi was set to start on May 3. Early indications were that it would last for a year or more.

SUSAN: The flight to the Netherlands was as bad as I expected. Worse actually, because where once I could have sat quietly in the airport and read, now television was inescapable, ruining my concentration. Since I had last taken an international flight, coach sections had been turned into the modern equivalent of steerage. The plane was cramped and crowded. If I got an hour's sleep, I was lucky. I tried to distract myself, but bombs and Theo and Theo and bombs were all I could think of.

We arrived at the Amsterdam airport exhausted and jet-lagged, but a contingent of reporters was there, so we started giving interviews as soon as we were through customs. Actually two AP reporters I had contacted found us even before we reached customs. Good thing too. I got lost in the airport looking for the big, colorful decorative cube where we were supposed to meet the OVC staff and the other Pan Am families. The AP reporters guided me there. I greeted the other families and gave a special hug to the Wolfes and Flynns.

A bus was waiting to take the families to our hotel. It had been cold and damp when we left. It was cold and damp when we arrived. Camp Zeist, the hotel we would be going to, Holland itself really—all were still unknowns, abstractions. The major highway we drove along could have been anywhere and the flat, soggy landscape looked so much like South Jersey that for one eerie moment I imagined I was back in the Garden State. But the lack of litter in tidy little Holland proved I was very far from home.

The families on the bus kept up low-key chatter, and there was even some banter about tulips and windmills, kind of whistling past the graveyard. All conversation came to a abrupt halt, however, when we reached the grounds of the Holiday Inn and saw a line of television cameras waiting for us at the front door. They were there because of my phone calls and faxes to assignment desks. And they were a reminder to everyone in the bus that we weren't here for tulips and windmills.

The hotel was very clean, very nice, and in a wealthy area. A golf course attached to the hotel provided a peaceful view from the hotel restaurant. Behind the golf course was a wooded area with expensive houses. But that was it. There was no place to go. No crowds to lose oneself in. No shop windows to stroll past. No easy way to escape when the pressure became too great.

The families would be together all the time. Bused together to and from Camp Zeist. Bused together in the evenings for sightseeing in nearby towns. Though being with the Flynns and the Wolfes meant a lot to me, I couldn't bear to be with all of the families always. I needed breathing room. I needed to be alone.

Now that we had seen the hotel, Dan and I were able to work out a survival plan. We would snatch what little privacy we could. The hotel was full of reporters and we were committed to talking to them, but we would skip the evening bus tours with the families and have dinner in the hotel.

On the day we arrived, we were given a tour of the court facilities at Camp Zeist. Shortly after we were driven through the gate, I saw an old Libyan man dressed in traditional North African robes. He was the first Libyan I had seen since I arrived, for there were no Libyans staying at our hotel. He was smiling and laughing. My heart sank.

The courtroom building was all spanking new, freshly painted, impressively done and totally sterile. State-of-the-art technology was pointed out to us with pride. It must have all cost a pretty penny. Who would foot the bill for this edifice created solely to get past the worst act of terrorism against civilians in U.S. history? I suspected it would be the American taxpayer. Some of the families were very excited about the trial, obsessed with it actually. Full of questions, they wanted to know every detail, walked around with pads of paper, took notes, made suggestions, cared about specifics. Not me. Not for one moment could I forget that the trial was merely a sideshow, and not the main event.

Because it was so new and so empty, Camp Zeist didn't look real. The old court building in Brooklyn where the civil trial against Pan Am had been held looked real. Many years of trials had been held there and you knew it the moment you stepped into the building. Zeist was like a stage set. Or better yet, a Potemkin Village. A false front.

Security was very tight. There were guards with submachine guns. I indulged in a little fantasy. I saw myself grabbing one of the guns, rushing down to the prison cells where Fhimah and Megrahi were being held and blasting away—and through this simple act of vigilantism getting a small measure of justice for Theo. The John Wayne fantasy lasted only a few seconds, but it felt good.

That night at the hotel, the U.S. Ambassador to the Netherlands held a reception for the families. Dan and I didn't attend. I had had it up to here with State Department blather. I did go in briefly before the reception to tell the ambassador and her staff what I thought of the trial, and to tell the ambassador one other thing.

The U.S. government had dropped this trial into the Netherlands and was running away from it at warp speed. Secretary of State Albright, for example, was nowhere to be seen at Camp Zeist. The Libyans would have observers at the trial. So would the U.N. We needed an American representative. We needed an American presence. I urged the ambassador to come to the trial herself. No underlings please. Her presence in the courtroom on the day the trial opened would be worth more than all the receptions, canapes, speeches and cooing in the world.

I climbed into bed at 10 P.M. Dutch time, giddy from exhaustion. Trial arrival day was over. The past twenty-four hours had been awful. The next twenty-four would be worse. I took a sleeping pill and asked only for a few brief hours of oblivion.

DAN: Shortly after the bombing, Susan and I had determined that if there was to be a human face put on this tragedy it would be Theo's. Though we lacked organizational skills and were probably the least diplomatic people in the world, we knew how the media operated. We knew how to get our story out. We knew, for example, that when the trial opened there would be a huge crush of world media. We also knew that as the trial progressed and there was day after day of technical and highly detailed testimony, the media crowd would melt away to nothing.

We made sure that our names were first on the list to attend the opening of the trial. As usual, Susan had gone through her press Rolodex and contacted everybody she knew. I prepared a press release that was faxed to all the wire services. I also had copies of Theo's picture made up. It was a publicity head shot taken her last semester at Syracuse. She was going to use it along with her resume when she applied for summer stock jobs in the summer of '89. Now it was to be used for a very different purpose.

When we stumbled off the plane in Amsterdam after a ghastly flight, the first people to greet us at the gate were the reporter and photographer from the Associated Press. I handed the photographer a copy of Theo's photo, and it went around the world. When we got back home, a friend who had been vacationing in Bermuda sent us a copy of the paper from Hamilton. It had Theo's picture on the front page. We had succeeded in putting a human face on the tragedy.

We went to the spot in the airport where family members were to gather to be taken to the hotel. A crowd of reporters and photographers had gathered there as well. By the time we got to the hotel that crowd had grown to a mob.

"OK," I kept telling myself, "this is what we're here for."

We were part of a group of about 30 American family members that had arrived the day before the trial was scheduled to begin. After our arrival we were bused over to Camp Zeist, where the trial would actually be held, for a sort of orientation.

It would be misleading to say that the trial was conducted in a remote spot. Camp Zeist was a Cold War–era U.S. Air Base—since closed—that had been given over to the Scots in a complex arrangement that, legally at least, made it a little bit of Scotland for the duration of the trial. It was located in the middle of a pleasant and wealthy area of homes and estates. But you couldn't just walk out of the courtroom and go anywhere else easily. It was an hour's drive from Amsterdam. Local accommodations were sparse and pricey. The court area was surrounded by a high and well-guarded chain-link fence. It was, in short, not the sort of place one could just drop into casually.

The court building itself was brand-new and very high-tech. The judges, defendants, lawyers and witnesses, etc., would be at the front of the court. The spectators' gallery—which seated about 200—was separated from the actual proceedings by a transparent, floor to ceiling, bulletproof, soundproof barrier. Television was everywhere. We were told that there were nine cameras in the court, and a full-time TV director was needed. Not only were the witnesses on television, but virtually all of the evidence was also displayed on screens.

Security was not merely obvious—it was downright showy. Scottish policemen and -women were everywhere—many carrying Heckler & Koch submachine guns, which they somehow did not look comfortable with. There were even dogs—bomb-sniffing dogs, I presumed, because they were far too friendly to be guard dogs.

The prisoners themselves were housed in what was described as underground cells in a building hidden behind twenty-foot-high walls of polished concrete topped with razor wire. It looked strong enough to repel a rescue attempt by the entire Libyan army. Details of the exact conditions under which the prisoners were being held were sketchy, but from what we gathered, their cells were much larger and more comfortable than those usually occupied by defendants on trial in a Scottish court.

For me there was an air of unreality and discomfort about all of this—as though I had just been taken into a large stage set, on which I was to have a minor role in a play, but I had never been shown the script.

We were then bused back to the hotel where, fatigued, jet-lagged, disoriented, and dispirited, I tried, with the aid of a couple of slugs of Dutch gin, to get some sleep before opening day.

Chapter 20

DAN: As the trial began, I was again struck by a sense of theatrical unreality. On the back wall, behind the judges' bench, was a large heraldic crest with a Latin motto: *"Nemo me impune lacessit,"* which means "No one dare attack me with impunity." The four judges (three who would decide the case and a spare in case one of the elderly judges dropped dead) were led into the chamber by an attendant carrying a silver mace. The judges wore full white wigs and flowing ivory robes embroidered with large red crosses. The lawyers for both sides wore shorter wigs and black robes. In sharp contrast to this archaic traditionalism, they were completely surrounded by television monitors and other electronic equipment and often had to take off their wigs to put on earphones to hear the translators. With all the customary "My Lording," the scene looked and sounded like an amateur production of Gilbert and Sullivan being performed in a computer lab.

The defendants added to the theatrical atmosphere. Previously we had only seen pictures of them wearing Western clothes. Now they appeared in what we were told was traditional Libyan garb: wide-sleeved white robes, embroidered waistcoats and dark caps. Some of their relatives in the audience also wore white robes and caps. When the judges entered, the victims' relatives all stood. When the defendants entered, the Libyan spectators all stood.

I had not expected to react strongly at the first sight of Fhimah and Megrahi. They were, after all, only the accused triggermen in a much larger plot. But when I saw them, I felt a rush of hatred. Mere cogs in the machine they may have been, but to me they were murderous cogs.

Unlike at most American trials, there were no opening statements. There was a reading of the indictment. Then the defense notified the court that as a "special defense" they would attempt to incriminate Palestinian terrorists for the bombing. After that, the prosecution began calling its witnesses and at this point the theatrical aura was shattered by brutal reality.

Early in the parade of witnesses was air controller Alan Topp, who was the first to see the radar image of Pan Am 103 break up into separate images. Topp recalled shouting across the room to his supervisor to come over and look at the screen. The supervisor shouted back that he was busy talking to the Dumfries and Galloway constabulary because another plane had reported sighting a large fire on the ground near the town of Lockerbie.

"That's when the penny dropped," Topp said.

What Topp saw on his radar screen—innocuous-looking green boxes on a map grid representing the final seconds of Pan Am 103—was displayed on monitors throughout the courtroom. Spectators gasped. I was one of them.

Then came witnesses from Lockerbie itself—people who had been on the ground when the pieces of the plane and its contents fell to earth. William Pattie told of how a flaming engine from the 747 slammed into a relative's house, destroying it so completely that the remains of the two people who had been inside could never be found.

Jasmine Bell described visiting her brother's house in Lockerbie when the debris from the plane came falling from the sky and all around her. She slipped in the darkened driveway of the house and her hand touched something. "It's just meat," her brother said as he pulled her away. "Just meat."

At Tundergarth, three miles from Lockerbie, the cockpit of the plane almost floated down over the house of Kevin Anderson. "There were bodies lying around the cockpit." He got a flashlight and looked inside. "I could see the pilot."

I had read many of these accounts before. But to hear them told firsthand, by the people who had experienced them, was entirely different. I had to keep reminding myself to breathe.

I tried to see if the defendants had any reaction to this grisly testimony, but they were almost entirely hidden from view behind their video monitors.

There was another dose of reality as the trial opened. Col. Gadhafi gave an interview to Britain's Sky TV network, and news of the interview quickly spread among the families at Camp Zeist. Gadhafi had airily brushed aside any suggestion that he or his government had had anything to do with the bombing. "The court is sitting to judge them (the defendants), not whether they are Libyan agents," he said. He insisted that he had made an "agreement" with the U.S. and Britain. In return for handing over the suspects, the court would not raise questions about Libyan government involvement in the bombing. "The agreement is to try these two suspects . . . these two suspects only."

He seemed quite confident that whatever the outcome of the trial in the Netherlands, it would not affect him at all. The Libyan government would not be "undermined." The colonel was going to be just fine.

SUSAN: There were no windows in the courtroom, and windowless rooms always make me feel trapped, a sensation that was worse now that the room was no longer empty. There were rows of reporters; then came rows of officials and victims' families. I deliberately sat as far away as I could from the section where the Libyan spectators were seated. It was bad enough looking at them. Then I looked at Fhimah and Megrahi. To my eyes, they perfectly fit the discription of the banality of evil. Two ordinary-seeming men. No horns grew out of their heads. They were impassive, even bored.

They were accused of being the hands used to place the bomb on the plane. "Theo, they killed you," I thought. And

I felt such hatred for Fhimah and Megrahi that I wanted to use my hands to strangle both of them.

DAN: At the rear of the courtroom were four special glass-enclosed booths reserved for observers. One was for Libyan observers. While we were at the trial, this booth was usually filled. The two center booths were for U.N. observers, and they too contained several representatives. The fourth was for U.S. government observers. The State Department, continuing its long-standing policy of downplaying the bombing and trying to pretend that this terrorist act had been directed at some other country, sent no one. After the U.S. Ambassador to the Netherlands was berated by Susan and others about this, she came to the trial briefly. Then a single low-level embassy employee sat in the U.S. booth for a while. The U.S. booth was occupied for less than three hours during the first week of the trial.

The only other representative of the U.S. government (aside from two Justice Department prosecutors) to actually attend the opening of the trial was Sharon Waxman from Senator Kennedy's office. The senator had persuaded the Judiciary Committee, of which he is a member, that the trial was of concern to the U.S. and someone ought to be there.

Sharon's presence created a nasty little rift between U.S. and British family members. There was a room set aside in the court building for family members. But the British families objected when Sharon came into the room, saying she was not a "family member." True enough—as far as it went—but she had been invited. It was just another sign that, in the view of some of the British families, the U.S. was somehow involved in the bombing.

We tried our best to prevent open confrontation by avoiding the Libyans and Jim Swire, as well as Bert Ammerman and Bruce Smith, who showed up for the trial start. There were a few hostile glares, but no shouting matches in the hallway.

SUSAN: I saw very little of the trial. When the testimony began, I couldn't believe what I was seeing and hearing. Though I knew when I left New Jersey that I was en route to a brutal experience, I hadn't expected it to be as bad as this. Back in America, I'd been told that the court (the lawyers, the judges, whatever) had agreed to skip the usual Scottish legal procedure of describing how each victim had died. Since the Pan Am civil suit and the British Fatal Accident Inquiry got a lot of sickening information on the record, I convinced myself they wouldn't go over all the gruesome details again at Zeist.

But they *were* going over many of them, the stuff of my worst nightmares saturating the courtroom. I couldn't endure it. When air-traffic controller Alan Topp was sworn in, Dan, who sensed what was coming, told me to "get out." I stood up in a panic. Immediately Ann den Bieman, a family liaison officer from the Scottish Crown Office who was sitting close by, leaped to her feet and led me out of the courtroom and took me to the family lounge. I told her I wanted to be alone.

The lounge was quiet. The occasional closing of a door or the sound of footsteps was all that broke the silence. I cried. I paced the room. I looked out of the window. I sat down on one of the new small sofas, buried my head in my hands, and tried not to think. But it was too late. Pan Am 103 was splitting apart before my eyes. There was Theo, amazed and terrified. I watched her die. I watched her fall. Saw her body hitting the ground in the sheep meadow. Now I was in Port Jervis getting the news. I was running downstairs. The television was on. 103. 103. Yes that was her flight. Wreckage. Fire. It was all happening again.

That night at dinner I spoke to a woman who lost her husband in the bombing, a quiet woman who kept to herself. "How was it for you in court today?" I asked. She lifted her hands in a pleading gesture. "It was pure torture," she said. "If this is what hell is like, we had better all repent now."

Once I practically collided with the U.S. Ambassador to the Netherlands outside the family lounge. The ambassador looked at me eagerly and announced, "Susan, I'm here." She seemed startled and disappointed when I barely responded, brushing past her to get to the lounge.

She probably expected me to say I was glad she was there. After all, I had urged her to come. But at that moment I could barely see the ambassador. Tears of grief were in my eyes and all my wounds were freshly opened. I had to be where they could bleed unseen.

Finally I gave up trying to listen to the testimony. When we arrived at Camp Zeist I would go straight to the family room and not even enter the courtroom, or I'd take a walk around the compound. It was during one of these walks that I stopped to talk to a prominent European reporter. In his rumpled, old-fashioned suit and with his gold-rimmed glasses he looked like a character out of an Eric Ambler spy novel of the 1940s. I was struck by his appearance because I met him on the day that marked the anniversary of the liberation of Holland from the Nazis and he looked as if he came right out of that era.

I gave him my analysis of the trial, how it was merely the result of a deal to get past Pan Am 103. The leaders of the world were eager to forgive Gadhafi's mass murder because there was money to be made. The reporter told me forcefully that I was absolutely right. In disgust he described a recent conference of European and African leaders that he had covered. European leaders from France, Italy and Germany had fawned over Gadhafi. Gadhafi's response? He lashed out at them in contempt, insulting them, humiliating them, swaggering like an ancient barbarian potentate. And what did these world leaders do after he insulted them? They fawned all the more, metaphorically kissing his feet. I walked away. European appeasement. Nothing new. And plenty of it emanating from the good old U.S. of A. too.

I did a lot of talking to the press. At one point a large heavyset man with a thick Scottish accent corralled me and introduced himself as the publicist for Jim Swire. He told me proudly that he'd gotten Swire a lot of interviews and added that he was doing publicity for Bert Ammerman and another American family that would be arriving the next week. He beamed. I glared. I don't know if he expected me to hire him or not, but I was sick of hustlers and hangers-on.

"I don't believe in handlers," I said. "I get my own interviews." I walked away. Later, I found out the big man was David Ben-Areah, a small-time journalist who had been on the fringes of the Pan Am 103 case from the beginning. He had worked for filmmaker Alan Francovich—Francovich who got money from the Libyans to make a propaganda piece about the bombing! Ben-Areah had written a eulogy for Francovich after his death. How could the family of any Pan Am 103 victim have anything to do with the likes of David Ben-Areah?

DAN: After the dramatic testimony of the Lockerbie witnesses, the trial began to bog down. Debris from the explosion and crash had been spread over hundreds of square miles. Scottish policemen testified in detail about how evidence had been collected, stored and examined. At first the defense seemed intent on questioning where every fragment was found and how each evidence bag had been sealed and marked. In cross-examination, repeated questions were asked about whether there were any FBI or CIA agents on the scene. I recalled the O.J. trial where the defense endlessly questioned and requestioned every bloodstain, every footprint, every fiber. I had a sinking feeling that estimates that this trial would drag on for a year or more might be optimistic. There was so much technical evidence.

At the end of the first week of testimony, the prosecution had the names and addresses of all the victims read into the record. When they got to Theo's name they had the wrong address, wrong town, wrong everything. I began shaking my head and saying, "No! No!" Seated right behind me was Ann den Bieman. She put her hand on my shoulder and asked me what had happened. "It's wrong," I told her. "All wrong. You have to get this fixed—you have to! I demand a correction, in writing!" I scribbled out the correct address and shoved it into her hand.

It was nothing—a simple clerical error, inevitable in an event that requires hundreds of pages of documentation—yet that little clerical error hit me harder than anything I had experienced during the week.

Theo had been taken from us. Now even her address, part of her identity, had been mangled. Somehow all the frustrations, anger, sadness and sense of irreconcilable loss were focused on that trivial error. It felt as if yet one more part of Theo's identity had been erased. Irrational, of course, but sitting there in the Netherlands just a few yards, and a bulletproof shield, away from the men accused of her murder, I wasn't feeling terribly rational. (It took three months to have the error corrected, but it finally was, and in writing. Theo's address wasn't the only one the records had wrong.)

The following morning we flew back to the U.S. The government would have covered expenses for several more days, but neither of us had any taste for a tour of the tulip fields. All I wanted to do was get the hell back to our animals and familiar surroundings. I was drained.

SUSAN: Holland might or might not be a nice country. I don't know and I don't care. I never want to see it again. Oh, was I glad to be getting away from the trial. Oh, was I glad to be going home. So I could buy Maryland crab at the Lobster House in Cape May. Then sit on the couch with the cats nestled around me and the dog's head on my lap. Turn on the television. Put on my Yankee cap and watch baseball. America, thank God, is not just its government.

DAN: As we were leaving the Netherlands, so were the press people. The day before we left, a court artist I had become friendly with announced he too was returning home. "Nothing more going on here," he said. Within a few weeks of the trial's start, the large media facility housed only a

couple of wire service reporters, the occasional accidental—like the New Jersey reporter who was following some
Jersey families attending the trial for a "local color" story—
and a regular contingent of reporters from Libya.

Though the Libyan media appeared to be well represented—at least there were a number of people there who
said they were Libyan reporters—press coverage of the
trial in Libya itself was minimal. A reporter who was in
Tripoli at the time told me that coverage of the opening
was limited to brief notices and a few government comments. Even this faded as the trial progressed. As far as the
Libyan government was concerned, it had nothing to do
with the defendants or what had happened at Lockerbie.

Press coverage in the U.S. became so sparse that some
family members began to suspect a deliberate press black-
out. But no sinister conspiracy theories were needed to explain what was happening. The trial was taking place a long
way from the U.S. If it had been in New York or even Ed-
inburgh the coverage would have been better. Pan Am 103
had been bombed a long time ago. Some of the reporters
we met had only been teenagers in 1988. No celebrity had
died on the plane. Much of the testimony in the trial was
technical and, frankly, boring. And most significant of all,
the trial was not being televised.

It wasn't that television executives didn't want to cover
the trial. The BBC actually sued to get that right—and lost.
The BBC suit was supported by all the U.S. TV networks.
Those TV executives we talked to—and we talked to several—were extremely anxious to have the trial televised.
Only a cable network like Court TV could possibly provide wall-to-wall coverage of such a lengthy trial, but significant excerpts might have appeared regularly on the
nightly news. And that competition would have, in turn,
stimulated the print media to do a better job.

The reasons the Scots offered for not allowing the trial
to be televised ranged from the stubborn to the absurd.
The basic reason was "We're Scottish and we don't do that
sort of thing." Well, they don't normally hold their trials in
the Netherlands either, and rarely are there many more

non-Scots than Scots involved in a Scottish mass murder case.

In discussions with the Scots, we were treated to many references to the "O.J. trial circus." As if there was any possibility that a well-guarded air base in the middle of Holland could be turned into central LA, or that a trial of a decade-old case without celebrity, sex and race could possibly attract that sort of attention, no matter how many people had died.

We were reminded that U.S. Federal trials are not televised. True enough, but U.S. Federal trials are held in the U.S. If a U.S. trial were being held, say, in a suburb of Warsaw, that rule would certainly be reexamined.

Another objection to television was that some witnesses, fearing for their safety, would not want to appear on television. But they do appear in court, and it is far easier to disguise the identity of a witness electronically than it is in person in open court. It's done all the time. Professor Robert Black weighed in with the objection that witnesses might be intimidated by cameras—a baseless objection since the cameras were already there. No new equipment would have to be introduced.

In fact, the daily proceedings of the court were already being shown at what were called "remote sites" in New York, Washington, London and the Scottish town of Dumfries, near Lockerbie. Because of the time difference, the U.S. sites were on a six-hour tape delay, and the tapes, we were told, were burned at the end of every session, so that there would be no video record of the proceedings.

Access to the remote sites was strictly limited to victims' family members and a few select others—like some Syracuse University law students. We were warned that if we tried to bring in a ringer we could actually be prosecuted. Lawyers, like Lee Kreindler, who were going to pursue a civil suit against Libya were barred. So were members of the U.S. Congress and their representatives, and most of all the press was barred. Reporters that we knew, whose employers would never pony up the funds to send them to the

Netherlands, desperately wanted to view the proceedings on television. This simply was not allowed, and the only reason we were given was that the Scots didn't want it.

Professor Black, who consistently spoke out against televising the trial, said airily that anyone could see the trial by going to Camp Zeist. That is, anyone who had many thousands of dollars to spend and no limits on his or her time. You see, another problem was that there was no firm schedule. On several occasions the lawyers just ran out of witnesses, and the next ones were in England or Malta or Germany or wherever, so the court session was canceled for a day or several days.

Even the remote sites were a lot less useful for family members than had originally been envisioned. Remote viewing sites for members of victims families had first been used in the Oklahoma City bombing trial. That trial had been moved to Denver, but there was a site in Oklahoma City where a closed-circuit TV feed was made available to victims and family members. The difference was that virtually all of the victims came from Oklahoma City. The Pan Am 103 victims came from all over the world. It wasn't easy or cheap for the mother of a victim from Minneapolis or Miami to get to Washington or New York. Pan Am 103 was not a planeload of rich Americans. There were few millionaires made from the civil suit. As a result, most of the time there was only a handful of family members at any remote site—and sometimes there were none at all. Most of us, quite simply, couldn't afford to go. One time we drove to Washington and booked into a hotel in order to see what we assumed would be important testimony. But when we got to the remote site, it was closed. The session had been canceled, and our trip wasted. Many other family members had identical experiences.

The reality was that in the twenty-first century people had less access to this trial than they would have had when Scottish judges first started wearing those wigs and robes and crimes were local.

The restrictions on the remote sites were so extreme, so illogical and so downright goofy that I couldn't help but

wonder if they were not part of a deliberate attempt or
agreement to play down the trial, to "keep it in the closet,"
in the words of one disappointed reporter.

People who read just the sketchy and often misleading
daily news reports could easily have gotten the impression
that the prosecution case was full of holes—witnesses who
contradicted themselves, witnesses who failed to remember important information or witnesses who simply did not
show up. But people who were sitting in the courtroom,
viewing the proceedings at the remote sites or receiving
transcripts were getting a different impression. The prosecution case was detailed, deep and, surprisingly, on most
points virtually unchallenged.

Take the testimony of Edwin Bollier, one of the most
significant prosecution witnesses, and one of the most difficult because his story changed constantly. Bollier was one
of the two heads of the small Swiss electronics firm called
MEBO (Robert Meister was the other—hence the name
MEBO) that had produced the timing device found in the
Pan Am 103 wreckage. His firm had supplied this type of
device to Libya; indeed Libya had been MEBO's best customer and MEBO was a virtual terrorist supply house.
During his testimony, Bollier described how his firm had
provided the equipment for making suitcase bombs to the
Libyans. Suitcase bombs are hardly conventional military
hardware. Over the years, MEBO products had been
found in the hands of a variety of Libyan-backed terrorists.

For years Bollier had been conducting a bizarre and
very public campaign to prove that Libya was not behind
the Pan Am 103 bombing. His campaign reached a
crescendo in the days leading up to the trial and his testimony.

On the stand, he rattled on about faked evidence and altered police reports. He even told a story about a mysterious man who came to his office and intimidated him into
writing a letter to the CIA on a Spanish typewriter.

Bollier was clearly a slippery and unreliable witness. But
there were certain things that he could not escape. Yes, he
had identified the timer fragment as one that his company

had sold to the Libyans. And yes, he had dealt directly with Megrahi, whom he identified as a Libyan "colonel or higher." He said he thought Megrahi might actually be a member of Gadhafi's family. This was testimony he had first given not to the CIA, the FBI, British Intelligence or even the Scots; it was given to the Swiss police. Moreover, key elements in his testimony were backed up by Meister and MEBO's chief engineer, who had preceded Bollier to the stand.

Then there was the testimony of Tony Gauchi, the Maltese shopkeeper who had sold the clothes found in the suitcase that contained the bomb. It had been widely predicted that Gauchi would be a weak witness whose memory was bad and who had actually identified a Palestinian terrorist and not one of the Libyans.

On the stand, Gauchi presented a very different picture. He was a lively and very sharp individual who appeared to be doing his very best to honestly recall an event that had happened quite a long time ago. He identified photographs of Megrahi as the man who most probably came into his shop early in December of 1988 and bought the random selection of items. He also identified Megrahi in a lineup or "parade," as the Scots call it, at Camp Zeist and pointed him out in court. Though his identification was not absolutely conclusive, he was a highly credible witness, whose finger pointed firmly at one of the defendants. The defense could do nothing to shake his testimony.

And there was more. Witnesses highlighted the sloppy security procedures at Malta's Luqa Airport. Passports and other travel documents showed that Fhimah and Megrahi were in Malta in Malta on critical dates. The movement of the bomb-carrying suitcase from an Air Malta flight to the first leg of Pan Am 103 was clearly traced in the computerized records of the Frankfurt airport. But the final connection—linking the Libyan defendants to the bomb itself—was not made before the trial broke for summer recess late in July.

Chapter 21

DAN: When governments have to release information they are not proud of, they try to do it at a time when the media and the public will not be paying attention. Friday afternoon one weekend before Labor Day weekend is just such a time. And so August 25, 2000, was when the U.S. and British governments finally released Kofi Annan's letter to Gadhafi and its attendant annex. So the documents that on various occasions the U.S. government had told us did not exist, could not be found, or could not be released were finally released.

Along with the documents there were additional letters about the documents and a two-page question-and-answer sheet prepared jointly by the British Foreign Office and the U.S. State Department that attempted to explain why these documents didn't really mean what they very clearly did mean.

There were no bombshells in the documents—they said pretty much what we already knew they said. But out in public, official and complete, they looked even worse than we had been led to believe. What was most telling about this entire episode was the ease, comfort, and utter lack of self-consciousness with which the U.S. and British governments had lied to their people. I don't think that government officials regard lying to ordinary citizens as lying at all—it's just part of doing their jobs.

Madeline Albright had told us, in person and in a voice throbbing with sincerity, that Gadhafi had been given a one-time, nonnegotiable ultimatum by the U.S. and Britain. Over and over she stressed there were no negotiations. Sandy Berger had agreed—no negotiations. Yet here was a letter signed by Kofi Annan that spoke of "lengthy negotiations which also involved the efforts on the part of the Governments of Saudi Arabia and South Africa."

We had been told the information could not be released because it was contained in official U.N. documents. But at a rather testy news conference at the U.N., Hans Corell, the U.N. official who had actually overseen the transfer of the two suspects, insisted that every word in the documents had been written and approved by the U.S. and U.K. and could have been released anytime, if the two countries had wished it.

The phrase that the trial would not be used to "undermine the Libyan regime" was explained away as assurance that the suspects had the "right to remain silent." But they had already been assured of that right—repeatedly and much more directly.

And then there was this little bit in the questions and answers supplied by the Foreign Office and Department of State.

Q: Does the *annex* set out special arrangements for the Libyan accused?

A: NO, THE ANNEX COVERS CLARIFICATIONS OF THE CRIMINAL JUSTICE SYSTEM IN SCOTLAND AND THE RIGHTS AND SAFEGUARDS WHICH ARE ENJOYED BY THE ACCUSED IN A CRIMINAL TRIAL.

Oh yeah. The annex provided that, if convicted, the accused would be housed in their own special prison wing at Barlinnie Prison in Glasgow under U.N. supervision, and that the Libyans could establish a consulate near the prison and have constant contact with the prisoners. How many other prisoners in Scotland are kept in their own special prison wing under U.N. supervision with their government representatives near at hand to make sure they are treated right, and incidentally, don't get itchy and start talking about their bosses?

I've never been given a straight answer to that question, but I'll bet the answer is none.

This was no regular Scottish trial, and it was never intended to be. As Lord Advocate Colin Boyd told me, these men were under no pressure to give up their superiors.

So much for the mantra that the prosecutors would "follow the evidence wherever it leads." It wasn't going to lead anywhere else, certainly not to Gadhafi. And everybody understood that—everybody, that is, except the families of those who were killed.

SUSAN: At least the word was now out that the trial was the result of a deal, a distinctly ugly deal at that. The State Department's propaganda campaign to present the trial as a mighty blow against international terrorism—the hottest thing to happen to Justice since Moses brought the Ten Commandments down from the mountain—had failed. Reporters now used the word "deal" routinely when they described the trial. Dan and I preferred accuracy and truth to lies and propaganda. We had done a lot to get the truth out about the deal—and we were proud of that.

After the start of the trial I had tried to distance myself from what was going on at Camp Zeist, in order to keep some perspective on it. I told myself that, win or lose, it was a reeking mess, so why should I get caught up in it? But I did. I developed quite a passionate desire to win. And whenever the case looked wobbly I'd pretend I was saying to the prosecutors, "Look, this trial is every bit the ordeal I knew it would be, so the least you guys can do after putting us through this is to win."

DAN: The Libyan defector Abdul Majid Giaka, a Libyan intelligence agent who worked at Malta's Luqa Airport posing as an employee of Libyan Arab Airlines, was scheduled to be the opening witness when the trial reconvened in late August. I had always assumed that this guy had come to the attention of the authorities many months after the bombing itself. Then about a week before he was scheduled to testify, press reports revealed that he had actually been a CIA double agent months before the bombing and had even met with his handlers on December 20, 1988, the day before the bombing!

That raised the horrifying possibility that the CIA actually had some advance warning of what was about to happen and did nothing. I immediately called Vince Cannistraro, who insisted that he had never even heard of Majid when he headed the CIA side of the Pan Am investigation. There were lots of CIA informants, moles, and double agents, and this guy was just too obscure.

Before the testimony began there was controversy. The CIA had turned over normally secret documents from Majid's handlers detailing his career, but these were heavily redacted—that means large parts of them were inked over so they couldn't be read, for "security reasons." The defense exploded, claiming that vital information was being withheld. It took weeks—during which the trial was recessed yet again—for most of the information to be revealed. It was not nearly as sensational as the defense had tried to make it sound.

According to the documents, Majid, a one-time auto mechanic, had been a low-level Libyan intelligence operative. The CIA reports indicated that the information he provided, while not inaccurate, was not particularly useful either. He was always asking for more money and the CIA agents wondered if he was worth it. There was no indication that he had any prior knowledge of the bombing and the importance of those fragments of information he could and finally did supply was not recognized until investigators had already focused on the Malta connection, months after the bombing itself, and incidentally after Cannistraro had left the agency.

Since this was information that would have come out in testimony or cross-examination anyway, it is difficult to understand why the CIA had tried to hide it in the first place. The resulting flap merely fueled the passions of the CIA conspiracy theorists.

After a delay of several weeks, the defector—the prosecution called him Majid—took the stand and I went to the remote viewing site in Washington to watch. Later newspaper accounts were to report that he looked and sounded nervous and frightened. On the television picture that I saw and the audio I heard, and presumably all that the observers in the courtroom could see or hear, none of this was apparent. His face was simply a blur, and his voice an electronically masked rumble—from which nothing could be discerned. The English translation was done alternately by male and female interpreters—and reflected as much emotion as a written transcript. I was told that, on the Libyan side of the courtroom, if an observer pressed up against the wall, he or she could just catch a momentary glimpse of the witness reflected in the glass that protected him, and on the Arabic-language channel, there were occasional fleeting scraps of his voice before the electronic alteration cut in. Whether one could really judge by appearance or voice, or whether the Libyans who claimed to observe this were merely seeing and hearing what they wanted to see and hear, I was in no position to judge.

According to his testimony, Majid was employed by the J.S.O. (Jamahariya Security Organization) working at the Malta airport under the cover of being a regular Libyan Airline employee. He had approached the CIA early in 1988 and offered to become a double agent. His motive, he said, was his growing disgust with the way the Libyan government operated, particularly in its treatment of anyone who dared to disagree with the Leader. But he also wanted to be paid for his services, though the amount of money he got seemed fairly modest considering that if he was found out he would be killed.

There was nothing in his testimony to indicate that he had any advance knowledge of the plot to blow up a U.S. airliner. He told of being asked by one Libyan official if it would be possible to plant a bomb on a British airliner out of Malta. He said that it would be. He also said that Fhimah kept explosives, identified in court as Semtex, in a drawer in his office at the airport. This was reported to the

CIA well before the bombing, but did not seem to set off any alarm bells.

Majid described Megrahi as a high-ranking Libyan intelligence officer—though posing as another airline employee—and described Megrahi's frequent contacts with Fhimah, who was station manager for Libyan Airlines at the Malta airport. He told of a scene in the airport the day before the bombing when Megrahi arrived on a flight from Tripoli carrying a dark Samsonite suitcase—the sort of bag that contained the Pan Am 103 bomb—and how Fhimah, because of his position, was able to guide his companion past various security checkpoints.

It wasn't smoking-gun testimony by any means. In fact, in his summation Chief Prosecutor Alistair Campbell noted that if Majid had been making up the story, as he was accused of doing, he could have made up a better one. Still the evidence added a good deal to the prosecution case, especially the case against Fhimah—if the judges believed him.

The defense lawyers, William Taylor for Megrahi and Richard Keen for Fhimah, tore into him. They didn't call him Majid, as did the prosecution. To Taylor, he was Giaka—no Mister here. Keen called him "Mr." but spat out "ja-KAH" so that it sounded like an obscene word. There were nearly three days of not so much cross-examination as abuse—repeatedly calling the witness a liar. The prosecution didn't jump up once to object to "badgering the witness." The assault apparently delighted the Libyan spectators in the courtroom. Sitting in front of a television screen thousands of miles away, I was horrified. A Justice Department lawyer viewing the proceedings also felt that this sort of assault could not have taken place in an American court. The Justice Department lawyer placed a call to the court in the Netherlands, but was calmly assured that in Scottish courts lawyers objected to this sort of questioning only when they believed the witnesses couldn't take it. They seemed quite satisfied with Majid's performance. He stood his ground and did not contradict himself. I was slightly reassured by this sunny optimism—but only slightly.

SUSAN: I didn't go to the remote site in Washington to watch Majid. When I read the wire stories on the Internet in my office that morning describing Majid's testimony, I shouted, "What!" so loudly that the dog started to bark. I was that stunned. I tried to calm down by reminding myself that the media coverage of the trial was often biased and inaccurate. Because American reporters couldn't get into the remote sites in the U.S., we had to depend heavily on stringers and the British press covering the trial from Zeist. Britain doesn't have a First Amendment, and as a result, the British (and Scottish) media, with a few honorable exceptions, aren't very respected or respectable. I'd watched the testimony of Tony Gauci, the clothing-store owner in Malta who had identified Megrahi as the man who bought the things later found in the bomb bag. When I read news reports later, I wondered if the journalists and I had been watching the same trial. I thought Gauci helped the prosecution a lot. The reporters said he was confused and ineffective. So maybe the news reports on Majid were just plain wrong.

Then Dan called. I didn't need to see him to know how agitated he was. I could hear the worry in his voice. He told me the reporters got it right. Majid was being pounded. And the prosecution was giving him no help. I begged Dan to come back quickly, but by the time he got home I was paralyzed with depression and barely noticed him. Deeply hurt, he became very angry, saying that knowing he was coming home to me was all that carried him through the long, tough day, and here I was acting as if he didn't exist. I felt he was being unfair to me since I couldn't help being depressed by Majid getting hammered. So I lost my temper too. We wound up shouting and yelling. It took several hours before we could apologize to each other and make up. The long trial's corrosive effects were beginning to take their toll.

DAN: There were other significant moments, not all provided by witnesses. Fhimah's diary was entered into evidence. Not only were there dates of a number of meetings with Megrahi but there was also the December notation to "Pick up Air Malta Tags" and next to that "OK." An Air Malta baggage tag would have been essential to getting an unaccompanied suitcase on an Air Malta flight. The defense fought hard to keep the diary out of the trial on the grounds that it had been seized illegally. But they did not dispute its authenticity.

To me the most surprising and significant witnesses came from Libya itself. One was an official of the Libyan passport office. He confirmed that Megrahi had been issued a special passport under a false name at the request of the J.S.O. Megrahi used this passport to travel to Malta just before the bombing and never used it again. So much for Megrahi's claim that he was just an ordinary airline employee.

The second surprising witness was a surly Libyan identified in court as an intelligence agent for Libya. His cover had been as a Libyan Airlines employee in Tripoli, and he was caught in Senegal carrying Semtex and timers—a full bomb-making kit—in his briefcase. He didn't say much, but his mere presence was dramatic evidence that Libyan intelligence was in the business of making bombs to blow up airplanes.

The prosecution also launched a preemptive strike against the "special defense"—the attempt to show that someone else, presumably Palestinian terrorists, had planted the bomb. Investigators from the German "Autumn Leaves" operation against the PFLP/GC terrorist cell in October 1988 testified that none of the material that they had seized during the raids matched the type of bomb used to bring down Pan Am 103. It was also made clear that the PFLP/GC was heavily infiltrated by agents from Jordan, Germany, and elsewhere—and there was no information linking that organization to the Pan Am bombing.

Some former members of the East German secret police, the Stasi, testified, their identities concealed by the same sort of electronic alteration that protected Majid. The Stasi had supplied equipment to the PFLP/GC in Germany, but these agents could not recall ever having any Mebo timers of the type used in the bombing.

The scariest witness was Mohammed Abu Taub—a Palestinian terrorist doing a life sentence in Sweden for setting off a bomb in a synagogue and other acts of violence. Taub was a dapper and unrepentant killer. He was not a member of the PFLP/GC, but early on, he had come to the attention of investigators because he had ties with Malta. Taub freely, indeed proudly, admitted to being a terrorist—but absolutely denied having anything to do with the Pan Am bombing.

The prosecution case was winding down and the final witness turned out to be someone we knew, Pierre Salinger. Salinger had been President John F. Kennedy's press secretary. Later he became a journalist working for ABC. He had been deeply involved in the 1989 *Primetime* broadcast, where we met him, and for several years had worked on the Pan Am story out of ABC's London office. Even after the indictments of Fhimah and Megrahi, Salinger had never believed that Libya was responsible, and from time to time we got letters from him reiterating his belief. Because of his contacts in Libya he was given a chance to interview the two defendants in 1991. On the tape of the interview Megrahi denied ever knowing Edwin Bollier or anyone else from Mebo and ever having traveled under a false passport. Both answers were clearly lies. Salinger had been called only to certify the conditions under which the interview tapes were made. But he wanted to do more. He interrupted the questioning by Megrahi's lawyer, saying, "I know these two Libyans had nothing to do with it. I know who did it and why they did it." Megrahi's lawyer wouldn't bite. He just said, "Thank you."

Prosecutor Alistair Campbell reminded Salinger that all he had was hearsay evidence, which was inadmissible. When questioning was finished and he was asked to step down, Salinger didn't want to go. "That's all? They're not letting me tell the truth." The Chief Judge told him politely, but firmly, that he ran the court and the witness had to step down. Looking somewhat confused, he finally did. And on November 21, 2000, the prosecution case ended.

Fhimah's lawyer routinely filed a motion to have the

case against his client dismissed for lack of evidence, and the motion was routinely denied. The general feeling was that the defense would not present a long case—and just possibly the whole trial would all be over by the end of the year. Then came the Norwegian connection.

A group of asylum seekers—Palestinian and Syrian—living in Norway claimed that they had information linking the PFLP/GC to the bombing. This had been turned over to the Scottish authorities, who turned it over to the defense, who declared that it was vital to their case. The defense had already received one adjournment to give them time to investigate further. Now they asked for another, and so the trial was adjourned again, until January 9.

That came as a huge disappointment. It meant that it would be another anniversary date—the twelfth—and another holiday season without any sort of resolution.

What made this so bizarre was that these "secret documents," as they were routinely called in the press, were utterly worthless and everybody knew it—or should have.

The document was supposed to be a report written by a now-dead PFLP/GC bomb maker named Mobdi Goben, nicknamed "the Professor." He operated out of Yugoslavia and had contact with the PFLP/GC cell in Germany. Investigators who looked at the available evidence concluded that the document was almost certainly bogus and contained nothing new about PFLP/PG activities.

The document of some thirty-plus pages was supposed to be an account of Goben's life and terrorist activities. It had only one brief reference to the Pan Am bombing. The writer complained that after the Pan Am bombing Yugoslavian security officers asked him so many questions that he had to leave the country, and this made him wonder if PFLP/GC members "in the Autumn Leaves cell had a hand in the affair."

Even in the unlikely event that this document could have been shown to be genuine the information it contained was so thin that it would not have affected the trial and probably not even have been allowed in because it was clearly hearsay.

All of this was well reported, yet the Libyan defense continued to insist that the document was vital, that they would call witnesses from Norway, even the United States, if they were able to get the original copy from Syria. The defense opened by calling a couple of very minor witnesses and then requested a delay.

The request was granted. The trial was going to drag on into the thirteenth year.

SUSAN: The trial was such a heavy burden, it set me back years and drove me into myself. Soon I was living my life within a tiny circle, and as the trial dragged on, the circle grew smaller and smaller, until it was about the size of a dime. I stopped watching birds. I stopped seeing friends. There was room only for Dan, pets, books, and walks inside the circle. Nothing more. Step out of it and I became moody and hostile, overwhelmed by responsibilities and petty irritations.

At first we were told that the trial was going so smoothly it might be over by late September. Maybe October. Possibly November. Halloween passed. The trial crept through Thanksgiving, Christmas, and New Year's. On bad days I asked myself if the trial had been endowed with eternal life. It certainly seemed endless. Forget about plans for the future. The trial was the future.

Every morning began with an obsessive search for news. Not an easy task since the trial arrangements made media coverage hard to come by. When the Flynns weren't at Zeist, they were at the New York remote site. The Wolfes went to the Washington site whenever what promised to be critical testimony was presented, and not a day passed that I didn't check in with either Kathleen or Rosemary. I kept calling the OVC in Washington and the OVC in Zeist, government officials, political ops, lawyers, anyone who knew or might know anything about the trial or had an opinion about it. We got the transcripts and read them closely.

For us, and for a lot of other American families, the remote sites were remote indeed. Our little corner of New

Jersey was too far from Washington or New York to provide us easy access to them. After one wasted trip, when we
arrived at the remote site in Washington only to learn the
trial was delayed, we agreed that Dan, the more energetic
of us, would go alone to see the trial when necessary, getting up at three in the morning to be at the Washington remote site when it opened at nine, driving back home when
the site closed.

I worried whenever Dan went off to watch the trial. Was
he too tired to drive safely? What time would he get
home? Would he be exhausted for days after he came
back? And I didn't need that extra worry. I cursed the
Scottish court and the U.S. and British governments for
putting us through this, when we should have been able to
sit in our living room and watch the trial on television. And
if this was what we had to go through to follow the trial,
where did that leave most Americans? In the dark, which
is exactly where the people at Foggy Bottom wanted them.

DAN: The trial finally reconvened on January 9, 2001. The
defense had never been able to obtain the Goben documents they requested from Syria, and it was clear the
judges were not going to grant them any more delays. So
Megrahi's lawyer called a couple of witnesses who were
hanging around—a Maltese weatherman and an FBI
agent—neither of whom had anything of significance to
add. Then Taylor said he had no more witnesses. Fhimah's
lawyer called no witnesses at all. And so, suddenly, surprisingly, almost shockingly, the Pan Am 103 trial, which for a
while felt as if it was going to drag on forever, was over.

The defense decision not to put on any case was hailed
by some observers as a sign of confidence. Robert Black,
who had somehow become the most visible legal inter-
preter of the trial, told the *New York Times,* "A conviction
is—I kid you not—impossible."

Summations began the next day. Alistair Campbell started
with a surprise. He announced the prosecution was dropping
the two lesser conspiracy charges and going only for the

most serious—and most difficult to prove—murder charge.
"I invite you to convict for murder," he told the judges.
Campbell also announced that the prosecution was dropping
the charge that Fhimah was a Libyan intelligence agent.

The case was, he admitted, a circumstantial one. But a
circumstantial case was like a rope built of many strands,
no single strand strong enough on its own, but when woven
together, strong enough to sustain the murder charge.

For the next day and a half Campbell dryly, but meticu-
lously, wove the strands together. It was a competent, but
not a riveting, performance. Next up was Taylor—
Megrahi's lawyer—a flashier orator. He took a full four
days to sum up a case he had never presented. Mostly he
picked away at perceived flaws and weaknesses in the
prosecution case and reran the alternate theories of how
the bomb got on the plane—including the old and quite
discredited one about the young Lebanese American,
Khalid Jaafar, having brought the bomb aboard in his luggage. Keen, Fhimah's lawyer, took about two days. Then on
January 18, 2001, the trial really and finally was over. It had
lasted over nine months, though with all the delays and re-
cesses there were only eighty-four days of actual testimony. There were also thousands of pages of documents
and photos and other physical evidence.

Lord Sutherland noted that there was "quite a bit" of
material to go through. He recessed the court and said it
would reconvene on January 30—not to announce a verdict, but to announce when a verdict might be announced.
The earliest date he said would be January 31, but he
added that would be very unlikely.

We had planned to go back to Camp Zeist. We wanted
to be on the scene when the verdict was delivered. The
OVC had enough money left in its budget to send some
eighty victims' family members to the Netherlands and we
made sure our name was at the top of the list. But when to
go? We didn't want to go to the Netherlands and then have
to spend a couple of weeks waiting. The OVC wasn't going
to pay for that and it would have driven us crazy anyway.
So we, and most of the other American families as well as

many members of the press, simply put our plans on hold. We would wait to see what the judges said on the 30th. Surely we would then have enough time to get to the Netherlands.

The phone rang at 4:30 in the morning on the 30th. It was Ann den Bieman from the Scottish Crown Office at Camp Zeist. "The Judges announced that they will deliver their verdict when court opens tomorrow morning," she told us.

That was totally unexpected. There was no way that we could arrange to get from where we lived to Camp Zeist in the Netherlands in under twenty-four hours. We had been virtually assured that the verdict would not come on the 31st. Now we had been double-crossed by the judges.

Kathleen Flynn was on the phone almost the moment Ann hung up.

"Have you heard?" she asked.

"Yes."

"It doesn't sound good."

"No, it doesn't."

It wasn't that we wouldn't be able to get to Camp Zeist that really worried us—it was the possible meaning of this abrupt and unexpected decision. Had the judges decided that both defendants would be found not guilty and wanted to make sure that they would not have to confront a courtroom full of hysterical American relatives? At that moment I was more convinced that we were going to lose the case than I had been at any time during the past nine months.

SUSAN: The phone call came from Zeist at 4:30 in the morning. The verdict would be announced the next morning. Everyone, from the OVC to the reporters, expected the verdict to come no sooner than the following week. We were on top of the list to fly to Holland on a couple of days' notice. It had been a hideous week. Dan was sick with the flu, and I was already exhausted from the preverdict stress, the extra housework and animal care, and looking after Dan, who could barely get out of bed. We assumed that with a few more days' rest he would be able to travel to Zeist with me, no matter how weak he felt, because he would at least be over the worst of the illness. It hit me now that I would have to go by myself to hear the judges' decision. Worse yet, it was to be announced at 11 A.M. Dutch time, 5 A.M. here.

Direct flights left for Holland at night and landed in Amsterdam in the morning. Even if I could get a seat on a plane at such short notice, I might never get to Zeist in time. I wasn't a kid who could dash out of the house with my sleeping bag, take a circuitous route to Holland, changing planes several times, and somehow make it by inches, breathless and at a run. Forget Holland. Zeist was out. It would have to be the Washington remote site.

I wasn't much of a driver to begin with, and even if I were queen of the road, I couldn't face driving to Washington alone. You want to talk road rage? If it was a not guilty verdict, then driving back, exhausted, depressed, and furious, I'd be a menace to myself and every driver who got near me.

I became frightened. Why this sudden verdict? Did it mean they were going to let the Libyans off and didn't want a roomful of American families wailing, grieving, and angry with television cameras lined up outside the court to show the world the families' reactions as soon as they stepped outside? Or was it just judicial arrogance? Proud Scotland refusing to budge an inch to please the big, powerful United States.

I got mad. How dare they keep us out? We deserved to be there. It was an American plane. Most of the victims were Americans. And the U.S. government was the big spender when it came to paying for the trial. At the very least why couldn't the verdict be announced at a decent hour our time? Damn those Scottish judges. But I didn't think about them for more than a few minutes. I had to get going.

It was well before 8 A.M. that I called the OVC. Its director, Kathryn Turman, had flown to Zeist a few days earlier, and I reached her assistant Barbara Johnson. I'd always found Barbara to be very kind and cooperative. The news that the verdict would be announced within twenty-four hours had sent her and the rest of the staff scurrying off to work indecently early. I begged her to send a car for me so I could get to Washington. She was very reassuring. Of course, they'd send a car. I thanked Barbara and hung up the phone, feeling very grateful to the OVC. Barbara and Melinda Lamont-Havers, who was in charge of logistics, worked ferociously throughout the day, notifying families, arranging transportation, and finding them places to stay. At short notice, all they could find for me was a car service from Atlantic City. My transportation was a white stretch limo with a liveried driver. The high-roller special. In my jeans and sweatshirt I felt foolish.

That Dan and I would be separated from each other when the verdict came was something that we had never thought possible, and it caused us a lot of pain. We were husband and wife, father and mother of Theo, and we belonged together at that moment. At least, I'd have the Wolfes and Stephanie Bernstein with me. It was comforting to know I would be with such very good friends when the word came in.

The bravest family member the day of the verdict was Kathleen Flynn. A week earlier she learned she had breast cancer and surgery could not be delayed. It was scheduled for January 31. Nothing could stop her from hearing the judges deliver the verdict, so on the morning of the 31st Kathleen went to the remote site in New York. After the verdict she went directly to the hospital. She handled all the terrible possibilities of the day with remarkable dignity and a total lack of self-pity. As she told me when she first learned she had cancer, "I've lost a child, Susan. That was the worse thing that could ever happen to me. Nothing else, no matter what, can be as bad." When Jack Flynn called me the day after her surgery to tell me the cancer had not spread, I felt wonderful. For twelve years I'd admired Kathleen's courage, but this was strength on a truly grand scale.

DAN: One of the networks called and asked if they could send a crew out to film my reactions as the verdict was delivered and then do a live interview later for one of the morning shows. We had started twelve years earlier vowing that we were going to put a human face on this tragedy—Theo's face. Flu or no flu, I wasn't going to change that now.

I was up at 3:30 in the morning, my pajamas and pillow drenched with sweat. Yet I felt much better. It was one of those "the fever has broken" moments. I felt ready for whatever the day would bring. I was even feeling a bit more confident about the trial's outcome.

SUSAN: In Washington I was up at 3 A.M., in the hotel lobby by 4 A.M., waiting with the rest of a large group of families for the bus that would take us to the remote site. Since we'd found out the date and time of the verdict, things had been incredibly frantic. The phone rang constantly. Calls from families. Calls from the media. I didn't get to Washington until nine at night, arriving at the hotel carrying one carelessly packed suitcase and a Wodehouse novel.

The bus came. It bore the ghoulish number 103, which set people talking. As the bus rolled through the Washington darkness the families were subdued. When we reached the remote site the media was already out en masse, with cameras, microphones, and satellite trucks. I had spent much of the day before making sure they would get there early and stay late. I needn't have worried. Because so many American families didn't have time to get to Zeist, coverage at the remote sites was massive.

Once inside, the atmosphere was edgy and gloomy, at least as far as the families were concerned. Rosemary and Jim had saved me a seat in the front row, nearest the TV monitor. Stephanie and her children were in the same row, a few seats away. There were Justice Department officials in the room. There would be a briefing session after the verdict. An FBI agent came up to me and shoved a card with his phone number in my hand, in case I had any questions about the verdict when I got home. I barely noticed him or his card. And I didn't notice that a couple of wheelchairs, and medical supplies, had been quietly brought into the viewing room in case anyone collapsed on hearing the verdict. Rosemary told me about that later.

I took out the yellow pad I'd brought with me, and a pen, and got ready to write down the verdict. Why? I certainly wasn't going to forget it. My hand shook as if palsied so that when I wrote the word *verdict* I couldn't read it. It was just an indecipherable scribble on the page.

Then the television monitor came to life. The judges walked into the courtroom. The Megrahi verdict came first. "Guilty," said presiding judge Lord Sutherland. "Unanimous." I glanced at Stephanie. She was smiling. Everyone in the room was smiling. A loud happy noise erupted from us all. Instantly I forgave the judges for getting me up at three in the morning. At that moment I dearly loved them and would have forgiven them anything, even the most outrageous sins. The verdict was literally music to my ears.

Then came the Fhimah verdict. "Not guilty. Unanimous." We all groaned. I just had to talk to Dan. There was a phone in a small office to the side of the room we were in. I rushed to it and tried to call him, but I couldn't remember my phone number. Barbara Johnson had to look it up for me on the OVC families list.

I was very depressed about Fhimah. Only after I talked to Dan did I realize: yes, he's right. The Megrahi conviction nails Libya. It nails Gadhafi. That's what matters. That's what I had to tell the world. I didn't bother to hang around for the briefing. I was the first family member to go down to the street and face the cameras. And that's what I did all day long.

DAN: For me the decision came in at about a minute after 5 A.M. on CNN. They didn't have a camera in the courtroom, but they had someone inside who was giving the word to correspondent Richard Blystone, standing outside.

On the first defendant Megrahi—"Guilty."

I was swept by a feeling not of joy, but of relief—tremendous relief. As I talked to other people later, I found they all had the same feeling—relief. I was so relieved that I barely noticed or cared that the verdict on Fhimah was "Not Guilty." They got the main guy—the guy who had been identified as a "fairly high" Libyan intelligence agent. His conviction pointed the finger of guilt right back at Libya and Gadhafi.

Susan called, her voice was so husky and fatigued I did not recognize it at first. "Fhimah got off," she whispered darkly.

"Yeah, but they nailed the number one defendant. Everyone in the media is saying that points to Libya itself."

That brightened her a bit. "I have work to do," she said. And she was off.

Fhimah got off, according to the court's written opinion, because the judges had not believed much of Majid's testimony. But still—we won. Yet looked at objectively, what had we won? Two hundred seventy people had been murdered. The case was the subject of the largest criminal investigation in history. It dragged on for over twelve years. The trial itself lasted nine agonizing months and cost over eighty million dollars. And one man had been convicted. Not the ring leader. Not the boss. A middle-level operative, the sort of disposable character every state possesses. If he actually serves his entire sentence it will be twenty years, under soft prison conditions. The wing of the Glasgow prison where Megrahi will be housed has already acquired the local nickname "the Gadhafi Cafe." That would work out to about twenty-seven days for each person murdered.

By any accounting, that isn't justice. It isn't even partial justice. It's a piddling excuse for justice. Though some in the State Department tried to portray the trial's outcome as the result of a successful policy, that claim is self-serving. Would any future terrorist be deterred by such an outcome? That seems doubtful. The reverse is more likely; you can pull off a murderous frontal attack on the most powerful nation on earth and pay only a minimal price.

Even some of those who originally crafted the policy of confronting acts of state-sponsored terrorism through the judicial system expressed doubts. Brent Scowcroft, who was national security advisor to George Bush senior, told the *Washington Post,* "This is an immensely frustrating process trying to deal with terrorists. We have to ask ourselves, 'Is this the best we can do? Is it a deterrent?' Maybe not."

And yet, despite all the reservations—despite all *my* reservations—I was feeling pretty good. What I had feared most of all was that a guilty verdict would be followed by a rush to "close the book on Lockerbie, and move on." Pay off the families, call that justice, and go back to doing business with Gadhafi.

But that didn't happen. All of the family members reacted with the same view: It isn't over. Gadhafi did it, and we have to get him too. No one was sure what should be done—but something. We would not allow the country to go back to business as usual. I was on a satellite hookup with another family member, a fellow I had not exchanged a civil word with in years. He began by saying, "I agree with Dan Cohen." I agreed with him too.

The Wall Street Journal, a traditionally antisanctions paper, came out with an editorial saying that Libya is so far beyond the pale in its international behavior that sanctions against the Gadhafi regime should be continued. Other papers followed suit. The new Bush administration reacted by saying all the right things. No specific actions were promised, but the tone was tough.

Gadhafi did his part. The first reaction of Libyan diplomats to the split verdict was muted. They deplored the conviction but said it was time to move on. But Gadhafi welcomed home the acquitted Lamen Khalifa Fhimah as a hero and martyr. He said the Scottish judges should "commit suicide" and that Libya would never accept responsibility for the bombing as required in the U.N. resolutions.

Increasingly large and emotional crowds began to appear in the streets of Tripoli. At one point three men tried to cut their own throats to protest the verdict. Gadhafi himself behaved like a crazed barbarian chieftain. He insisted that he had "proven evidence" that Megrahi was innocent, and then he literally shut down the entire country of Libya so everyone would be forced to hear what he had to say. He didn't really have anything to say. He just ranted against the verdict for over two hours. All of this political theater was aimed at showing the world that Libya wasn't going to accept responsibility for the bombing in any way, shape, or form. I wonder if Gadhafi felt he had actually been promised complete exoneration, rather than mere protection from punishment, and now believed himself to have been betrayed.

Certainly the television images of the wild-eyed Libyan leader and the chanting Libyan crowds would not play well in the U.S. No politician who wanted to keep his job was going to say, "He's changed. We can deal with him."

I know these are all reactions of the moment. In the weeks and months to come the diplomats will be dealing behind the scenes, looking for new and creative ways to once again "get past the Lockerbie problem." The lawyers will be there too, with their sugarplum visions of millions of Libyan dollars in "compensation" and tales of how money is really punishment, the "hit 'em in the wallet" theory of justice. And how if we just accept the money and go away, that will be a "sign" that Libya has accepted responsibility.

Even our friends have urged us to "take the money. You deserve it after what you've been through." They love us and want the best for us—but they don't really understand us. They don't understand the cold and unappeasable fury and hatred we have, and will always have, toward those who murdered Theo. It is self-delusional to say that money in any way represents punishment to a state that has annual oil revenues in excess of $12 billion. If in any way taking the money helps Libya escape blame and return to being a respected member of the international community, and incidentally increase its oil profits, far beyond whatever it will pay out—then to hell with the money. It's blood money.

But all that is yet to come. At the moment I'm feeling pretty good—and I'm going to savor this moment.

Chapter 22

DAN: What's the point of going on, year after year, with a fight you can't ever win? Not long ago I picked up our copy of *Their Darkest Day,* a book about Pan Am 103 written by a couple of Syracuse newspaper reporters who had covered the story extensively in the early days. We talked to them many times. On the flyleaf, Tom Foster wrote: "Your perseverance has been an inspiration. Thank you both for all you have done for us and for everyone who steps on an airplane." Nice thought, Tom, but wide of the mark.

We aren't crusading for improved airline security, the better treatment of crash victims' families, or the victims of crime. Our objective hasn't been world peace, personal peace, reconciliation, closure, or any of the other objectives that have been attributed to us from time to time. And justice? After more than a decade, and a million lies, I don't even know what justice means to me in this case. It certainly wasn't a bunch of old Scotsmen in robes and wigs sitting around in the Netherlands, handing out a twenty-year sentence for mass murder.

What drives me is something much less abstract, more personal, basic, primitive. My daughter was murdered, and I want to get the bastards who killed her, and the bastards who planned her murder, and the bastards who let it happen, and the bastards who are helping all the other bastards get away with it. Revenge is a word I do understand.

I'm not going to pick up a gun and try to shoot the people responsible. I'm not trained for that sort of thing. Besides, the real villains are too well protected. But I admit, I do think about it a lot. Forgiveness in this case is not a word in my vocabulary.

The best I can do is wield the weapons I have—my writing, my talking, sometimes my shouting—to prevent people from forgetting what happened. I realize that in time people forget everything, but I'm working to keep the story out there and to stop all the above-named bastards from pretending that it never happened, or that they had nothing to do with it, or that they did their very best.

"Theo would want you to find peace and forgive," people have told me—people who never knew Theo. I often think of something that happened when she was about five years old. She was born and spent her earliest years in the country. We moved to Port Jervis so that she could get to school more easily and meet more children.

Late one afternoon I looked out my office window and saw Theo surrounded by a group of neighborhood children. I guess they had been teasing her. It wasn't serious. She was the new kid on the block, and she was being tested to see where she ranked in the pecking order. Kids are like that. Theo was also the shortest kid in the crowd. She was *always* the shortest kid in the crowd. But this time she had a weapon, a stick, and not an ordinary stick, a piece of lath from a nearby construction site, with a large nail sticking out of the end. And she was swinging it at her tormenters. They backed off, half in jest but half in fear.

I rushed out and took the nail-studded stick away from her. I said all the words expected of a good father, like "You could have put someone's eye out." "The next time they bother you, come to me. I'll talk to their parents." But in truth I was immensely proud of my daughter, and she knew it. Nobody was going to push Theo around, and if they tried, they were going to pay. That's the way she lived her life.

She was murdered by some faceless goons, thousands of miles away, for no reason other than that she was an American. She didn't even have a chance to swing a stick at them. I don't have a stick, but I'll use whatever weapons I have to get at them, not because I can defeat them, but just to let them know I'm there.

I hope Theo would be proud of me, as I was of her. I think she would. I owe it to her memory.

SUSAN: I know you can't hear me, Theo. You are ashes in a graveyard now. Yet I am going to pretend to myself that you can because I have a few things I want to say to you.

I have changed a lot since you were here, Theo. I don't know how much of what I taught you was true. The world is a much more dangerous and brutal place than we imagined back in the days when you were alive and we were happy and idealistic. The world is cold, cruel, and evil, a breeding ground for betrayal. I don't think the world will ever change, not really. A lot of days I don't want to be on this earth anymore. And I don't much care what happens to it. Sometimes I want to run away to some far-off place, just to escape. But wherever I ran, I couldn't leave behind the bombs that keep exploding inside my head. Wherever I went, I'd still be lost and lonely.

The only place I can escape to, Theo, is inside the books of P. G. Wodehouse, who created the best make-believe world there is. There's a beautiful castle in his world called Blandings, where it is always and ever a perfect summer's day. Well, you know that, of course. No daughter of mine could grow up without knowing about Blandings Castle. I visit it as much as I can, and I've told your father that when I die I want to have the words, "You can go to Heaven if you want, I'm going to Blandings Castle" put on my head-stone. You would like the Wodehouse fans I've met in the past few years, Theo. They are your kind of people.

Both Fergie and Hugo have died. Clumbers are not a long-lived breed. But we have another one, called Maudie. She's shy but very devoted to us. Her favorite hobbies are eating and sleeping. There is one exception. On warm days she does like to go to the beach for an hour or so and chase seagulls. She's not very good at it, and I never let her off her lead, but being a Clumber she enjoys herself anyway. Maybe it's all those wonderful smells at low tide.

I would bring her on the ferryboat to Lewes, Delaware, but it's a trip I can't take. I remember those ferryboat rides we took with you to Nantucket and how much you enjoyed them. I can still see you, pigtails and all baby, showing off Rupert the dachshund superstar to all his admirers on the boat. He always found admirers everywhere, didn't he? The two of you had an awful lot of fun, and I had an awful lot of fun watching you. I can't take the ferry because the memories would get to me before we ever reached Delaware, and I'd break down.

Want to know how the cats are doing? Max, of course, is as flawless as when you first saw him. At least he thinks he is, and I'm not sure he isn't right. Hope still adores him, and tolerates us. Sometimes I think she really likes us, but just has trouble showing it. Monty has taken over my office, so I have an animal with me wherever I go in the house. I have a computer now instead of a typewriter, and Monty seems drawn to it. Since he chews books, I tremble to think what he'll do to the computer, but the animals have always done whatever they wanted and got away with it. You know that.

Oh, yes, there is another cat too, though he still hasn't quite made it all the way into the house. That's because his full presence might be too much for the other cats. We found him in the attic over the garage, and we couldn't locate his owner, so we kept him. He's big and good-natured, and we call him Ollie. Whoever owned him had him declawed, so he can't catch anything. He'd never survive on his own. Probably somebody just threw him out when they got tired of him. The things people do, huh, Theo? He sleeps in your father's office at night or on cold days. Otherwise, he stays outside. There's lots for a cat to see outside here. I like it myself. No matter how depressed I get, the sight of a hawk always awakens in me, if only for a moment, the joy in life.

I talked to Annie Lareau recently, Theo. She's the same wonderful person you knew in college. She moved to the

West Coast. You always thought she would. She misses you a lot. Years ago I gave her your diary. I never read it. People don't want their mothers reading their diaries. I respected your privacy in death as I did in life. Your friend Megan is married now and has a little boy. I am so sorry you never had a chance to know him. You would have been his honorary aunt. Theo, there are so many might-have-beens. Would you ever have gotten a lead in a play in New York? Would you have married? Had children? Your life is one big question mark.

I think I'd better tell you why I fought so hard for justice all these years. Somehow I think you know, but I want to make sure. I don't care about traditional memorial services, or stone monuments either. They have their place. But I had another kind of memorial in mind for you. One that's all my own. You deserved the best I was capable of, no matter what the cost to myself, because you gave me so much happiness. If it hadn't been for you, my darling, I would never have known how deeply I could love.

Very few people ever fight back, Theo. Fewer yet fight back when they know they're going to lose. That's why the world is the mess it is, because victims crumple up in corners, lie to themselves, and run away, or crawl into holes. And when terrible things happen, the people who aren't victims avert their eyes and cover their ears and never say a word. It's a victim's duty to shout the truth, to confront those who refuse to see and make them see, and to seek justice even when justice will never come. I made my fight, knowing I could never win. I built it, day by day, stone by stone, until to me it is as solid as a medieval cathedral. But my shrine wasn't built for the glory of God. Mine was built in honor of you. In honor of your charm, your talent, your bright eyes, your beautiful voice, your passion for life. This book is part of my memorial to you.

So where do I go from here? What do I do with the rest of my life? I will keep fighting, of course, as long as I can. You know that. But my personal future? I have no illusions. Without you the future will be what the past has been since December 21, 1988. Still, I will carry into that future the knowledge that I did everything possible to punish those who murdered you and to force the world to remember Pan Am 103. I will take the strength the fight has given me, the dignity and honor, the clear conscience I earned from it into the time to come. Maybe that's not much of a talisman against the bleakness and emptiness, but it is something. I am not just a victim.

I will never forget your last words to me, "I miss you and I love you." Well, I miss you and will always miss you. I love you and will always love you. So please understand how proud I am that in parting my very last words to you are simply these: Theo, I have been true.